T5-DIG-944

Anti-Racism in European Football

Anti-Racism in European Football

Fair Play for All

EDITED BY CHRISTOS KASSIMERIS

LEXINGTON BOOKS

A division of
ROWMAN & LITTLEFIELD PUBLISHERS, INC.
Lanham • Boulder • New York • Toronto • Plymouth, UK

LEXINGTON BOOKS

A division of Rowman & Littlefield Publishers, Inc.
A wholly owned subsidiary of The Rowman & Littlefield Publishing Group, Inc.
4501 Forbes Boulevard, Suite 200
Lanham, MD 20706

Estover Road
Plymouth PL6 7PY
United Kingdom

Copyright © 2009 by Lexington Books

All rights reserved. No part of this publication may be reproduced,
stored in a retrieval system, or transmitted in any form or by any
means, electronic, mechanical, photocopying, recording, or otherwise,
without the prior permission of the publisher.

British Library Cataloguing in Publication Information Available

Library of Congress Cataloging-in-Publication Data

Kassimeris, Christos, 1974-
  Anti-racism in European football : fair play for all / edited by Christos
Kassimeris
       p. cm.
  Includes bibliographical references and index.
  ISBN 978-0-7391-2611-0 (cloth : alk. paper) -- ISBN 978-0-7391-2612-7 (pbk. :
alk. paper) -- ISBN 978-0-7391-3822-9 (electronic)
  1. Racism in sports--Europe. 2. Mass media and sports--Europe. 3.
Soccer--Europe--Public opinion. 4. Public opinion--Europe. 5. Europe--Race
relations. I. Title.
  GV706.32.K358 2009
  796.334094--dc22   2009020292

Printed in the United States of America

♾️ The paper used in this publication meets the minimum requirements of American
National Standard for Information Sciences—Permanence of Paper for Printed Library
Materials, ANSI/NISO Z39.48–1992.

Contents

Chapter One

Introduction

Christos Kassimeris

The mass appeal and mesmerizing effect of playing or watching football aside, the jovial nature of the popular game has long been distorted for racism allows no room for its proper development. The popularity that football has enjoyed since its very inception, in tandem with the usually exuberant atmosphere surrounding football matches, has for many years been disrupted as large groups of people clearly feel otherwise. Similar to the symptoms of the game's other societal disease, hooliganism for that matter, racism in football has been successful in discouraging people of certain religious convictions, skin color and ethnic origins from participating more actively. Often attributed exclusively (mistakenly so) to the sheer presence of extreme elements on the terraces, the seemingly festive setting of a football stadium every now and then reveals a not-so-welcoming environment, particularly for non-white people. Racial abuse, monkey chants and flying bananas generate jungle-like emotions that insult the innermost principles of humanity.

Combating racism in football is not a difficult task merely because the adversary concerned reflects a social phenomenon deeply rooted in European history that dates back to the times of colonialism and the despicable need to justify the supremacy of "white culture" over primitive, non-white civilizations. Rather, the intricacy of racism in football and, therefore, the discovery of a suitable remedy stems for its manifold shapes. Despite the huge numbers of non-white football players and their presence in every single European football league, particularly in west Europe, the percentage of non-white spectators remains alarmingly low; representation in football governing bodies is virtually a non-issue and non-white football managers have yet to emerge from obscurity. There is little doubt that racism in football constitutes an unsettling phenomenon that dictates immediate attention for the integrating values of sports, in general, present national authorities with an exceptional opportunity to complete assimilation with effect.

Most sources indicate that racism in football was acknowledged in the late 1960s and early 1970s, even though relevant evidence suggests otherwise. Lurking in the shadow of hooliganism, racism in football remained undetected for an admittedly extended period of time, since the occasional racist incident was more often than not attributed to football violence alone. Further European integration, the revival of nationalism and far-right politics, however, have recently highlighted the resurgence of ethnocentrism across the continent, hence separating racism from hooliganism. Heralding a new era in European affairs is not regionalism, supranationalism or any concept denoting amalgamation, as far as inter-cultural relations are concerned, but xenophobia, extremism and racial segregation. While the anonymity that a football crowd offers appears to relax whatever defenses may persuade one against engaging in racist activity, under normal conditions, thus ascribing fan culture manipulative characteristics reminiscent of mob rule; other forms of racism in football seem to evade equally coherent interpretations. The absence of black managers, the failure to appreciate the talent of Asian players and the nonexistence of non-white officials in football governing bodies all conspire at the expense of the beautiful game.

My first expedition in the world of football concerned racism in European football. Recently printed by the same publishing house, the book delves in the history of football, assesses the impact of nationalism on the popular game, produces a detailed account of racist incidents related to football, discusses the response of certain anti-racism organizations and supranational football governing bodies and, finally, makes reference to anti-racist legislative instruments at the national and European Union level. While the overall contribution of all pertinent anti-racism organizations has been fundamental to the campaign against all forms of discrimination, my research revealed that little is available about their initiatives, particularly within the academia. The sheer magnitude of the cultural and educational events organized by them, not to mention their determination to eliminate bigotry from football, prompted the present author to invite these organizations in an endeavor to raise awareness about racism. In this respect, the present study provides a detailed account of football-focused anti-racism organizations across the European domain, with particular emphasis on the anti-racist campaign in England as the undisputable pioneer in this field.

To this end, the following chapter produces a brief historical account of racism in European football. More precisely, chapter 2 provides an overview of how distinct European nations interpret the same disturbing phenomenon and, most importantly, how they are eradicating racial discrimination from the beautiful game. Evidently, different European states have carried out a wide range of government-sponsored anti-racism activities for the purpose of combating racism while promoting inter-cultural relations. Those west European states featured in this chapter have been intentionally selected, given that their football leagues receive far more publicity by virtue of the game's development in these countries. Consequently, no matter what anti-social phenomena take place there, they are more likely to attain Europe-wide exposure or, indeed, any attention whatsoever. As far as the rest of Europe is concerned, it is addressed collectively not so much because football's publicity in these countries rarely transcends national borders, but because of the apparent lack of sources devoted to the examination of racism in football in east Europe and the Balkans. Despite the intrinsic value of the information available in these sections of chapter 2, it is the prejudice regarding a non-white footballer's potential playing positions that the present author considers most disruptive. Needless to say, the contribution of the European football governing body (Union of European Football Associations) is also discussed, as is the interest of the European Parliament in safeguarding the main principles of football, as well as employing the popular game for the cause of further European integration.

Chapter 3 concerns the Football Against Racism in Europe organization and some of the anti-racism organizations that comprise it from across the continent. As the only pan-European organization solely dedicated to the elimination of all forms of discrimination from the beautiful game, Football Against Racism in Europe enjoys Europe-wide support from Europe's football governing body, football associations, clubs and even groups of people not officially connected to football, particularly during the so-called Week of Action that is usually held during the second half of October every year. The participation, too, of Football Against Racism in Europe in recent European Championships and, of course, in the 2006 World Cup in Germany has been instrumental in the campaign against racism in football. The same chapter also produces some information with regard to certain associated anti-racism organizations, namely, Bündnis Aktiver Fussballfans, Progetto Ultrà, Schalker Fan-Initiative, Nigdy Wiecej, Kick It Out, Football Unites, Racism Divides and Show Racism the Red Card. While the nature and scope of the latter three anti-racism organizations, all based in Britain, is further elaborated in relevant chapters reserved exclusively for the pioneers in combating racism in football; information in relation to their continental partners is confined to chapter 3 alone.

As already stated, chapters 4, 5 and 6 concern the activities of Kick It Out, Football Unites, Racism Divides and Show Racism the Red Card in their attempts to rid football of racism. Although it is not definite that racism in football originated in Britain, it is certain that the three aforementioned organizations led the way, and continue to do so, in the campaign against racism in football. Generally, all three are heavily involved in projects that enhance community cohesion, have obviously invested much energy in raising awareness about racism through relevant schemes and are constantly seeking new, alternative methods to bring closer together people from distinct ethnic backgrounds. Naturally, in most of the initiatives football remains the main protagonist, thus utilizing the game's positive qualities. Even though these anti-racism organizations appear to employ different approaches that are all concentrated upon the disturbing phenomenon of racial discrimination, one particular strategy is common to all three. Not surprisingly, perhaps, they all place a great deal of emphasis on education and, therefore, regularly organize educational events at schools or during football training sessions for children.

Having illustrated the involvement of certain anti-racism organizations devoted to the eradication of all forms of discrimination from the beautiful game, the following chapter produces a critical analysis focused entirely upon the contribution of all pertinent actors. It suffices to say that the agenda and activities of all anti-racism organizations that concern the heart of this volume are assessed in chapter 7 within the relevant theoretical framework. In spite of the fact that the participation of all the anti-racism organizations mentioned above in the campaign against racism in football—and in society more generally—has been quite successful, it is widely agreed that anti-racism campaigns are difficult to orchestrate, particularly when the all-important support (physical and financial) for the initiation of any such project is too little to even consider promising. In any case, the core mission of these football-oriented organizations is thoroughly discussed in this final chapter, providing the reader with the opportunity to better digest the information presented in preceding sections.

While notions pertaining to the study of anti-racism are comprehensively addressed in chapter 7, it is imperative that we briefly divulge certain aspects of this subject, particularly since anti-racism has yet to receive proper scholarly attention. Considered little more than well-intended practices, anti-racism campaigns are often merely regarded as yet another tool for combating discrimination in society. In point of fact, anti-racism is often defined by—if not exclusively dependent upon the definition of—racism per se, thus mystifying our subject matter to an extent where deeper social, cultural and political connotations are exposed. What is more, the sort of diversity that characterizes the approach adopted by organizations devoted to the eradication of racial discrimination without doubt ties in well with the diverse interpretations of anti-racism. The significance of identifying, for epistemological purposes, the various forms and shapes of racism extant notwithstanding, it is unreservedly fundamental that one takes into account the fact that different anti-racism organizations employ equally different strategies while targeting prejudice, for the phenomenon of racism is often mistakenly perceived as a singular concept. Racism in modern Europe seems to have discarded whatever biological overtones it has long been associated, only to be accorded a cultural guise too complex to locate with accuracy. Those biological interpretations that originated during the times of Europe's apparent intellectual supremacy were easily dismissed when science failed to placate the alleged superiority of the "white race" over the dark-skinned "primitive creatures" encountered outside the very continent that was once the epicenter of imperialism. Nowadays, racism has acquired a cultural dimension so complex that European societies have yet to realize its magnitude, let alone discover the all-important remedy that would further promote integration by means of eliminating discrimination altogether. Needless to say, anti-racism too has altered along similar lines. It is in this context, therefore, that the present volume examines the practices of all pertinent actors discussed herein.

Except for several documents and public announcements condemning racist incidents in football, the supranational authorities of the game have only recently become seriously involved in anti-racism activities. The Union of European Football Associations has supported relevant campaigns and organizations over the past few years, whereas the attempts of *Fédération Internationale de Football Association* to combat racism materialized during the 2006 World Cup in Germany and will be extended over the next tournament in South Africa. On the contrary, anti-racism organizations devoted to football—highly praised for their contribution to the popular game—have been remarkably active. These organizations came into being in the mid-1990s, thus their response to racial discrimination and xenophobia in football was timely enough to adopt novel measures intended to eradicate these issues and reach out to ethnic minority groups. It is no coincidence that all anti-racism organizations have been commended for various successful, innovative schemes such as the Streetkick game designed by Football Unites, Racism Divides and the phenomenal Mondiali Antirazzisti organized by Progetto Ultrà in Italy. Likewise, Kick It Out and Football Against Racism in Europe are also unique in that both collect information related to racist incidents in European football.

However, to maintain such high levels of efficiency, it is imperative that the attempts of these anti-racism organizations attract the necessary support of national governments and football associations alike, not to mention clubs and players. In any other case, their endeavors will be irreparably harmed. Hence, this book not only aims at making an original contribution to academia, considering the lack of sources regarding these anti-racism organizations, but also intends to raise awareness about their very existence and encourage more people to take part in their activities in any form possible. On the whole, this volume should appeal to general readers, professionals in non-governmental organizations—primarily those related to sports—and, of course, to academics and students with an interest in social sciences and humanities.

As a final remark, the editor would like to note that while chapters 2 and 7 include endnotes, as is common practice within academia, the remaining contributors come from non-academic organizations, thus the inconsistency in citations.

Chapter Two

Racism in European Football

Christos Kassimeris

The constant expansion of the European Union (EU) and the massive waves of migration that today epitomize the cultural diversity of the continent are often considered as negative developments in the otherwise sophisticated and advanced environment that is the wider region of Europe. Naturally, the demographic character of most Western European states has changed rapidly, ever since the collapse of communism, thus enhancing multiculturalism at the national level. Even the apparently homogeneous societies of Eastern Europe, particularly during the Cold War era, have now welcomed scores of migrants that wish to improve their living standards. The imperial legacy of Europe coupled with unemployment and a strong sense of white supremacy has encouraged the propagation of xenophobia to an extent where discrimination, abuse and violence—all conveniently centered around racism and prejudice—have come to typify Europe's extreme nationalism and the kind of intolerance that many European societies reflect. What is beyond doubt a rather disturbing phenomenon has penetrated most aspects of societal life, including sporting activities. The beauty and popularity of the game notwithstanding, football too has suffered much from the same disease. Taking into account the usually massive stadiums where the game is played, the mass appeal of football presents to all racist elements a hardly unexpected advantage in expressing their anti-social, bigoted feelings nonchalantly—anonymity.

Racism in football takes shape in an appallingly wide range of forms, considering the sheer number of all pertinent actors: fans directing their sickening racist chants to non-white football players and spectators alike; political parties recruiting members in football stadiums, strengthening xenophobic trends by promoting their racist views; the well-documented lack of representation of ethnic minorities at all levels of the game, including the structure of football governing bodies (referees, managers, national football association officials, club officials, etc.); and, of course, the overall intimidating atmosphere perpetuated by a section of fans who appear, often deceivingly, to defend extreme right-wing values, all together conspire at the expense of the beautiful game. On quite a few occasions, non-white players have threatened to leave the football pitch amidst

7

a relentless bombardment of monkey chants and bananas. Similarly, non-white spectators who have witnessed the shocking degradation of like-colored football players have decided to refrain from attending football games in order to avoid unpleasant confrontations with the game's worst supporters. Furthermore, considering that in the past, particularly in Britain, "the style of the coverage did not lack certain racist undertone, especially when the media used terms like 'negro players,'"[1] it becomes evident that racist remarks during a football match—whether unintentional or not—were probably as natural as the skin color of the player they were addressed to, thus transforming football stadiums from a festive arena to an inhospitable environment for all those fans who are members of distinct ethnic communities.

The rapid expansion of the European Union should have facilitated the reconciliation of seemingly incompatible cultures, nationalities, religions and all other elements of segregation for the purpose of promoting a new Europeanized identity while serving the cause of continental supranationalism. On the contrary, the core mission of the European superstructure has clearly failed, considering, for example, the European Union citizens' negative response to the EU-sponsored constitution, which so far renders the Europeans' *unity in diversity* almost unfeasible. Despite Europe's prevalent multiculturalism, there is little doubt that "racism is a serious question across Europe, one that European football has not only been slow to address, but one which still awaits a sustained and powerful rebuttal."[2] Emphasizing the polymorphism of this unsettling phenomenon is the fact that racism in Europe during the 1990s was somehow perceived "as a 'coded, sophisticated reconfiguration of racist attitudes' which is able to cloak itself in a respectability its more aggressive and overt predecessor never could."[3] What should have definitely prompted all pertinent actors to concentrate their efforts toward the elimination of all forms of discrimination, however, must have escaped the attention of the authorities, for racism was allowed to grow with minimal resistance. Any other interpretation would allow room to speculate over Europe's apparent chauvinistic predisposition.

Probably encouraged by the revival of nationalism that followed the aftermath of the Cold War and the collapse of communism across the Eastern Bloc, racism in the new millennium continues to disrupt the European Union's campaign to attain further integration and cultural assimilation. It is, therefore, imperative that racism be confronted decisively. In reference to the popular game, it has become evident that "football racism is particularly acute during periods of political and economic restructuring."[4] Mirroring recent political trends, racial discrimination in the game of football—in terms of fan behavior—is, arguably, encouraged by representatives of extreme right-wing parties, who purposely occupy the terraces of football stadiums with the intention of recruiting new members. While pointing fingers and criticizing the extreme right provides an obvious outlet in our search for a credible culprit, thus holding a particular political stream culpable for all relevant anti-social convictions, the dangers emanating from such simplifications may prove far more threatening to the cohesion of any given society. It is worthy of note, nevertheless, that the "weakness of some campaigns is their concentration on the perceived racism of hooligans, but this exaggerates the prevalence of racist or neo-Nazi groups within hooligan networks, as few hooligans are ideologically racist or members of extreme right-wing movements."[5] Undoubtedly reflecting the overall complexity of racism as a social phenomenon, "a team of academics from Leuven University in Belgium, having conducted research into the causes of the Heysel stadium disaster, concluded that fascist groups across Europe were using football as a cover for networking, exchanging information and recruitment. Far-right groups seem keen to target football matches to attract recruits. . . . The major reason for this has been the 'traditional' demographic make-up of football crowds as overwhelmingly male, large numbers of whom are young and from working-class backgrounds. Whilst it is simplistic to generalize about either the potential political allegiances of such broad sections of the population or the typical socioeconomic background of a fascist, it remains the case that the stereotype of the football fan seems to overlap quite broadly with that of the far-right street activist."[6] Given the diversity of views concerning the impact of extreme right-wing parties on racism in football, one thing is certain: more research is necessary.

The ideological standing of football supporters notwithstanding, football racism has already plagued a significant number of European states that are now required to take concerted action in order to eradicate the beautiful game's modern disease. Football racism, more often than not, reflects discrimination in society; however, the anonymity that dominates mob-like crowds, such as the supporters that occupy a stadium's terraces, may persuade certain fans to engage in racist conduct. Much unlike the context of everyday conditions, within which one is expected to behave in a socially acceptable manner (individuals often do, out of sheer apprehension at the prospect of being pilloried), the heated atmosphere of a football stadium may dictate a wholly different pattern of behavior through which the very same individual who once refrained from openly embracing intolerance no longer hesitates to express racist views (safety in numbers). Yet not all countries experience the exact same features of this distressing phenomenon, given that racism at the national level seems to express, and somehow coincide with, the historical and cultural background of the nation in question.

Belgium

The population of Belgium is reasonably heterogeneous, which comprises a considerable proportion of migrants that nears 9 percent. While cultural diversity is nothing new to Belgian citizens, authorities at the national level are constantly seeking the appropriate means to strengthen integration at home. In this respect, the Royal Commissariat for Immigration Policy, *Le Commissariat Royal a la politique des émigrés* (CRPI), was established in 1989 following an alarming increase in the electoral support of extreme right-wing parties the year before. The main task of the CRPI is to encourage integration by eradicating discrimination at the expense of ethnic minorities and, particularly, migrants. Supported by the Centre of Equality, schemes that aim at multiculturalism and all pertinent institutions, the CRPI has excelled in the field of assimilation. Worthy of note is the success of the Institute for Sports Management in organizing the Neighborhood Ball campaigns annually. Along the same lines, the national football federation of Belgium, *Koninklijke Belgische Voetbalbond* (KBVB), has been instrumental in promoting integration among young people, while combating racism at the same time. The Fighting Racism in Football campaign commenced in the 1990s with the participation of professional football clubs from across the country. The anti-racism campaigning of the Belgian football federation was suitably strengthened with a number of *Fédération Internationale de Football Association* initiatives, namely, the United Colors of Football and Show Racism the Red Card programs.

Despite the age-old rivalry between Flemish and Walloons, racial discrimination seems to overshadow the nationalistic sentiments that separate the two main ethnic communities of Belgium. Large waves of migrants arrived in Belgium during the 1960s, when the home economy was in need of cheap manual labor. Much later, the Bosman affair, coupled with the free movement of population from one European Union member state to another, would add a different perspective to the steady influx of foreigners in Belgium—cheap football players. Interestingly, during the mid-1990s Antwerp Football Club had "the highest percentage (36 percent) of foreign players and yet Antwerp is the city where extreme right-wing and racist and xenophobic ideologies attract the highest number of votes in Belgian politics," which clearly demonstrates "that there is no correlation between the number of foreign players in football and the degree of integration in society."[7] Predating the Bosman ruling by almost a decade, the King Boudewijn Foundation, *Koning Boudewijn Stichting*, promoted anti-racist campaigns throughout the country. In fact, the Neighborhood Ball scheme was originally instituted by the King Boudewijn Foundation, thus emphasizing the unique qualities of the "king of sports" early on. This anti-racist campaign concentrated on "instituting local, informal football competitions and targeted economically deprived young people particularly from ethnic minorities. The 'local sports initiatives' campaign supported existing small-scale projects focusing on deprived neighborhoods containing immigrants and minority ethnic groups."[8] Another similar initiative concerned the "sports clubs show their colors" campaign, which sought to promote anti-discrimination policies among clubs.

Britain

Britain has been susceptible to migration much because of her imperial past, as a large number of migrants coming from the Commonwealth reached her shores in the twentieth century. In terms of race equality, the interests of ethnic minorities in Britain are well accommodated with the relevant policies that were originally developed in the 1960s. Disturbing events at Nottingham and London in 1958 and Oldham in 2001, however, serve to expose the occasionally uneasy relations between the native white population and members of distinct communities. Nowadays, "a plethora of governmental and non-governmental agencies provide general services targeted at ethnic minorities, together with sporting initiatives such as *Sporting Equals* (Commission for Racial Equality & Sport England 2001) and the *Equality and Diversity Strategy* of UK Sport (2004). The focus on ethnic minority sports participation is evident in the commissioned research by Sport England (Sport England 2000) and Sport Scotland (Scott Porter Research & Marketing Ltd. 2000) and by the development of a system of good practice guidelines for national sports governing bodies by Sporting Equals (Sporting Equals 2000). In addition the need for action to achieve equity is acknowledged in the *Government's Plans for Sport* (Department of Culture Media and Sport 2000)."[9] The Labor government of Tony Blair, nonetheless, sought to implement hard-line policies that discourage migrants from entering the country, inspired to a great extent by the "war on terror" that succeeded the tragic events of September 11. Surprisingly, "Trevor Phillips, Chairman for the Commission on Racial Equality, in April 2004 argued that Britain's policy of multiculturalism had gone too far, and that there was a need to ensure that a core of British values remained intact. Thus there is evidence, in some areas of government and the quasi-government sector, of a shift from dominantly multicultural or intercultural positions to the monocultural and assimilationist position with an emphasis on protecting cohesion rather than diversity."[10] Cultural diversity remains one of the dominant characteristics of British society, but this should not suggest the absence of ethnocentric attitudes.

Although it is not entirely certain whether or not it was British football that suffered from racial discrimination first, it is beyond doubt that the pioneers in combating racism in football are of British origin. Racist abuse and violence in and around football grounds reached a peak during the 1970s. Viv Anderson, becoming in 1978 the first black football player who represented England, did not alleviate the predicament of English football. Racist abuse throughout the 1970s blemished the beautiful game, as "the fans—almost exclusively white at this point in history—considered soccer to be a 'white' game. An occasional successful black player was acceptable. However, the rise of dozens of black players, including England internationals Viv Anderson, Garth Crooks and West Bromwich Albion's triumvirate, Cyrille Regis, Brandon Batson and Laurie Cunningham, posed a more sinister danger; that the game was in the early throes of an alien takeover. This has to be considered against the social background of England during the late 1970s: high youth unemployment; a right-wing Conser-

vative government; the resurgence of the far right (National Front) and especially the virulent skinhead movement, which had had a strong presence in English soccer stadiums for a decade."[11] Margaret Thatcher rose to power having
first "attracted much of Britain's racist vote when she claimed to understand the
fears of those who felt 'swamped' by an immigrant culture,"[12] thus benefiting
from the exploits of the main British fascist party already in decline. The National Front had been moderately successful for the most part of the 1970s and
was, reportedly, taking advantage of the mass appeal of football to impress
young people, thus expanding its membership. Supported by the British Movement and similar neo-Nazi groupings, the racist chants that were once invented
by National Front members continued to echo in football stadiums across the
country. London-based clubs such as Arsenal FC, Charlton FC, Chelsea FC,
West Ham United FC and the notorious Millwall FC, all enjoyed significant
racist support. Still, "despite the activity of fascist groups at football grounds
around the country, there is little evidence to show that many people were recruited into political activity. This is particularly so with the hooligans who generally proved too ill-disciplined and independent for groups such as the NF. As a
result, recruitment amongst the hooligan fraternity was never systematic or
widespread. Despite agreeing with the political agenda of the racist groups, the
bulk of hooligans only turned up when there was a chance to fight."[13] Similar
views are held by Les Back, Tim Crabbe and John Solomos, who concluded
"that the involvement of right-wing political groupings in football culture is limited,"[14] given that "the relationship between the far-right and football culture is
instrumental rather than organic."[15]

Nevertheless, the influence of those groups was substantial in terms of
shaping fan culture and attitudes when taking into account that "in 1981 the
youth wing of the NF launched Bulldog, a magazine aimed at attracting young
people through music and sport. One page was always devoted to football with
reports of racist chanting and violence. Of particular interest to some fans was
Bulldog's "League of Lout," a table charting racism within the game. Leeds
United, West Ham, Chelsea and Newcastle fans would regularly battle to be
labeled the most racist in Britain. Certain grounds became known for racism
among large sections of the fans and Leeds, Chelsea and Newcastle were among
the worst of the big teams. Leeds had been a centre for strong NF support for
many years and this moved into the football stadium in the 1970s."[16] Immensely
worrisome was the case of Leeds United FC, since its support was virtually
"synonymous with the rising political influence of the National Front and other
neo-fascist groups within football by late 1970s."[17] That racist segment of the
Leeds United FC supporters did little to disperse their negative image, forcing
the club's official to adopt drastic measures—a hotline for reporting racist offenders—when the football governing body threatened to expel the club. Leeds
United FC made the headlines for all the wrong reasons, once more, when some
of its more eponymous players attacked an Asian student on 12 January 2000.

Interestingly, while the club proclaimed the innocence of its footballers, the national football association removed the accused from the England national team until the legal aspect of the case was resolved.

The atmosphere in quite a few football stadiums in England must have been anything but welcoming for non-white spectators, regardless of the ever-increasing numbers of black football players. In comparison to the size of the respective communities, however, Asians footballers are conspicuous by their absence, while few black former football players are making their living as managers. For the record, Ruud Gullit became the first black manager at the helm of a Premier League club when he managed Chelsea FC, even though it is quite likely that he was probably considered first as a "foreigner" and then "black." Should the above fail to convince the reader regarding the apparent dimensions of racism in English football as a natural extension of its society, one needs only consider that "the notion 'British' is widely held to be less racially or culturally exclusive"[18] than "English" is. As for Scotland and Northern Ireland, they suffer from racial discrimination in football, too, yet sectarianism clearly overshadows all other phenomena that have the capacity, theoretically at least, to compromise the cohesion of their society.

France

Similar to the composition of the population in Britain, France is yet another west European state that features a strong sense of multiculturalism. Except for the Basque, Breton, Catalan, Corsican and Roma national minorities, French society has long been receiving migrants from third countries. While authorities at the national level focus much on assimilation, since "policy measures in all domains will be seen as 'general' in their target, rather than specifically focusing on given minorities," "the spatial or social concentration of ethnic minorities in particular contexts (parts of the city, or among groups such as *les jeunes en difficulté*) means that services may be de facto delivered largely to ethnic minority elements by virtue of their spatial or social concentration. In relation to sports services, Lionel Arnaud (1999) illustrates this point excellently in his book *Politiques Sportives et Minoritiés Ethniques*."[19] In general, the degree of multiculturalism in France is well reflected in the establishment of the national Islamic Congress and the first Islamic School in Lille, not to mention certain important appointments at the political level.

Although immigration in France increased in the 1970s, racism in football was almost non-existent—in terms of fan behavior—before the late 1980s, when extreme right elements started to infiltrate the "kops" representing, if you will, extreme right-wing groups such as the *Mouvement National Républicain* (National Republican Movement) and the *Front National*. During the 1980s and 1990s, the Front National, in particular, and other far-right groups enjoyed considerable support, which was often demonstrated during electoral periods. Despite their declining popularity from 2002 onward, these political formations rarely overlooked opportunities for racist propaganda. For instance, both the 1998 and 2000 successes of the national football team of France were publicly castigated by Jean-Marie Le Pen, for the composition of the team lacked the necessary homogeneity. More accurately, the leader of the *Front National* obviously failed to appreciate the football-based ascendance of his country, as World and European champions in 1998 and 2000 respectively, since the national football team comprised "foreigners" and non-white players. Sadly enough, what should have been a definite triumph of multiculturalism over racism was undervalued by those who shared Le Pen's ideals. In any case, "nations such as France, who won the 1998 World Cup with a multi-racial side that reflected her colonial past, and the Netherlands, where Surinam is found on the birth certificates of some of its most lauded players, have always tended towards greater sporting inclusiveness."[20] As far as the truly commendable achievements of the French national football team are concerned, it is important to note that "football players from immigrant communities excelled because for them the usual access to social mobility, through school and work, were closed. What these players gave an earlier era of French football was the will to succeed and the desire to be recognized. The youth training schemes continue to attract disproportionately the children of immigrant families because they are encountering problems in the education system."[21]

Yet racism in French football is not limited to the occasional unethical statement of party leaders; it is far more severe as the accidental death of a Paris Saint-Germain fan in November 2006 denotes. With regard to the eradication of racism in sports, however, little has been achieved over the past years. To a great extent, "the cause of the sports associations and the political world's passivity with respect to taking action against racism in football appears to lie in the French hesitancy to 'politicise' sport. Both the sports associations and government are against exclusion in sport in general, but believe that an anti-racist attitude and politics are inappropriate to sport. Taking an anti-racist viewpoint is generally regarded as engaging in politics, which, according to many people, is not appropriate in football. A few groups are openly anti-racist and the majority of clubs and supporters support this anti-racist ideology. At the same time, clubs and supporters' groups claim that they would never undertake any anti-racist initiatives, because they do not want to engage in political activity."[22] No matter the standpoint of football clubs and relevant governing bodies in France, it is highly recommended that all pertinent actors adopt the much needed measures to curb this upsetting phenomenon effectively.

Germany

The term "guest worker" is almost self-explanatory, given that "the distinction which has traditionally been made in policy commentary has been that between 'German' and 'foreigner.'"[23] The main national minorities in Germany concern people of Danish, Friesian, Roma, Serb and Sinti origins; nonetheless, migrants from distinct ethnic backgrounds also reside in the same society, ever since the German economy welcomed them in the 1960s. Reflecting the exact same response of other west European states, central to the German authorities' understanding of multiculturalism-oriented policies is, bizarrely enough, the need to assimilate all "foreigners" to German culture. In this respect, "although legal rights for national minorities are provided for and the rights of 'foreigners' to take on German citizenship have been liberalized to some degree, provision for ethnic minorities in German sports policy is fragmented and limited. Much of such policy relates to activity at Länder level. Some schemes are targeted not simply at the minorities themselves, but at xenophobic youth such as the *Street Soccer for Tolerance* project promoted by the German Football Association and Länder organizations in Brandenburg, which aims to resocialise young people prone to violence by playing in mixed teams with negotiated rules."[24] Here, it is worthy to note that racism in football is far more regularly witnessed in the deprived areas that once constituted part of the former German Democratic Republic due to the social and economic inequalities that continue to describe conditions in the eastern part of the now unified Germany.

August 1963 has come to represent a significant date in the contemporary history of German football for it symbolizes its very revival. The division of Germany had definitely taken its toll on the proper development of the popular game, nevertheless, when the German *Bundesliga* kicked off that summer the sheer essence of football was fully restored. The presence of five foreign football players almost went unnoticed, as they were too few to jeopardize the all-important German identity of the game. However, "racism, xenophobia and the most vicious nationalisms have arisen in those societies least confident of themselves, or in those most divided. Nationalism is never so intense as among people whose national identity has been cast into doubt, has not been fully developed or is challenged by a group within."[25] Years later, German football, too, would fail to escape the ugliness of racism as Julio Cesar negotiated a peculiar contract with the officials of Borussia Dortmund that featured an opt-out clause in case the player was ever subjected to racist abuse while playing before a home crowd. As it happens, a section of Borussia Dortmund supporters was, at the time, affiliated to the *Nationaldemokratische Partei Deutschlands*. Naturally, the first foreign players to experience racial discrimination in football were members of the Turkish community. While German legislation prohibits the use of symbols that make reference to the shameful past of the Nationalist Socialist period, it is believed that the "use of Nazi symbols and slogans reflects a deeper alienation towards wealthier Westerners rather than a political ideology. Punks during the 1970s were similarly interested in using swastikas to upset and shock rather than to signify fascist sentiments."[26] Even though racism in Germany continues to blemish the beautiful game, local authorities did well in ensuring a safe environment for those that attended the recent World Cup.

Italy

Migration is a fairly recent experience for Italian society with the majority of migrants originating from Albania, Morocco, the Philippines, Romania and Tunisia, making up some 3 percent of Italy's population. Likewise, racism in Italian football is a new phenomenon first witnessed during the 1990s. As it happens, the "ultra" groups that emerged in the 1970s declined in significance during the 1980s, but were soon succeeded by extreme right groups that became progressively more active in targeting immigrants by means of racist rhetoric throughout Italy's football grounds. Despite the fact that the Italian government has done little to combat racial discrimination at football matches and, generally, in football, the Ministries of Education, Internal Affairs and Social Solidarity have facilitated the integration of immigrant communities through a variety of sporting schemes. One that certainly commands our attention is the *Unione Italiana Sport Per Tutti* for having developed a range of programs that promote inter-cultural dialogue, while bringing native Italians and migrants closer together. Central to the objectives of *Unione Italiana Sport Per Tutti* is the organization of sporting activities. On the whole, the *Unione Italiana Sport Per Tutti* has five sets of aims:

- to promote recreational, cultural and sport activities that aim at maintaining specific cultures and identities of immigrant communities in Italy
- promoting inter cultural dialogue, in particular the project of Centro Olympic Maghreb in Genoa aiming at immigrants from North Africa, South America, Eastern Europe
- promotion of events such as the Anti-racist World Cup which involves mixed teams (men and women) from different ethnic minorities
- initiatives to combat ethnic and social prejudices such as the "Ultra Project" targeting football fans at national and international level
- projects at the international level, for example:
  a. the Peace Games which aims to promote peace through sport and other recreational activities in areas of crisis in Africa, Middle East and the Balkans
  b. the campaign '*Una speranza per il futuro*' (A hope for the future) which provides funds for the reconstruction of a sport camp in Mostar.[27]

Before the influx of migrants to Italy, racism in Italian football was, oddly, re-served for separating, at least geographically, fans supporting clubs based in the north from those in the southern part of the country. The *mezzogiorno* clearly reflects an unusual racial ideology, according to which northern Italians call, indiscriminately, their neighbors in the south "*Negro di Merda*." Political parties like the *Lega Nord*, which promoted the secession of Italy's northern provinces, ascribed to the notion of regionalism a wholly different interpretation, thus add-ing a new dimension to football rivalries. With the notable exception of these regional antagonisms, however, the only visible form of racism concerned the anti-Semitic sentiments of SS Lazio fans against city rivals AS Roma. While SS Lazio fans would openly express their antithesis to the Jewish past of AS Roma, supporters of the latter would gradually incline to the extreme right too, since a "long struggle took place over the 'control' of Roma's curva sud, with a shift towards extremist far-right politics."[28] Eventually, fans of the capital's dominant football clubs would revert to an inherently racist conduct as black players in the Stadio Olimpico were always greet with banana missiles, monkey chanting and fascist salutes, particularly from SS Lazio fans. At this point, it is important to note that the *curva* denotes a part of the stadium's terraces that is occupied by a club's fanatic supporters, a sort of sacred territory that necessitated protection from all things foreign to the game, therefore, encouraging racist and xenopho-bic stereotypes. The following account is telling:

> From the end of the 1980s, simultaneous to the rise of political movements overtly including a xenophobic component such as the Northern League (due to the increase of intolerance in Italian society towards new immigrants), and together with the growth of skinhead and extreme rightist movements, stadia saw the expotential growth of racist choruses, the exhibition of Nazi or fascist symbols and of open-ly anti-Semitic banners. Outside the stadia the increasingly system-atic involvement of ultra groups in actions characterised by racial or political intolerance could be detected (beatings of black people and leftist militants, fire attacks against hostels for foreigners or social centres etc.). In this period the racist and xenophobic tendencies that had long been latent in the civil society started to explode and to be-come more visible. This happened in the curve of certain stadia of Northern Italy, where the growth of an anti-Southern feeling in stadia preceded and accompanied the birth and development of an openly xenophobic and separatist movement such as the Northern League, also acting as booster in the strengthening of identity based on ethnic differences. In Italian curve, this local racism coexists with classical racism against those who are considered to be strangers who do not belong to the national community. Insults against people from the South are not chanted exclusively by groups supporting the Northern League; on the contrary, they are also adopted by the Northern sup-porters of the nationalistic (as opposed to separatist) tendency, such as Verona, Inter, Piacenza and so on.[29]

Sadly, racial discrimination mirrored the methodical recruitment of fans to right-wing parties as well. Markedly, "the demonstration of the evident mixture between right-wing politics and football comes from the numerous career opportunities offered to some ultra leaders because of their ability to supply votes and gaining a consensus among young people. There are, for example, Parliamentary Members belonging to National Alliance who come from the Verona curva supporters. But it is above all inside the local governments that the presence of subjects connected to xenophobic and racist movement is observed. In Rome, for example, during the administrative elections of November 1993, a total of thirteen elected representatives belonging to right-wing lists came from the Roma and Lazio curva supporters."[30]

The involvement of political movements in Italian football materialized in the 1970s, when both the right and left infiltrated fan groups, thus producing the necessary grounds for the emergence of the *ultras*—groups of fans that should not be confused with hooligans, since their formation was much dependent on political ideology. The *ultras* initially reflected political developments in Italy, but when order was restored these groups of fans reverted to extremism, ultimately culminating in racism against immigrants. One such group in particular, SS Lazio's *Irriducibili*, never hesitated to advertise its inclination to fascism (SS Lazio was supposedly supported by the Italian dictator Benito Mussolini) by means of displaying racist banners and degrading black football players. Interestingly, "the increasingly politicised racism of this group emerged just as immigration to the region of Lazio itself increased,"[31] thus rendering the *Irriducibili* "a prominent example of a politically motivated racist ultra group," eager to make use of "standard nationalistic and supranational notions of race and whiteness."[32] In an attempt to eradicate racism from football, the Italian Football Federation introduced relevant measures prohibiting "all banners bearing racist slogans in the stadiums in 2000. The measure itself, however, has never been applied, and no match was ever suspended because of racist banners or abuse, even if banners still continue to appear."[33] It suffices to say that racism, too, continues to blacken the reputation of the popular game in Italy.

Netherlands
The population of the Netherlands, yet another west colonial power, is heterogeneous. Reflecting her political system is multiculturalism and relevant initiatives for the integration of distinct ethnic communities. Nevertheless, the rise of right-wing parties in the late 1990s signaled a new era whereby "local authorities began to reduce activities and resources spent on multicultural sports initiatives. What had been the twin objectives of the integration of ethnic minorities into mainstream Dutch sports provision on the one hand, and the promotion of ethnic sporting groups on the other, gave way to a simple emphasis on the former approach.

Schemes such as *Als racisme wint, verliest de sport* (If racism wins, sport loses), a multimedia campaign and development of a special commission for complaints on racism in sport; and the provision of advisors by provincial and municipal governments in the 1990s, have all been subject to financial cutbacks in the current decade. Also in the 1990s, the National Olympic Committee and national sports federations, in close cooperation with NPS, a Dutch national broadcasting service, broadcast a series of programmes entitled *Nieuwe sporters; Nieuw kader* (New sportsmen; new volunteers). These were television documentaries about the ways in which sport clubs operate (practice, rules, costs, subscription fees, volunteering, decision making, etc.) which were broadcasted during hours reserved for minorities."[34]

Similarly to France, the Dutch national football team underlines the multicultural depth of the Dutch society, given that a significant number of players claim Surinamese origins. However, this should not suggest that racism in Dutch football is non-existent or, at least, limited to insignificant proportions. On the contrary, it has been reported that "at the 1996 European Championship white and non-white Holland players had such a public quarrel that, according to news reports, on the pitch they preferred to pass to members of their own cliques and did not speak to each other off the pitch."[35] It is worthy of note, nonetheless, that the overall impact of Surinamese footballers on Dutch football has been, and still is, immense, if one takes into consideration the football geniuses that answer to the names of Davids, Gullit, Kluivert, Rijkaard and Seedorf. As a matter of fact, the athletic performance of non-white players was duly noted, since in 1960 the first Surinamese footballer made his debut sporting the colors of the Dutch national team. Even though migrant football players play for Dutch clubs ever since the 1950s, it was really the 1980s that saw their numbers rise rapidly, particularly following the independence of Surinam in 1975. It was the 1990s, however, when Dutch football witnessed unprecedented numbers of migrants playing their football for Dutch clubs, immediately after the Bosman affair. Still, "people of immigrant descent continue to be significantly underrepresented in the referee corps and in positions outside of the playing field."[36]

Anti-Semitism, too, continues to mark Dutch football. Ajax FC, in particular, is often targeted by rival fans—usually those supporting Feyenoord Rotterdam—because of the club's alleged Jewish past. Elsewhere in the country, anti-Semitism continues to jeopardize the multicultural identity of the Netherlands, therefore, highlighting the ambivalent stance of the Dutch people in the times of Nazi occupation.

Spain

Immigration in Spain is a relatively recent phenomenon and so are the relevant integration policies that are in place today, particularly those concerning sporting activities. Evidently, "there appears to be little or no published literature on policy and provision of sporting services for ethnic minorities in Spain at the national level. At the regional level, each Community decides its own policy regarding sport provision for immigrants, refugees and asylum seekers. The Communities with highest levels of immigration have been among the first to include immigrants in sport policy formulation. It must be stressed that these are the first examples of including immigrants in sport policy, and policy development is still in its infancy. There were no clear examples of sport and immigration programmes as such. Rather, ad hoc collaborations existed between voluntary and regional/local level public sector organisations. In Catalonia, for example, "the Generalitat (regional autonomous government for Catalonia) has included immigration in its sports policy, stating that: *'sport is probably one of the most effective means of integration. When we take part in sport we are all equal, and so cultural, ethnic and racial differences disappear. Thanks to sport, we are able to create links with immigrants that can be maintained in day to day life.'*"[37]

However, the Spanish Football Federation remains inactive, if not apathetic, to the racist incidents that have thus far troubled football players and officials during match day. One black footballer who has suffered much from racist abuse while playing for FC Barcelona away from home is Samuel Eto'o. The player from Cameroon has been decorated for his football skills on quite a few occasions, yet his credentials seem to vanish the moment he steps onto the pitch of another club, as rival fans rarely waste time in degrading the gifted footballer. In a far worse incident, the manager of the Spanish national football team never hesitated or regretted insulting another football superstar, Frenchman Thierry Henry, as mentioned below.

Eastern Europe and Balkans

Much unlike their western counterparts, countries in east Europe and the Balkan peninsula remained comparatively homogeneous throughout the Cold War era and have only just been experiencing the effects of globalization as a result of the fall of communism. Fans supporting clubs from Bulgaria, Croatia, Hungary, Poland, Romania, Russia and Serbia, to name a few, have recently demonstrated their racist conduct on more than one occasion, more often than not denigrating black football players with horrific remarks. Needless to say, as with west European states, fans in these parts of the continent frequently express their extreme nationalistic sentiments—a likely derivative of the Cold War oppression—that are occasionally accompanied by anti-Semitic views. As one might expect, racist behavior is also extended to games involving national sides, particularly when facing opposition from west Europe, since the latter are more likely to field a non-white football player. Furthermore, taking into account the fact that nationalism has only recently been revived in the countries that were once under the influence of the former Soviet Union, it is anything but surprising to ascertain that football matches at the national level symbolize more than a game. Restricted to supporting their country in an orderly fashion that evokes dictatorial measures, the termination of authoritarianism generated enough enthusiasm among these people so as to communicate their national identity in the most despicable manner. While such conduct should not be condoned in any way, it is just about understandable, given the conditions in which extreme nationalism was allowed to grow.

International level
Football matches at the international level differ little from those games contested between clubs, as far as the teams' composition is concerned. The sheer fact that even the more homogeneous, predominantly "white" countries, such as Greece, Italy and Sweden, have in the past featured black players speaks volumes of the diversity that characterizes the majority of European nations. Yet the more nationalistic east European populations, particularly the more fanaticized fans, seldom let the opportunity to emphasize skin-color differences pass when attending football matches at the international level. The same "imagined communities" Benedict Anderson considers nations to represent become very real and vibrant when confined to the terraces of a football stadium, habitually resorting to xenophobic rhetoric in order to stress their supremacy, albeit deceivingly.

Black players representing England have been racially abused in Spain, Slovakia, Spain and the Former Yugoslav Republic of Macedonia, for example, just as black footballers that represented France and the Netherlands in Euro 2004 were degraded by Croatian and German fans respectively. Unfortunately, the same football tournament witnessed the ill-conceived display of fascist symbols from Spanish, German and Italian fans. Interestingly, the English fans who abused the supporters and players of Turkey's national football team while playing at home in April 2003, which forced the European football governing body to fine the English Football Association, were not much different from the fans who condemned the humiliation of their players during matches abroad. The incident that deserves attention, nevertheless, concerns the racist remarks of Spain manager Luis Aragones. Prior to facing England at the Bernabeu stadium in Madrid, the Spanish coach had called Thierry Henry a "black shit" in a bizarre attempt to build the confidence of Cesc Fabregas, Henry's teammate at Arsenal FC. When the friendly game between the two nations took place, the Spanish fans erupted in an unprecedented cacophony redolent of racism. While Aragones never really apologized to the Frenchman, the Spanish Football Federation was merely fined 100,000 Swiss francs.

Playing positions

Should one decide to excuse the racist conduct of fans in an endeavor to comprehend their patriotic sentiments and frustration that results from the threat that
migrants (mistakenly) seem to pose to society or, at least, attribute their obvious
anti-social behavior to ignorance and the apparent fear of the unknown, the supposed advocate of those fans would surely find it difficult to defend the position
of certain managers who question the biological suitability of non-white players
to the game of football.

As derogative and unintelligent as they may appear, some managers are
likely to make observations that clearly reflect their limited understanding of a
player's qualities, now and then commenting that "black players can't play in
cold"; "while skillful they lack the grit and determination of their white counterparts"; "black players have attitude problems, are lazy and give insufficient application to the game."[38] To make certain that this issue attracts the attention it
deserves, it is imperative to quote a few authors who have already explored this
delicate matter before this astonishing form of racism is properly discussed.

Liz Crolley and David Hand argue that

> a characteristic frequently ascribed to black footballers as a group is
> that of physical power. Their strength is frequently commented upon,
> with references to their physique being commonplace.[39]

The two authors also report that

> one of the most enduring myths of white, Western civilisation, is that
> of naturally athletic, strong, powerful, aggressive and frightening
> black male—the origins of this myth may be traced to the colonial era
> when media accounts and cultural representations of blacks portrayed
> them as aggressive, potentially savage and uncivilised, providing the
> spurious moral justification for colonisation. The stereotype forever
> associating blacks with the body is often brought into sharper focus
> by modern media sports texts' insistence on contrasting black foot-
> ballers' physical attributes with their implicitly superior white col-
> leagues' disciplined capacities. Just as the vocabulary of physical
> power and strength is made to work overtime in sections of match re-
> ports and articles describing black players, it is conversely the vo-
> cabulary of discipline, control and the intellect that features highly
> when white players are discussed.[40]

Collin King, in his turn, stresses that

> this propensity to adopt a biological approach to racism and sport has
> led to the placement of black players into specific positions on the
> sports field because of their racial attributes. This practice of placing
> black players in limited intellectual positions has been noted in the

playing positions of English soccer, where a high percentage of black players placed on the wing or in centre-forward positions. They [Merill and Melnick (1988) and McGuire (1991)] suggest that white coaches see the black body as only operating through natural speed and physical strength and unable to be trusted to make decisions in vital positions in midfield.[41]

Richard Giulianotti, therefore, has good reasons to believe that

> fan racism is less problematic to black players than their maltreat-ment by more powerful football figures, since football coaches and officials decide when the non-white player can play. Soccer players are stacked into "central" or "non-central"/ "peripheral" positions. Central players form the team spine of goal-keeper, sweeper, mid-field play-maker, centre forward. They represent its "intelligent cen-tre," shaping the pattern of play according to the team's ability and the demands of each match. Peripheral players, such as full-backs and wingers, are valued intellectually, although their athleticism and indi-vidualism are vital in exploiting width, especially in attack. Black players tend to be "stacked" into these peripheral positions due to their coaches' racial beliefs that they cannot match the decision-making skills or consistency of white players, although their speed and unpredictable style are essential on the wings. Thus, football coaches and the media tend to assume that black players possess er-ratic qualities ("natural ability"), while white players have more con-trollable capabilities ("hard work" or "dedication").[42]

Regarding another group of non-white footballers, Giulianotti main-tains that

> Asian players that advance to the youth leagues or to trials with pro-fessional clubs find that they are played consistently out of position by white coaches who expect little from them. One problem in eluci-dating player stacking is that football coaches and players have long associated particular nationalities with specific playing qualities. Fu-ture research into positional segregation and racism would do well to recognize the complexity of this issue.[43]

Gianluca Vialli and Gabriele Marcotti's line of thought, too, reflects much the same perspective as the authors mentioned above. However, their contribution probably merits more weight, for Vialli displays a wealth of experience, having been both a player and manager in England. The two suggest that

> there is clear belief that black footballers are more athletic. This idea is rarely discussed publicly in England, unlike Italy, where, in many ways, it is accepted as fact. I don't think it's hard to understand why: England is a far more diverse and multi-racial society than Italy and

> it's a more sensitive issue because of the underlying implications. If blacks are naturally better athletes than whites, it's as if they have a God-given advantage, and this belittles their achievements: it implies that whites must have to work that much harder to compete with blacks. Or that blacks can afford to be lazy.[44]

They also add that

> this is close to ugly, long-held racial stereotypes and understandably makes people uncomfortable, particularly because of what some might see as the next logical step in this thinking: if blacks are more blessed in one department (athletic ability) surely they must be deficient in another (intelligence). Of course, this thinking is very far from the truth and highly dangerous. But there are differences between black and white players.[45]

Censuring the likes of these managers for their unethical approach to the beautiful game or even seeking legal retribution by reason of their noticeable lack of professionalism is no remedy to the problem. Despite compromising the whole notion of impartiality here, bar the odd remark revealing some empathy, the present author feels compelled to indicate that comparing white athletes to black or Asian—based entirely on biological practices—could only resemble veterinarians having a discussion over distinct breeds of dogs in an attempt to determine properties such as fitness, strength and speed.

Evidently, Giulianotti has every reason to argue that this form of racism is far more problematic. The ignorance and lack of understanding—as regards the professional relationship between manager and player—would, indeed, be a major obstacle to overcome for any colored footballer. However, there are notable examples of black football players exceeding "expectations" at the ultimate level football competitions. The four semi-finalists, for instance, of the 2007-2008 Champions League competition involved three English clubs and Spanish giants FC Barcelona. The latter featured the much-admired Samuel Eto'o (a great striker with unsurpassable football skills), Thierry Henry (yet another talented forward), Lilian Thuram (central and right-wing defender), Éric Abidal (left-wing defender) and Yaya Touré (central midfielder), all coached by Surinamese manager Frank Rijkaard, who celebrated two Spanish league titles (2005 and 2006) and the 2006 Champions League during his stay at the Catalan club. As for the English clubs, Manchester United FC featured Patrice Evra (left-wing defender), Louis Saha (forward), Wes Brown (right-wing and central defender), Anderson (central midfielder), Nani (left-wing midfielder), Rio Ferdinand (central defender) and Mikale Silvestre (left-wing and central defender), as well as two Asian football players, namely, Ji-Sung Park (right-wing and central midfielder) and Fangzhuo Dong (forward); Chelsea FC included Ashley Cole (left-wing defender), Michael Essien (central midfielder), Claude Makelélé (central midfielder), Mikel John Obi (central midfielder), Shaun Wright-Phillips (right-wing midfielder), Florent Malouda (left-wing midfielder), Salomon Kalou (forward), Nicolas Anelka (forward) and Didier Drogba (forward); and, finally, Liverpool FC had a roster that contained Jermaine Pennant (right-wing midfielder), Damien Plessis (central midfielder), Charles Itandje (goalkeeper) and Ryan Babel (forward). Just as there is no question about the caliber of any one of the football clubs mentioned above, considering their success at home and abroad, the competence of the footballers employed by them is beyond doubt. Moreover, the fact that the aforementioned players cover all possible playing positions on the football pitch is evidence enough to suggest that all myths and stereotypes associating race to skill and intellect are utterly inaccurate and unsubstantiated.

Union of European Football Associations
As Europe's supreme football governing body, the Union of European Football Associations (UEFA) stresses that "national associations have a vital role to play in acknowledging problems that may exist, encouraging the implementation of the UEFA ten-point plan for professional clubs, and setting out clear codes of conduct against racism, including disciplinary sanctions against players, clubs or officials who contravene those codes."[46] One would assume that UEFA has had little contribution to the campaign against racism, since it recommends the mere implementation of the recently devised ten-point plan, at the same time transferring the burden of responsibility on the national football associations. It goes without saying that the involvement of UEFA in the campaign against racism is instrumental. What is noteworthy, concerning the role of UEFA in the elimination of racism from football, is the organization's clearly identifiable understanding of not only the phenomenon of racism in football, but also the potential remedies available. Three issues, in particular, deserve mention here. First, it is important to note that UEFA's officials are aware of the role fans and fan culture can play in all anti-racist campaigns. More precisely, UEFA argues that

> while it's undoubtedly true that some football supporters are perpetrators of racist abuse against players and other fans, it would be too easy to stereotype fans in general as "the problem". In fact, as most people will acknowledge it is always a minority among supporters who take part in racist activity, whether it's abuse and chanting or something more physical and menacing. However, it is also true that football fans have always been at the start of attempts to combat racism. If, sometimes, they are the problem, they are also the solution. In many European nations it has been the actions of fans that have kick-started other members of the football family into taking notice, and taking action. Fans create the atmosphere and passion that make football unique. It's their culture and it's from the spirit of this culture that the most effective attempts to combat racism arise.[47]

Equally important, from UEFA's standpoint, is the role of football clubs. In this respect, UEFA brings to our attention the fact that

> as football clubs become larger organisations with multi-faceted operations so their responsibility as employers and exemplars of good community relations grow. Many are also employers and it is important that they operate "equal opportunities" policies, that they encourage people from ethnic minorities to apply for jobs, involve those communities in outreach work and develop community partnerships. In parts of Western Europe some clubs are looking beyond the moral reasons for working for equality and are increasingly aware of the potential commercial benefits of engaging with previously excluded communities.[48]

As a final point, with reference to the all-important concept of integration, UEFA acknowledges that

> involving ethnic minority fans and migrant groups in campaigns against racism in football is vitally important. One of the most striking aspects of all European football is the discrepancy between the high number of black players on the field and the lack of black faces in the crowd.[49]

Unsurprisingly, UEFA has been anything but apathetic in the campaign against racism in football. As the relevant documentation suggests, UEFA has already explored the issue of football-related racism across the continent; however, the European football governing body is not entirely well-equipped in combating racism alone, thus the need to involve the national football associations in a far more committable scheme such as the implementation of the ten-point plan.

UEFA's *Ten Point Plan of Action for Professional Football Clubs*, as is formally recognized, stipulates the following recommendations:

> 1. Issue a statement saying the club will not tolerate racism, spelling out the action it will take against those engaged in racist chanting. The statement should be printed in all match programmes and displayed permanently and prominently around the ground.
>
> 2. Make public address announcements condemning racist chanting at matches.
>
> 3. Make it a condition for season ticket holders that they do not take part in racist abuse.
>
> 4. Take action to prevent the sale of racist literature inside and around the ground.

5. Take disciplinary action against players who engage in racial abuse.

6. Contact other clubs to make sure they understand the club's policy on racism.

7. Encourage a common strategy between stewards and police for dealing with racist abuse.

8. Remove all racist graffiti from the ground as a matter of urgency.

9. Adopt an equal opportunities policy in relation to employment and service provision.

10. Work with all other groups and agencies, such as the players union, supporters, schools, voluntary organisations, youth clubs, sponsors, local authorities, local businesses and police, to develop proactive programmes and make progress to raise awareness of campaigning to eliminate racial abuse and discrimination.[50]

The intention of UEFA to rid football of racism notwithstanding, it suffices to say that not all football clubs, if any, will adhere with much vigor to the scheme proposed by the European football governing body.

The first item of the ten-point plan requires minimum resources; nevertheless, it is almost certain that a significant number of clubs simply fails to include such a statement in the match day programs for various reasons that will not be addressed here. The same probably applies to the second and third points, as the public address announcements are more likely to be reserved for advertisements, while monitoring the behavior of season ticket holders is not always feasible. Similarly, patrolling the stadium to avoid the dissemination of racist material is again difficult, as stewards and police officers are expected to maintain the safety of spectators, players and other match officials by searching all fans, particularly, known hooligans. From the same point of view, the seventh item is deemed equally complex to implement, given the stewards and police officers' priorities before, during and after a football game. Further down the list, contacting "other clubs to make sure they understand the club's policy on racism" is unnecessary, since no club can provide guarantees regarding the conduct of the visiting crowd. Removing racist graffiti and drafting a document that would stand for the "equal opportunities" policy of a club are, presumably, the only items on UEFA's ten-point plan that could be widely applied throughout the continent with relative ease, though the present author reserves the right to remain skeptical. On the whole, the vast majority of UEFA's recommendations have probably never been endorsed extensively, even though carrying out these points necessitates little energy.

Points five and ten were only briefly set aside, for they deserve our uninterrupted attention. The need to "take disciplinary action against players who engage in racial abuse" is imperative, yet the implications arising from measures like this may prove detrimental to players and club alike. The player is likely to invite criticism from rival fans and football players when playing away from home, whereas the club will probably witness the value of its "asset" decline. In either case, both club and player will suffer much, financially and emotionally, thus the apprehension toward item five of the UEFA-sponsored ten-point plan. The final item is equally significant, merely because should any club decide to improve its standing within its immediate environment, the attempt alone would bring closer together people otherwise segregated in society. Apart from serving the club's publicity and increasing its revenue, conditional on success in increasing ethnic minority attendance, collaboration between football clubs and all pertinent actors is surely welcomed for it can only benefit the game—provided that the ultimate objective is to promote integration, along with raising awareness about racism. In this respect, the campaign against racist abuse and discrimination is less likely to fall short.

From the above, it stems that further action was necessary from the side of Europe's football governing body. Following the second Unite Against Racism conference, therefore, UEFA published the "Tackling Racism in Club Football" report, which was, in essence, a guide concentrated upon the following principles:

> UNDERSTAND THE PROBLEM—It is easy to argue that issues such as racism are not within the domain of your club, that they are broader societal issues which should be left to other authorities. Most clubs will find it helpful for key staff to undergo an awareness training programme.

> BE CLEAR ABOUT YOUR OBJECTIVES—Are you running a campaign to tackle racist chanting, or to reach out to local ethnic minority communities, or both? Develop principles for action that can be widely publicised, that all internal and external stakeholders within the club can support. Encourage publicity and ownership of these ideas.

> WRITE A PLAN OF ACTION—Include practical outcomes for implementing your objectives. Use the UEFA ten-point plan as a basis for the measures your club can take. Set targets for progress and monitor regularly.

> DEVELOP A CLEAR IDENTITY for your campaign, to help recognition and spread ownership among supporters. You may wish to develop a specific brand name.

> MONITOR AND REPORT PROBLEMS—Develop systems for monitoring and reporting racial abuse and discrimination in all areas of your club.

PARTNERSHIPS—Work with fans, players, stewards, NGOs and community organisations with expertise in the field to implement your action plan. Make sure you involve ethnic minority and migrant communities.

FAN CULTURE—Use the culture and traditions of fans to help get your message across. Use message boards and other media associated with fans.

USE YOUR ICONS—Draw on the support and appeal of players to endorse anti–racist and anti–discriminatory messages.

MEDIA ACTIVITIES—Work with the media to publicise your activities.

ENCOURAGE NEW AUDIENCES—Work towards making your club as open as possible. Take specific measures that encourage ethnic minorities, migrants and women to get involved as fans, players and employees.[51]

All in all, the contribution and commitment of UEFA to the eradication of racism from football seem praiseworthy; nonetheless, its relevant policies remain largely ineffective, predominantly due to their lack of application and the sheer absence of harsh measures that would, hopefully, prevent such racist conduct in the future.

The European Union response
Xenophobia, intolerance and discrimination of all forms jeopardize the stability of the superstructure better known as the European Union. Considering that cultural diversity is central to the aspirations of European Union officials—*"united in diversity"* is the European Union's catchphrase—the elimination of racism has already become the dominant feature of those policies pertaining to further integration. Continuous enlargement and the amalgamation of populations from new member states have long defined the purpose of the European Union, however, political forces persist on challenging the interpretation of 'ever closer Union' inasmuch as certain parties, not to mention governments, oppose supranationalism, while attributing an almost authoritarian meaning to the concept of assimilation. As you would have thought, reducing this seemingly undesirable, if not destructive, political influence—including its impact on sports—is imperative.

In the case of sports, football in particular, social inclusion may be facilitated through relevant activities by means of encouraging members of ethnic minorities to strengthen relations with the native population. There is no question that "part of the social function of sport is to foster integration and to bring people together from different cultural or ethnical backgrounds. Nevertheless, it cannot be ignored that sports events have often witnessed outbreaks of racism and xenophobia. This is part of a more general problem in society, also sometimes related to the problem of hooliganism. In addition to the essential work that must be done on an educational level, racism and xenophobia have to be dealt with through a combination of criminal (state) laws and disciplinary (sporting) measures (e.g., sanctions against clubs) in order to effectively deter such conduct."[52] Hence, the European Union must move heaven and earth to obliterate with effect whatever differences separate distinct groupings of people, for the notion of integration may otherwise be held captive of the same dynamics that currently undermine it. In this direction, the European Parliament produced on 14 March 2006 a written declaration on tackling racism in football. The declaration reads:

> The European Parliament,
> having regard to Rule 116 of its Rules of Procedure,
> A. recognising the serious incidents of racism that have occurred in football matches across Europe,
> B. whereas one of the objectives pursued by the European Union under Article 13 of the EC Treaty is protection against discrimination based on ethnic origin and nationality,
> C. whereas football players, like other workers, have the right to a racism-free working environment, as set down in the case-law of the Court of Justice of the European Communities,
> D. whereas football's popularity offers a new opportunity to tackle racism,
> 1. Strongly condemns all forms of racism at football matches, both on and off the field;
> 2. Commends the excellent work that organisations such as UEFA and FARE (Football Against Racism in Europe) have done in tackling these problems;
> 3. Calls on all those with a high profile in football to speak out regularly against racism;
> 4. Calls on national football associations, leagues, clubs, players' unions and supporters' groups to apply UEFA best practice, such as the UEFA Ten-Point Plan of Action;
> 5. Calls on UEFA and all other competition organisers in Europe to ensure that referees have the option, according to clear and strict guidelines, of stopping or abandoning matches in the event of serious racist abuse;

6.   Calls on UEFA and all other competition organisers in Europe to consider the option of imposing sporting sanctions on national football associations and clubs whose supporters or players commit serious racist offences, including the option of removing persistent offenders from their competitions;

7.   Instructs its President to forward this declaration, together with the names of the signatories, to the Council, the Commission, the governments of the Member States and UEFA.[53]

What prompted the Members of the European Parliament to adopt the above resolution, other than the unmistakable need to cleanse the popular game, was the determined lobbying of the Football Against Racism in Europe (FARE) staff and their relentless Europe-wide campaign against racism in football. While the following chapter discusses in detail the nature and scope of the Football Against Racism in Europe anti-racism organization, it is important to note at this point that the pan-European organization that is FARE is sponsored by the European Commission and was, in fact, established at the initiative of the latter.

Naturally, the European Union and, particularly, the European Parliament— as, perhaps, the most "democratic" of all EU institutions—cannot possibly allow racial discrimination to grow, thus their commitment to combat racism in football. Making good use of the game's mass appeal should provide officials at national and supranational levels with the opportunity to promote further interaction among people from different ethnic backgrounds.

Notes

1. Roman Horak, "Austrification as Modernization: Changes in Viennese Football Culture," in *Game Without Frontiers: Football, Identity and Modernity*, ed. Richard Giulianotti and John Williams (Aldershot: Arena, 1994), 63.

2. Gerry Finn and Richard Giulianotti, eds., *Football Culture: Local Conflicts, Global Visions* (London and Portland: Frank Cass Publishers, 2000), 261.

3. Liz Crolley and David Hand, *Football, Europe and the Press* (London and Portland: Frank Cass Publishers, 2002), 43.

4. Richard Giulianotti, *Football: A Sociology of the Global Game* (Polity Press, 1999), 160.

5. Giulianotti, *Football: A Sociology of the Global Game*, 161.

6. Jon Garland and Michael Rowe, *Racism and Anti-Racism in Football* (Basingstoke and New York: Palgrave, 2001), 93.

7. Bart Vanreusel, "Football, Racism and Xenophobia in Belgium: Racist Discrimination and Anti-Racist Responses," in *Racism and Xenophobia in European Football*, ed. Udo Merkel and Walter Tokarski (Aachen: Meyer & Meyer, 1996), 70.

8. Vanreusel, "Football, Racism and Xenophobia in Belgium: Racist Discrimination and Anti-Racist Responses," 74.

9. European Commission, DG Education & Culture, Studies on Education and Sport, *Sport and Multiculturalism*, Final Report (A Report by PMP in partnership with the Institute of Sport and Leisure Policy, Loughborough University, August 2004), 10.

10. European Commission, DG Education & Culture, Studies on Education and Sport, *Sport and Multiculturalism*, Final Report, 11.

11. Jacco van Sterkenburg and Eelco Westland, "United Kingdom," in *Football and Racism: An Inventory of the Problems and Solutions in Eight West European Countries in the Framework of the Stand Up Speak Up Campaign*, ed. Jacco van Sterkenburg, Jan W. Janssens and Bas Rijnen (Nieuwegein: Arko Sports Media, 2005), 34.

12. Nick Lowles, "Far Out with the Far Right," in *Hooligan Wars: Causes and Effects of Football Violence*, ed. Mark Perryman (Edinburgh and London: Mainstream Publishing, 2002), 109.

13. Lowles, "Far Out with the Far Right," 113.

14. Les Back, Tim Crabbe and John Solomos, *The Changing Face of Football: Racism, Identity and Multiculture in the English Game* (Oxford and New York: Berg, 2001), 106.

15. Back, Crabbe and Solomos, *The Changing Face of Football: Racism, Identity and Multiculture in the English Game*, 107.

16. Lowles, "Far Out with the Far Right," 110.

17. Richard Haynes, "Marching on Together: Leeds United Fans and the Media," in *The Passion and the Fashion: Football Fandom in the New Europe*, ed. Steve Redhead (Aldershot: Avebury, 1993), 15.

18. Back, Crabbe and Solomos, *The Changing Face of Football: Racism, Identity and Multiculture in the English Game*, 255.

19. European Commission, DG Education & Culture, Studies on Education and Sport, *Sport and Multiculturalism*, Final Report, 11.

20. Nick Harris, *England, their England: The Definitive Story of Foreign Footballers in the English Game Since 1888* (East Sussex: Pitch Publishing, 2003), 146.

21. Patrick Mignon, "Le Francais Feelgood Factor," in *Hooligan Wars: Causes and Effects of Football Violence*, ed. Mark Perryman (Edinburgh and London: Mainstream Publishing, 2002), 168.

22. Jacco van Sterkenburg and Sylvain Ferez, "France," in *Football and Racism: An Inventory of the Problems and Solutions in Eight West European Countries in the Framework of the Stand Up Speak Up Campaign*, ed. Jacco van Sterkenburg, Jan W. Janssens and Bas Rijnen (Nieuwegein: Arko Sports Media, 2005), 52.

23. European Commission, DG Education & Culture, Studies on Education and Sport, *Sport and Multiculturalism*, Final Report, 11.

24. European Commission, DG Education & Culture, Studies on Education and Sport, *Sport and Multiculturalism*, Final Report, 12.

25. Udo Merkel, Kurt Sombert and Walter Tokarski, "Football, Racism and Xenophobia in Germany: 50 Years Later—Here We Go Again?" in *Racism and Xenophobia in European Football*, ed. Udo Merkel and Walter Tokarski (Aachen: Meyer & Meyer, 1996), 154.

26. Giulianotti, *Football: A Sociology of the Global Game*, 161.

27. European Commission, DG Education & Culture, Studies on Education and Sport, *Sport and Multiculturalism*, Final Report, 23.

28. John Foot, *Calcio, A History of Italian Football* (London: Fourth Estate, 2006), 310.

29. Carlo Podaliri and Carlo Balestri, "The Ultrás, Racism and Football Culture in Italy," in *Fanatics! Power, Identity and Fandom in Football*, ed. Adam Brown (London and New York: Routledge, 1998), 96.

30. Podaliri and Balestri, "The Ultrás, Racism and Football Culture in Italy," 97.

31. Anthony King, *The European Ritual: Football in the New Europe* (Aldershot: Ashgate, 2003), 235.

32. King, "The European Ritual: Football in the New Europe," 236.

33. Jacco van Sterkenburg and Ashley Green, "Italy," in *Football and Racism: An Inventory of the Problems and Solutions in Eight West European Countries in the Framework of the Stand Up Speak Up Campaign*, ed. Jacco van Sterkenburg, Jan W. Janssens and Bas Rijnen (Nieuwegein: Arko Sports Media, 2005), 82.

34. European Commission, DG Education & Culture, Studies on Education and Sport, *Sport and Multiculturalism*, Final Report, 12.

35. János Bali, "Ferencváros, Hungary and the European Champions League: The Symbolic Construction of Marginality and Exclusion," in *Fear and Loathing in World Football*, ed. Gary Armstrong and Richard Giulianotti (New York: Berg Publishers, 2001), 259.

36. Jan W. Janssens, "The Netherlands," in *Football and Racism: An Inventory of the Problems and Solutions in Eight West European Countries in the Framework of the Stand Up Speak Up Campaign*, ed. Jacco van Sterkenburg, Jan W. Janssens and Bas Rijnen (Nieuwegein: Arko Sports Media, 2005), 52.

37. European Commission, DG Education & Culture, Studies on Education and Sport, *Sport and Multiculturalism*, Final Report, 16.

38. Back, Crabbe and Solomos, *The Changing Face of Football: Racism, Identity and Multiculture in the English Game*, 174.

39. Crolley and Hand, *Football, Europe and the Press*, 40.

40. Crolley and Hand, *Football, Europe and the Press*, 41.

41. Colin King, *Offside Racism: Playing the White Man* (Oxford and New York: Berg, 2004), 10.

42. Giulianotti, *Football: A Sociology of the Global Game*, 162.

43. Giulianotti, *Football: A Sociology of the Global Game*, 163.

44. Gianluca Vialli and Gabriele Marcotti, *The Italian Job: A Journey to the Heart of Two Great Footballing Cultures* (London, Toronto, Sydney, Auckland and Johannesburg: Bantam Press, 2006), 33

45. Vialli and Marcotti, *The Italian Job: A Journey to the Heart of Two Great Footballing Cultures*, 34.

46. UEFA and FARE, *Unite Against Racism in European Football, UEFA Guide to Good Practice* (UEFA Communications and Public Affairs Division, June 2003), 12.

47. UEFA and FARE, *Unite Against Racism in European Football, UEFA Guide to Good Practice*, 16.

48. UEFA and FARE, *Unite Against Racism in European Football, UEFA Guide to Good Practice*, 25.

49. UEFA and FARE, *Unite Against Racism in European Football, UEFA Guide to Good Practice*, 26.

50. UEFA and FARE, *Unite Against Racism in European Football, UEFA Guide to Good Practice*, 37.

51. Second Unite Against Racism Conference, *Tackling Racism in Club Football, A Guide for Clubs* (Produced by FARE for UEFA, 2006), 14.

52. Jose Luis Arnaut, *Independent European Sport Review* (2006), 84.

53. European Parliament, Tackling Racism in Football, Written Declaration of the European Parliament on Tackling Racism in Football (Texts adopted at the sitting of 14 March 2006), 87.

Chapter Three

Football Against Racism in Europe

Kurt Wachter, Susanne Franke and Jacek Purski

History

We want to see the beautiful game played without the cancer of racism. Football is the biggest sport in the world and belongs to us all. It should be the right of every person to play, watch and discuss freely without fear. Unfortunately, at all levels of the game, from amateur to international, there are incidents of racism. Be it from fans, players, clubs or other football bodies, Football Against Racism in Europe (FARE) believes that such behavior, on and off the field, is unacceptable and unwanted by the majority of fans and players. Football Against Racism in Europe aims to rid the game of racism by combining the resources of anti-racist football organizations throughout Europe. It helps to support and nurture groups and coordinates efforts on a European scale. By working together, Football Against Racism in Europe helps organizations share good practice and present a united front against racism in football. We believe the color of a player or fan and from where he or she originates does not matter. Unfortunately, at all levels of the game, from amateur to international, there are still incidents of racism. These can take the form of abuse directed at a "foreign" player to the mass "monkey" chants of supporters. Football Against Racism in Europe will fight through football all forms of discrimination in football: in the stadium, on the pitch, in the changing room, at the training ground, in the office and classroom; by fans, players, managers, coaches, administrators or educators. Therefore in February 1999, on the initiative of supporters' groups from different regions of Europe, a meeting, which included football associations and players unions, was held in Vienna to develop a common strategy and policy against racism and xenophobia. Out of this emerged Football Against Racism in Europe—a network of organizations from thirteen European countries—and a plan of action. The Football Against Racism in Europe network dedicated itself to fighting racism and xenophobia in football across Europe. Through coordinated action and common effect, at local and national levels, we will bring together all those interested in combating discrimination in football.

35

Football Against Racism in Europe calls upon football governing bodies and clubs to:

- recognize the problem of racism in football;
- adopt, publish and enact anti-racist policy;
- make full use of football to bring people together from different communities and cultures;
- establish a partnership with all organizations committed to kicking racism out of football, in particular with supporters groups, migrants and ethnic minorities.

Football Against Racism in Europe commits itself to:

- challenging all forms of racist behavior in stadia and within clubs by making our voice(s) heard;
- including ethnic minorities and migrants within our organization and partner organizations;
- working together with all organizations willing to tackle the problem of racism in football.

The beginning of the 1990s saw the formation of various groups of differing backgrounds in response to the reappearance of racist organizations at many football grounds across Europe. All these groups had one thing in common: instead of looking the other way when a racist incident took place, they were determined to do something about it. In February 1999 many of these groups joined together to form the anti-racism network Football Against Racism in Europe. Football Against Racism in Europe now consists of more than three hundred groups in thirty-seven countries, including supporters' clubs, anti-racism organizations, migrant associations, players' unions and football clubs, etc. The aim was to develop a common strategy against the widespread phenomenon of racism in football and to link up for the purpose of organizing joint campaigns. FARE combats racist and sexist attitudes at every level of the game, be they in the stands, on the pitch, in the dressing rooms, on the training ground or in the directors' box. For the last seven years Football Against Racism in Europe organized Action Weeks Against Racism, and each year thousands of fans and clubs in almost every European country contribute a wide range of activities. The next Action Week takes place in October of 2009—get involved! Football Against Racism in Europe's work has since gained the recognition of several high-level organizations, with awards being received from UEFA, MTV and the European Monitoring Centre Against Racism and Xenophobia.

With the kind support of the Union of European Football Associations (UEFA), the Portuguese players' union and the Football Supporters International, a number of Football Against Racism in Europe staff were for the first time in attendance throughout the tournament. In several host cities Football Against

Racism in Europe, through its partner Football Unites, Racism Divides, will be setting up the Streetkick game in the immediate vicinity of the fans' embassies set up by the Football Supporters International. Here, fans from all over Europe will be able to join together with local people from the host venues in an atmosphere of tolerance and mutual respect. Of the three hundred or so Football Against Racism in Europe partners, ten are currently members of a core group that coordinates existing projects as well as launching new ones. For example, the *Bündnis Aktiver Fussballfans* (BAFF) from Germany, formed in 1993, is an alliance of more than two hundred individual members and fifty supporter groups (fanzines, projects, fan clubs, etc.) from different clubs. BAFF campaigns for the interests of supporters—it opposes all-seater stadia, the increasing repression of fans by police and stewards, the omnipotence of television, unreasonable kick-off times, price rises, pre-match entertainment etc.—and, in particular, against racism and discrimination in football. BAFF was the first organization to draw up a nine-point plan against racism, a standard anti-racism clause for inclusion in stadium regulations and a catalogue of demands against homophobia in football. The Target Stadium exhibition on the subject of racism and discrimination in football has been raising eyebrows since 2001.

The plague of football
Each season, national and European football competitions provide examples of the most blatant forms of racism and xenophobia. Racist incidents are witnessed on a weekly basis: the racial abuse of players by other players, xenophobic chants by fans and insults directed at black and other minority players, the display of racist banners and symbols in and around stadiums, and the dissemination of far-right messages all form part of an ever-recurring problem in football, one which is particularly prevalent in, but not limited to, Europe. Alongside these open forms of discrimination, there is a whole host of more subtle types of racism. These take the form of institutionalized or structural racism. In this type of racism, migrants and other minorities are excluded from all levels of football. To this day, ethnic minorities are underrepresented throughout Europe, whether as fans or spectators in the stadium, as active participants on the football pitch, or in the decision-making bodies of clubs and associations. Some European countries even have institutionalized forms of discrimination against foreigners in amateur football. In Austria, for example, rules have been in force since 1 July 2004 limiting the number of foreigners in amateur football to three per team. Under these rules, EU nationals are also considered foreigners. International institutions such as the Council of Europe and UEFA have called on the Austrian football authorities to amend these discriminatory rules. Similar rules apply in Italy and Spain.

Nowadays, open racism is primarily a feature of the lower leagues, in contrast to the 1980s, when a growing number of successful black players (e.g., Yeboah, Hartwig, Sané and Baffoe) emerged in Germany. Nonetheless, it remains a serious problem in premier league football. The UEFA EURO 2004 in Portugal proved racism was not a thing of the past in major events such as the Euro Championship or World Cup. The championship reached a low point during the group game between Croatia and France. During the game, up to 1,000 Croatia fans made repeated "jungle noises" directed at Sylvain Wiltord. Two Croatian banners featured the Celtic cross, a symbol of the international "white power" movement. During the Denmark-Italy game in the Guimarães stadium, a group of Italian fans gave the Italian fascist salute while their national anthem was being played. Racist "jungle noises" aimed at Edgar Davids could also be heard during the Germany-Holland match. Throughout the game, a crowd of German fans could be heard chanting the homophobic "Schwule, schwule Holländer" (Queer, queer Dutchmen). Finally, while the Portuguese line-up included several black players, among the spectators or stewards in the stadiums, ethnic minorities were conspicuous by their absence.

In the absence of quantitative data on the scale of racism in football, the situation in a number of countries and regions will be examined on the basis of recent events there. During the current football season, the Football Against Racism in Europe network has received dozens of reports of racist and right-wing extremist incidents in European football stadiums. Even the European football association UEFA and the international federation FIFA have issued fines and closed stadiums this season following racist incidents. The rise in the number of reported incidents could be seen as signaling a new wave of xenophobic behavior in stadiums. In most cases, however, increased awareness in the media and among the "silent majority" of fans may have led to a growing perception of the problem. Racist incidents that were once simply ignored or seen as "part of the game" now increasingly come to the attention of the public. This is partly the result of efforts in European football to raise awareness of, and campaign against, racism.

The most recent reports of racist incidents on a large scale come from Spain. First, faint monkey noises could be heard at a friendly match between Spain and England in Madrid on 17 November 2004, directed at black England players Cole, Jenas and Wright-Phillips. One week later, on 23 November, Roque Junior and Juan of Bayer Leverkusen were the target of racist abuse at the Champions League game against Real Madrid in the Bernabeu Stadium. Even one of the best players of the moment in Spain's premier division and African footballer of the year, Samuel Eto'o of FC Barcelona, regularly has to endure monkey noises directed at him during away games. At a match against Real Zaragoza on 12 February 2005, peanuts were thrown at him. Finally, FC Seville has also been penalized by UEFA for racist incidents during the UEFA Cup. In Italy, SS Lazio—notorious for its racist, far-right fans—is hardly ever out of the news. Lazio has been penalized by UEFA on three occasions for racism at European competitions, most recently following incidents at a match against Partizan

Belgrade on 23 November 2004. However, even during home games, racial abuse is par for the course at Lazio, something FARE staff saw for themselves when they visited the club in January 2005. True to form, on 6 January 2005, Lazio captain Di Canio greeted his fans with the fascist salute. Few remember events back in 2001, when, having been relegated by Hellas Verona, Lazio's president succumbed to pressure from fans and stopped signing dark-skinned players, and fans hung a black doll from the stand with a rope around its neck.

In France, Paris Saint-Germain fans used the start of Nike's anti-racism campaign on 6 February 2005 as an excuse not just to protest against the company, but also to direct monkey noises at black players from RC Lens and to wave racist banners. Poland striker of Nigerian descent Emmanuel Olisadebe was the victim of racist monkey noises during a match against Olympiakos in the terraces of Panathinaikos Athens on 4 December 2004.

Czech Republic Sparta Prague had to answer to UEFA for the racist behavior of its fans during the Champions League on 29 September 2004, while Poland's football scene is riddled with right-wing extremist groups. Fans regularly hurl bananas onto the pitch in order to provoke African players. In Romania, Rapid Bucharest is derided as a "gypsy" club. In Slovakia, racist incidents at a Euro championship qualification match against England received global coverage in October 2002. Meanwhile, in Hungary, black players for FC Millwall were the target of racial abuse during their UEFA Cup away game against Ferencváros Budapest in October 2004.

In Denmark, a campaign known as "Brondby supporters against racism" was launched in the summer of 2004 following repeated incidents in Brondby IF's stadium. The Gambian goalkeeper of Swedish team Djurgården has to endure constant racial abuse. Immigrant club Assyriska is a ray of light, having made it into the premier league. Because of its success, however, its players and fans wage a constant battle against discrimination. In Norway, there were reports of six racist incidents in its premier division in 2004.

Dutch team Ajax Amsterdam, which is seen as a "Jewish" club, has had to contend with the rising tide of anti-Semitism in Dutch football witnessed in recent years. Opposition fans can be heard chanting "Hamas, Hamas/Jews to the gas," or making hissing sounds to imitate gas being released. In October 2004, a match between ADO The Hague and PSV Eindhoven was called off following anti-Semitic chants, the first time such action was taken.

In Greece, the home of the European championships, an Albanian immigrant was stabbed to death on the island of Zakynthos by an enraged football fan following his country's defeat by Albania in September 2004.

Even England, which boasts a long tradition of combating racism in football, saw incidents of racist abuse in its premier league in November 2004. The victim was Dwight Yorke of Birmingham City.

"Xenophobic chants are increasingly common among the public, including in football stadiums. It is now becoming a greater problem in Germany again." That was the finding of sociologist and violence researcher Professor Gunther A.

Pilz in an interview with Spiegel online in December 2004. Pilz advises the German Football Federation (DFB) on fan behavior and culture. When it comes to regional differences in racism in German stadiums, he points out that "in the former East German states, chanting is much more blatant and aggressive." Racism in German football takes many forms. It ranges from blatant racial abuse against black players and blatant extreme right-wing displays to structural discrimination against immigrant players. To this day, professional football is affected by racism, which is particularly worrying given its cultural and political status. Nigerian Victor Agali—former player of FC Schalke 04—reported numerous incidents of racial abuse to the club's anti-racist fan's association Fan-Initiative e.V. "When I was 18, I couldn't understand it, I had no idea what these monkey noises meant. I had never come across it before." Brazilian player for Dortmund, Dede, even considered abandoning his career in Germany following racist incidents in 2002: "Once I don't feel safe here any more, I'll leave." Dede's team mate at Dortmund, Otto Addo, related an incident in Cottbus: "With Hannover 96, I had a match deciding promotion to the second division in Cottbus. My team mate Gerald Asamoah and I were subjected to a torrent of abuse, which was a traumatic experience for both of us." While he was the Nuremberg coach, the present-day trainer of Bayer Leverkusen criticized the racial abuse hurled by his own fans: "For me, some of our best players, Jacek Kryznowek, Anthony Sanneh and Louis Gomis, are given a very hard time just because they have a different skin color. It is unfair how they are treated."

Black players are not the only victims of racism in German national league stadiums. The Kaiserslautern forum www.der-betze-brennt.de reported the following racist incident at a match between FC Kaiserslautern and Hertha BSC in the Fritz-Walter stadium on 23 November 2003: "Unfortunately, there were a few more racist and Nazi chants from home fans. Apart from anti-Gypsy chants, vociferous anti-Turkish abuse was also hurled (the background to this was the Germany-Turkey under-21 match, in which FC Kaiserslautern goalkeeper Tim Wiese in particular was abused by the Turkish side). Fans began chanting 'We hate Turkey,' among other things." The forum of www.der-betze-brennt.de also reported cries of 'Sieg Heil' from home fans. The homepage of a project entitled "The ball doesn't care who kicks it" gives the following description of a cup match between Berlin's Hertha Amateure and Schalke 04 in the summer of 2004: "Well before the game got underway, numerous shady characters were stationed near the guest stand. For over 90 minutes, all they did was hurl insults at Schalke players. A string of long-forgotten anti-asylum seeker and gypsy chants, and one instance of the racist and homophobic 'You're so queer, asocial and queer . . . go home to Istanbul' could be heard from the mouths of many supporters."

Numerous German football clubs have links to far-right groups and skinheads, whose racist and violent chants can be heard more outside than inside the stadium. These groups continue to attract young football fans. One striking example is the far-right "Borussenfront" in Dortmund, which peaked toward the late 1980s: "By 2002, the Dortmund 'Borussenfront' had renewed links with the club. In May 2002, it attended a demonstration by fans against commercialization and repression in Berlin." On 23 November 2003, local newspaper the *Bürsche Zeitung* carried the following report on a trip by fans from Rostock to Gelsenkirchen (Schalke 04): "Police arrested sixteen Hansa Rostock fans said to have been bawling Nazi songs as they made their way from the station to the stadium." The professional German football scene continues to attract the far right and racism. However, with increased monitoring in the top two divisions, a worrying trend has emerged: racial abuse has shifted to the lower leagues in recent years. The following is just one example of many: "At the Berlin fourth division derby last week between Türkiyemspor and BFC Dynamo, BFC supporters, recognizable by their far-right uniform, hurled insults at Turkish guests, ranging from 'dirty wogs' to 'Allah is a pig.' Examples of repulsive behavior can be found throughout the country, down to the lowest division."

In Germany, many professional and amateur clubs and their fans have become active members of the FARE network in recent years. A good example is FC Schalke 04, who hosted the FARE conference in 2004. Well known for their commitment to the fight against racism, FC St. Pauli fans have been involved in FARE initiatives from the very start. Other clubs from Germany's top two divisions also organized anti-racist events during the two most recent pan-European FARE campaigns. These clubs include Borussia Dortmund, Borussia Mönchengladbach, Eintracht Frankfurt, 1. FC Kaiserslautern, FC Mainz 05, Hannover 96, 1860 Munich, Werder Bremen and MSV Duisburg. Events of this nature are still very much in demand, as can be seen by the success of the poster campaign organized by FC Schalke's fan association in North Rhine-Westphalia in October 2003. Some thirteen national, premier and women's league clubs took part in the campaign, and the teams posed for photographs under the motto "Show racism the red card."

The European football season of 2007-2008 had barely started when we witnessed a series of serious racist, xenophobic and far-right incidents. In Italy, notorious Lazio fans racially abused and attacked Senegal's international Dame N'Doye during a friendly match with Panathinaikos. Newcastle United supporters directed Islamophobic chants at Middlesbrough forward and Egyptian star Mido. In Hungary, former national coach Kalman Meszoly remarked during a TV interview about African players at Hungarian clubs saying, "they have barely come down from the trees." When Croatia played Bosnia and Herzegovina in Sarajevo, Croatian fans formed a human U symbol representing the fascist *Ustase* movement responsible for mass killings of Serbs, Jews and the Roma during World War II. Other incidents have been reported from Austria, France, Germany, Lithuania, Montenegro, the Russian Federation, Scotland, Serbia and Slovakia.

The FIFA conference against racism held in Buenos Aires in July 2001, attended by all 202 national football associations, demonstrated that racism, xenophobia, anti-Semitism and related forms of intolerance are a problem not just for European football, as the following overview demonstrates.

South America

Afro-Brazilian players have been allowed to play in professional clubs since 1918 and have been represented on the Brazilian national team since the 1950s, which does not mean Brazilian football is color-blind. There may be numerous black professional players, but Afro-Brazilian trainers, referees and officials are conspicuous by their absence. In Argentina, anti-Semitic abuse in stadiums by particular fan groups ("hinchas") is nothing unusual, especially in games involving Atlanta, a club from a Jewish area of Buenos Aires. Nor are officials free from prejudice: in July 2003, when asked in a television interview why there were no Jewish referees, the president of the Argentinean Football Association (AFA), Julio Gordona, replied: "To be a referee, you need to work hard, and Jews don't like this type of work." In all Latin American countries, indigenous population groups are underrepresented in the world of football.

Asia

At a friendly international football match between Iran and Germany in Teheran on 9 October 2004, thousands of Iranian fans greeted the German team with a Nazi salute. Without going into detail, only the Middle East conflict is mentioned here, which has had a major impact on football in a variety of ways. For example, the Iranian government banned Iranian FC Bayern player Hashemian from playing during the Champions League game between Maccabi Tel Aviv and Bayern Munich in September 2004.

Australia

To this day, "soccer" is as white-dominated a sport in multicultural Australia as the local Australian rules football. Racist graffiti and verbal abuse targeted at Aborigines pose a problem. As a result, the Australian players' union has been involved in anti-racism campaigns since 1999.

Africa

The South African Football Association was admitted as a member of FIFA after it ended its racist association policy in 1992. Since then, the South African football authorities have made strenuous efforts to open what is a traditionally "black" game to a white and Asian audience. In some sub-Saharan countries, ethnic conflicts have had an impact on football policy and the running of the game. A positive counterexample is Rwanda, which, ten years after the genocide there, qualified for the Africa Cup 2004 in Tunisia with a multi-ethnic team.

European support

Each season in national and European football, racism and xenophobia occur on a weekly basis. Abuse of players by other players, supporters chanting racial abuse inside and outside stadiums and the presence of far-right organizations trying to use football to disseminate their message are ongoing historical problems.

In an attempt to tackle this disturbing phenomenon, the first European anti-racist football network, Football Against Racism in Europe, was founded at the European Commission sponsored seminar "Networking Against Racism in European Football" in February 1999 in Vienna. More than forty different organizations including anti-racist sport projects, fan clubs, players' unions, football associations and ethnic minority groups from thirteen European countries affirmed their commitment to fight racism and all forms of discrimination throughout football. The Vienna Football Against Racism in Europe Plan of Action states clearly that "every individual has the right to participate at all levels of football free of discrimination, regardless of ethnic origin, nationality, color, religion, gender, sexuality or disability." Therefore, from its beginning Football Against Racism in Europe stressed not only the need for anti-racism, but also to tackle discrimination on a number of grounds and to take into recognition the diversity of approaches toward discrimination. The global passion for football and the intrinsic values of sports (team work, fair play etc.), together with the enormous media attention, makes football an ideal tool for anti-discrimination issues. The new Football Against Racism in Europe work program 2002-2004 was sponsored by the Community Action Program Against Discrimination, which took practical steps to address the taboo of discrimination based on sexual orientation in sports. With the support of the European Commission and the entire football family, Football Against Racism in Europe will continue make a positive and lasting impact on the problem across Europe and achieve its ultimate aim: to keep the people's game free from racism and discrimination.

European football's governing body, UEFA, is backing the European Parliament's drive to tackle the problem of racism in European football. A group of Members of the European Parliament has launched a declaration in Brussels commending the work of the Football Against Racism in Europe network and calling for tougher action. The declaration strongly condemns all forms of racism on and off the field, calls upon high profile players and coaches to speak up against the problem, and urges action programs by Football Associations, leagues, clubs, players' unions and supporters' groups. The declaration achieved the rare status of a motion, as the majority of the 732 Members of the European Parliament gave their backing. In a statement, the Members of the European Parliament said, "It is a sad reflection on our world that racism continues to blight the beautiful game. Football is not the cause of racism, but it is in our stadiums and on our pitches that some of the most visible and violent abuse takes place. We should see this as an opportunity. The massive popularity of football presents us with the means to reach millions of people and, we must hope, to promote tolerance and understanding. By winning hearts and minds on the terraces and on the pitch, we make a crucial breakthrough in the bigger battle to free society of racism. No one government or organization can fight racism alone.

It demands the support of every part of society, of every individual. It is a problem that requires close co-operation between the public and private spheres.

"In the world of football, a similar picture exists. Each member of the family—the associations, leagues, clubs, players, referees and supporters—has its role to play. That is why our declaration calls for a joint effort from everyone that cares about football. We take great encouragement from the work of UEFA, FARE and the other organizations that are committed to fighting racism in football. They have understood that football has a special responsibility—and again, an opportunity—to tackle the problem." The Members of the European Parliament concluded with a cautionary warning on complacency, "But now is not the time to relax. We can and must do more. The European Parliament should call on all those with a stake in football to join the fight against racism, and to do what they can in their community."

Similarly, UEFA stressed its desire to toughen sanctions against clubs with racist fans. In additional to UEFA's existing portfolio of sanctions, clubs, players and national associations could now face expulsion from the game's competitions. UEFA vice-president Per Ravn Omdal, said, "We are prepared to implement the necessary sanctions, from fines and closure of stadium, and even to not allow teams to participate at all." The start of the 2001-2002 football season was also the promising kick-off for a new partnership between the governing body of European football, UEFA, and organizations fighting the problem of racism in football. At the annual UEFA Gala in Monaco, CEO Gerhard Aigner presented its charity a check for 1 million Swiss francs to Football Against Racism in Europe, which was accepted by Juventus and France defender Lilian Thuram on behalf of Football Against Racism in Europe. The presentation of the UEFA charity award is recognition of the achievements of the cross-European work of Football Against Racism in Europe. It was also a vital step to sustaining anti-racist practices in countries where progress has been made, and developing new work in nations that are suffering problems.

The idea to campaign against racism in and through football was much less accepted back in January 1999, when the Football Against Racism in Europe network was founded. Fan groups, anti-racist non-governmental organizations (NGOs) and migrant and ethnic minority organizations from fourteen European countries came together for a seminar in Vienna to discuss the widespread neglect of the problem. The year 2001 saw a significant step forward, as football started to take responsibility for dealing with the issue. FIFA gathered all member associations in Buenos Aires for an anti-racism conference, whilst UEFA introduced stricter measures such as fines and stadium bans for racist behavior. Finally, UEFA awarded Football Against Racism in Europe with their charity check and started to work actively with Football Against Racism in Europe, which included, for instance, the familiarization of UEFA venue directors and match delegates with racist symbols inside stadiums. The year after Football Against Racism in Europe assisted UEFA in issuing a ten-point plan of action, which offers national associations, clubs and leagues a set of practical guidelines designed to prevent and combat racism in the game. UEFA also introduced a scheme to support anti-racist projects to be implemented by their fifty-two national member associations. With the support of UEFA, the European Commission and the entire football family across Europe, Football Against Racism in Europe will continue to make a positive and lasting impact on the problem across Europe.

While there may be positive progress to report in stadiums on issues of fan racism—and problems such as racially abusive chants and the growing presence of the far-right in stadiums—the more complex side of the problem also needs urgent action. These issues include the under-representation of ethnic minorities in stadiums, in administering the game and even as players. Some associations also strictly limit the number of "foreigners" in amateur football, therefore excluding migrants from playing in officially sanctioned leagues. A future part of Football Against Racism in Europe work is to engage closely with national associations and leagues to advise on how these problems can be overcome.

The campaign in Eastern Europe
Problems of racism, and anti-Semitism in particular, are a part of everyday life in Eastern Europe to an extent no longer encountered in Western states. The racist abuse directed at England's players in Bratislava was a high-profile case that brought the issue to the attention of the international football community. However, the problem of widespread racism in Eastern European football stadiums had existed long before and there had been warnings about the scale of the phenomenon, not least through the Football Against Racism in Europe network. Under those difficult circumstances there is a room for improving the situation. Football Against Racism in Europe is in a unique position to influence the situation in Eastern Europe by being able to use good experiences from Western European countries as well as local anti-racist expertise and contacts in the region. The large number of events in the framework of the 2003 Football Against Racism in Europe Action Week is an encouraging sign.

The "Let's Kick Racism out of the Stadiums" campaign of the Polish Football Against Racism in Europe member "Never Again association" promotes anti-racism at football grounds and aims to challenge racist attitudes prevalent amongst Polish fans. Activities include regular monitoring and reporting of incidents, production of two anti-racist magazines (*Stadion* and *Never Again* magazine) and the organizing of an annual anti-racist football tournament. The Never Again association has succeeded at raising the awareness of the Polish Football Association and club officials to the issue of racist symbols displayed in stadiums. An anti-racist manual has also been produced jointly by Never Again and the Polish Football Association which provides guidance for club officials and game observers. In November 2003 Never Again gave a presentation at a high-profile conference on stadium security organized by the Polish Football Association. The activity of Never Again has been endorsed by, among others, Emanuel

Olisadebe, Poland's first black international. It is hoped that anti-racist work in Polish football can be sustained and new successful projects can be inspired and supported in other Central and Eastern European countries, too.

Anti-racist initiatives in Eastern Europe are very much needed but there is often little chance for them to obtain local funding. In October 2003 it was decided that the funds received by the Football Against Racism in Europe network from the MTV Free Your Mind Award would be used to aid anti-racist football projects in this region. The Never Again Association has been mandated to use the funds both for the enhancement of its own activities in Poland and for the expansion of the Football Against Racism in Europe network and promotion of anti-racism in and through football in the region. Never Again is well qualified for the task: it has highly competent activists and it has accumulated years of experience working at both the national and the international level. It has also experienced being active in a hostile environment, coming a long way from the initial refusal to acknowledge the problem of racism by authorities and media alike, to the gradual acceptance of the need for anti-racist measures. Never Again has a good overview of existing anti-racist initiatives in the region, not least through its close cooperation with United for Intercultural Action, the largest pan-European anti-racist network. Among others, Never Again hosted the large-scale United network conference in Poland in November 2003, with about seventy anti-racist groups from all over Europe being represented, many of them from central and Eastern European states. It is hoped United will assist in the implementation of this project.

The Never Again Association will serve as a contact point for the development of anti-racist football initiatives in Eastern Europe with a special emphasis on Lithuania, Latvia, Estonia, Belarus, Ukraine, Russia, and Moldova. In each of these countries a study visit is to be conducted with the aim to present and share the experiences of Never Again and Football Against Racism in Europe in combating racism in and through football, to encourage the development of local football-related anti-racist initiatives and to identify possible partners for long-term cooperation with Football Against Racism in Europe. Throughout the duration of the project, the Never Again Association will provide assistance to organizations in the region in terms of guidance, advice, inspiration, and material to be used in local activities. The existing activities in Poland will also be strengthened with an office and paid staff. In addition, an Eastern European Project Pool has been established for the support of local initiatives. It operates on the model of the already existing Football Against Racism in Europe Small Scale Project Pool, using the same criteria for the support of projects, taking into consideration the specific local situations where appropriate. Never Again advises and evaluates each project proposal, while Fair Play in Vienna will administer the funds.

It is expected the project will result in a growing number of initiatives from central and Eastern Europe taking part in Football Against Racism in Europe activities and in raising awareness of the problem of racism in football and in society in general. When the Football Against Racism in Europe network was established in 1999, activists and fans called on football bodies "to specifically address the issue of the rise of the extreme right, and their manifestations in football stadiums, in Eastern Europe." Today problems of racism and anti-Semitism are still part of everyday life in many parts of central and Eastern Europe. At the same time national associations and NGOs started several initiatives to foster a non-racist football and fan culture. Football Against Racism in Europe is in a unique position to influence the situation in Eastern Europe being able to use good experiences from Western European countries as well as local anti-racist expertise and contacts in the region. The large number of events in the framework of the 2004 Football Against Racism in Europe Action Week was an encouraging sign. Action took place in Armenia, Azerbaijan, Belarus, Bulgaria, Croatia, Czech Republic, Hungary, Poland, Latvia, Former Yugoslav Republic of Macedonia, Romania, Russia, Serbia and Montenegro, Slovakia, Slovenia and Ukraine. The three-year Stand Up, Speak Up campaign is also worthy of note.

However, many migrant and ethnic minority groups in Eastern Europe find it extremely difficult to run activities on a continuous basis and do not enjoy sufficient support from football institutions and the public sector. In Hungary, for instance, the African Star FC, which is made up of talented players from Nigeria, Cameroon, Rwanda, Liberia and Vietnam, as well as a Hungarian goalkeeper, struggles to get a license to play in a higher league. Since several players have refugee status or are asylum-seekers, the football association refuses to issue permission to play. In Poland Football Against Racism in Europe partner Never Again association runs an annual anti-racist football cup at the Przystanek Woodstock music festival, where they closely cooperate with the Association of Asylum Seekers. Their founding member Simon Mol received the "Anti-fascist of the Year 2003" award. In FC Africa United the Association of Asylum Seekers gathers African players from all over Poland to play in tournaments; some of them are playing in the two top leagues. People Against Racism (PAR) in Slovakia monitors the human rights situation for international NGOs and cooperates closely with the FC Roma. The football club is made up of Roma players who regularly play for amateur clubs in Slovakia. FC Roma has been formed to fight discrimination in Slovak football and society. Due to its ongoing fight against racist and right-extremist groups PAR suffered an arson attack on its office. Since 2003 Football Against Racism in Europe lends support to a range of other initiatives in the region, using the funds received from the MTV Free your Mind Award.

Football Against Racism in Europe partners
Mondiali Antirazzisti
The *Mondiali Antirazzisti* (Anti-racist World Cup) is a five-a-side football festival created by the Football Against Racism in Europe founding member *Progetto*

Ultrà—UISP Emilia Romagna, in cooperation with *Istoreco*. Since its inception in 1997, the event brings together fan groups, migrant and local communities, anti-racist organizations from all over Europe, for five days full of football, music and anti-racist activities. Celebrating old and new friendships, meeting new people, exchanging information and creating common projects together: this is what the Mondiali is all about! The 2005 edition was held once again in Montecchio, near the city of Reggio Emilia, from 6 July to 10 July, with a record participation of 192 teams and more than 6,000 participants.

Apart from football and basketball tournaments, the Mondiali offers important moments for debate on various topics, broadcasting of videos and documentaries, and gives a chance to all groups to bring in their self-produced material on anti-racism, displayed in the Piazza Antirazzista (Anti-racist Square). In the evenings, music concerts and other shows contribute to create the atmosphere which has made the Mondiali so unique during the years. The involvement of some ultras groups and migrant communities in the organization and management of the event is essential: these groups not only play in the tournament, but actively contribute to the festival, working in the camping areas or in the restaurants and bars, and helping out in any possible way.

Fairplay. Many Colours. One Game—Austria

A part of the Vienna Institute for International Dialogue and Cooperation (VIDC), Fairplay has been planning and organizing anti-racism and anti-discrimination football projects since 1997, specializing in campaigning and education work throughout Austria. This includes providing support for the Migrant Workers Tournament in Vienna, staging panel discussions on current issues and publishing its own magazine, *Fairplay*. In 1999 Fairplay played a major role in the formation of Football Against Racism in Europe and has since been responsible for coordinating the Football Against Racism in Europe pan-European work program and, in particular, the Football Against Racism in Europe Action Week, which takes place all over Europe every October.

Nigdy Wiecej (Never Again)—Poland

Never Again is an independent anti-racism organization that has been documenting racist incidents in Poland since 1996. Never Again publishes the country's only anti-racism magazine. It also puts out an anti-racism fanzine called *Stadium*. With its Let's Kick Racism out of the Stadiums campaign, Never Again attempts to counter the racist, and in particular anti-Semitic, attitudes prevalent among Polish football fans. Never Again organizes football tournaments and has also produced an anti-racism information brochure for the Polish Football Association. One of the campaign's most prominent supporters is Polish international Emanuel Olisadebe.

Show Racism the Red Card—England

Show Racism the Red Card sets out to use professional footballers as anti-racist role models and has already won hundreds of top European players and officials for its education work. The campaign produces posters, videos and CD-ROMs featuring statements by leading players who have joined together to make a stand against racism. In England and Ireland, Show Racism the Red Card also organizes national school competitions against racism.

Football Unites, Racism Divides—England

Football Unites, Racism Divides was formed in 1995 by a group of Sheffield United fans and works in particular with ethnic minority men and women in Sheffield and the local area. Football Unites, Racism Divides helps football clubs with strong ethnic minority involvement by organizing coaching sessions and courses and by providing logistical support. In doing so, Football Unites, Racism Divides enjoys a close working relationship with Sheffield United and their local rivals, Sheffield Wednesday. Football Unites, Racism Divides also delivers anti-racism education in schools and youth clubs and runs the Resources and Information Centre on discrimination in football and sport in general.

Kick It Out—England

Kick It Out is an English anti-racism campaign supported by the Football Association, the Premier League, the Football Foundation and the Professional Footballers' Association. For more than ten years now, Kick It Out has campaigned against discrimination in football at professional, amateur and youth levels. Its core priorities in recent years have included working with professional clubs and local ethnic minority groups, highlighting the exclusion of Asian players in professional football and carrying out educational work with young people by organizing discussion events with leading players, nationwide tournaments and school competitions. In England, Kick It Out is responsible for coordinating the National Week of Action, in which all ninety-two professional English clubs, four hundred other clubs, fan groups, schools and NGOs take part every year.

Progetto Ultra & Unione Italiano Sport per Tutti—Italy

Progetto Ultra works with groups of ultras from all over Italy. In Bologna it runs a pan-European documentation center on the subject of racism and discrimination in football. Once a year, in cooperation with *Unione Italiano Sport per Tutti*, *Progetto Ultra* organizes the *Mondiali Antirazzisti*, the anti-racist World Cup.

FARE Continental partners—An overview

Progetto Ultrà

Progetto Ultrà was born in 1995 as part of U.I.S.P. Emilia-Romagna (*Unione Italiana Sport Per tutti*—Italian Sports for All). *Progetto Ultrà* has two main goals:

- to protect football supporters as a relevant social phenomenon and popular culture and

- to limit violence and intolerance using community programs and social work aimed at football supporters and run with their assistance.

At the same time, the organization has various other functions. *Progetto Ultrà* uses its own financial resources and external contributions (Emilia Romagna Region, European Commission) to carry out its various functions. External contributions are provided on projects submitted to promote youth organizations and sport, or to fight racism and discriminations.

Football fan archive
Progetto Ultrà collects documentation on a European level. The material (up to now we've collected more than 18,000 titles) includes books, fanzines, newspaper articles and press cuts, researches and dissertations, magazines, photos of football supporters and Ultras. The archive also includes documents relating to violence, racism and youth culture. The archive is a rather unique resource throughout Europe and a genuine mirror of football supporters. Therefore, it has become a library, research center and meeting place for fans, academics and students.

Information and communication among supporters
The organization publishes and distributes information concerning laws and rights for supporters. We have prepared research dealing with the excessive commercialization of sports. Looking at other experiences and models in other countries we try to suggest alternative solutions for modern football's problems (stadium planning, excessive power of television in determining kick-off times, overpriced tickets, etc.). We organize meetings between rival fans to discuss specific topics (special laws against violence in football, ticketing, reduction in violence, etc.). We try to suggest and coordinate various initiatives to defend football supporters' popular culture, from the criminalization of organized football supporters and from the excessive commercialization of football.

Information and communication with other organizations
We are constantly involved in awakening public opinion, which often dismisses football support as an exclusively violent phenomenon. The purpose is to provide a less superficial and prejudiced interpretation of organized football supporters. Activities in this area include projects in schools, organization of and/or participation in meetings and seminars, publication of articles or essays, interviews with the media, exhibitions, videos and so on. On an institutional level the organization tries to alter the misconstrued conception of supporters inside the stadium being simply a problem of public order. We attempt to depict Ultras for what they really are: a very relevant social phenomenon which may lead to vio-

lence but has also been a source of powerful energy and community spirit throughout the years. For this reason we have suggested (and will continue to suggest) changes in legislations to mitigate the excesses of the current laws (too repressive) and other measures which include community programs as part of the aforementioned legislation.

Mediation between rival supporters and other organizations
Progetto Ultrà is a meeting place for the various components that form spontaneous gatherings (fan groups, including rival ones) and facilitates communication between fans and institutions. Therefore, we attempt to act as a mediator when we can or if we are requested to do so. This mediation involves rival fans, when disputes or misunderstandings have arisen, to clarify positions so as to avoid unnecessary altercations and eventually violence. We also try to mediate between fan groups and institutions, including the police, to possibly resolve problems due to conflicts between the parties. Thanks to our mediation, many stadium bans, issued far too heavy-handedly, have been lifted.

Assistance for supporters abroad
We also operate on an international level to provide support for fans abroad. *Progetto Ultrà* is a founding member of the Football Supporters International (FSI). During EURO 2000, held in Belgium and Holland, we set up a fan embassy for Italian fans to provide assistance in solving the various problems encountered (tickets, accommodation, mediation, information). EURO 2004 in Portugal has seen FSI set up for the first time seven fan embassies (Italy, Great Britain, Germany, Holland, France, Czech Republic, Switzerland) for fans traveling abroad to follow their national team. *Progetto Ultrà* organized the whole project and put up an Italian fan embassy.

Anti-racism campaigns
Progetto Ultrà is also a founding member of Football Against Racism in Europe. FARE is a network of European organizations and associations fighting against discrimination in football. Every year we are responsible for coordinating FARE's Action Week in Italy, in order to mobilize fans, football teams and organizations on racism in and out of European stadiums. *Progetto Ultrà* also organizes annually the Anti-Racism World Cup, which has become an extremely popular event throughout Europe. For about four days, approximately 5,000 people—of different nationalities, origins, religions, cultures and fan groups—gather side by side at the World Cup's campsite in order to play together non-competitive, five-a-side football, but more importantly, to meet each other, party together and send out a very important message against racism and discriminations. FARE received the 2002 Europe MTV Award, Free Your Mind, as best network of antiracist campaigning.

Bündnis Aktiver Fussballfans

The *Bündnis Aktiver Fussballfans* (BAFF) is currently the only national-based supporters' organization in Germany. It is made up of some forty groups representing fans of various clubs (independent supporters associations, fanzines, fan projects) and more than one hundred individual members, who act as multipliers among the supporters at their own clubs. Since *Bündnis Aktiver Fussballfans* was formed in 1993, supporters of different clubs have worked together on a national basis against racism and discrimination in football grounds, against the excessive commercialization of football, and for the retention of standing places. The organization is open to all fans who identify with these objectives. Members and contacts meet twice a year at different venues for the purpose of exchanging information on what is happening at their clubs and building up the network. In 1994 the first *Bündnis Aktiver Fussballfans*-organized national fan congress took place in Düsseldorf. At the second fan congress, which was held in Oer-Erkenschwick in 1997, some three hundred fans from forty-eight different clubs all over Europe were in attendance. The highlight was a podium discussion in which the German Football Association, the Professional Footballers Association, the television station SAT.1 and representatives of the police participated. From then on, the summer fan congress has occupied a permanent place in supporters' calendars and has become a well-publicized event in the German media.

Since its establishment *Bündnis Aktiver Fussballfans* has attempted to draw the attention of the competent institutions, clubs and supporters to the ever-present racism and discrimination in grounds, to encourage them to stand up in opposition to these phenomena and to perform corresponding information and educational work. To this end *Bündnis Aktiver Fussballfans* drew up a symbolic nine-point plan featuring proposals for clubs—an early template for the program recommended to clubs by the German FA in 1998 and the anti-racism paragraphs in the Specimen Stadium Regulations (*Musterstadionordnung*). Meanwhile, *Bündnis Aktiver Fussballfans* has linked up with supporters' organizations from across Europe in the network known as Football Against Racism in Europe (FARE). *Bündnis Aktiver Fussballfans* also supports the annual Anti-Racism World Cup held in Bologna, Italy, the British video campaign "Show Racism the Red Card" and the Internet magazine www.farenet.org. FIFA has now expressed an interest in some form of collaboration and now invites FARE representatives to workshops, for example. *Bündnis Aktiver Fussballfans* sees the live stadium event football as a form of culture with high social integrative value that has developed historically and is worthy of preservation. Yet current developments in the game toward a media-packaged, entertainment-sector marketing product are increasingly alienating fans (especially young fans), culminating in the exclusion of lower-income groups from football. A program drawn up by *Bündnis Aktiver Fussballfans* on the supporter-friendly organization of major international events was presented to the European Parliament in Brussels last year.

Bündnis Aktiver Fussballfans places special emphasis on the retention of movement-oriented standing places as an indispensable setting for established fan culture. As early as 1994 *Bündnis Aktiver Fussballfans* organized a demonstration in favor of standing places in front of the headquarters of the German FA in Frankfurt and followed this up a year later with a similar demonstration at the UEFA headquarters in Geneva. In the planning of new stadia ahead of the 2006 World Cup, which is being held in Germany, clubs are involving local *Bündnis Aktiver Fussballfans* groups and taking into account the inclusion of safe standing places (e.g., Schalke 04, MSV Duisburg, FC St. Pauli, Eintracht Frankfurt). In a process that has taken many years, *Bündnis Aktiver Fussballfans* has been able to draw attention to these and other issues in numerous local and national newspaper articles as well as radio and television programs. *Bündnis Aktiver Fussballfans* spokespeople are regularly consulted on current developments and events, be it the introduction of a European league, the centenary celebrations of the German FA or racist trends in German football grounds. Also worthy of mention are the fanzines produced locally by *Bündnis Aktiver Fussballfans* members. These constitute an important reflection of supporter opinion and serve as a creative counter-pole to right-wing extremism and violence. In 1996 *Bündnis Aktiver Fussballfans* organized a fanzine festival in Recklinghausen to allow fans to discuss the production of fanzines and to provide young fanzine editors with important tips, an idea that lives on today in individual working groups at *Bündnis Aktiver Fussballfans* fan congresses.

Individual *Bündnis Aktiver Fussballfans* groups, such as the Schalke Fan-Initiative, which boasts over three hundred members, attempt to become involved in local sport- and club-related decision-making processes in order to gain an ear for the interests of fans, for example, or to gain acceptance as a partner on safety issues, instead of being considered a safety risk. This involves committee work, meetings with club representatives/players in supporter-run, drop-in centers and fan-project offices, but also the integration of fans in club structures. The head of organization at FC St. Pauli, for example, is a *Bündnis Aktiver Fussballfans* founder member, and supporters already sit on the Supervisory Board there and in Schalke. Since 2001, *Bündnis Aktiver Fussballfans* is supporting the "Pro 15:30" campaign against television interference in the fixing of kick-off times and is organizing a traveling exhibition on the subject of racism and discrimination in football. The exhibition was funded by the European Union and part of the FARE-working program till the end of 2004. It was shown in more than twenty-five towns and more than fifty thousand people visited the venues until November 2004. For its work, *Bündnis Aktiver Fussballfans* won the Ambassador of Tolerance 2001 award, presented by the Association for Democracy and Tolerance of the German government. In 2003, *Bündnis Aktiver Fussballfans* released the music-CD-sampler *Music for the Terraces*, an antiracist football compilation that attracted much attention from all over Europe.

As far as the exhibition is concerned, "Target Stadium Racism and Discrimination in Football," organized in association with the European Union, provided an overview of racist and discriminatory incidents and developments in and around football grounds since the 1980s. The problems addressed by the exhibition were manifold. As in society as a whole, xenophobic or racist slogans (and banners, for instance, in the stadium) are a current problem, as is anti-Semitism and sexism. The exhibition showed that the aforementioned problems repeatedly led to acts of violence. Racism and discrimination are European problems that cannot be reduced to individual countries, national associations or clubs. We also offered an insight into the links between hooligans and right-wing fan groupings to neo-fascist ideology and political groupings. Besides the focus on football fans, the exhibition also centered on clubs, national associations and players. Whereas the main emphasis was placed on fans and football in Germany, the exhibition also established links to football in the rest of Europe. Furthermore, the exhibition documented the opposition mounted by fans, clubs and national associations. A number of alternatives were put forward highlighting the type of work that could be done against racism and discrimination in the stadium (fans, clubs, national associations, political parties) and how the capacity of football for bringing people of different nations together could be utilized. The exhibition aimed to awaken football fans, followers and, in particular, young people, but also national associations, clubs and the general public to the problem of racism and discrimination in our stadia. It also bolstered the work of local independent supporters' groups by integrating them further in the Football Against Racism in Europe network. Visitors were offered creative alternatives and perspectives. Where possible, fringe activities such as football tournaments against racism, podium discussions or readings were organized in the various host cities.

Schalker Fan-Initiative[1]

No member of the Schalker Fan-Initiative believed that politics have a place in football. Yet when the initial members of the initiative were gathered in 1992, the increased hostility toward foreigners in our country, our region and, in particular, the Parkstadium compelled us to take action, thus "Schalkers Against Racism" was born. A number of match-going Schalke friends decided to take part in the commemorative demonstration on 9 November 1992, the anniversary of the anti-Jewish pogrom of 1938, with a "Schalke fans against racism" banner and distribute a leaflet they had produced. In light of the massive support they received for their actions the leaflet was reprinted in a local sports paper (*Revier-Sport*) and the response was so great that the initiators hardly had time to draw breath. The media showed great interest and a host of information meetings, leaflet campaigns, and television, radio and newspaper interviews followed. As the vast amount of work involved could no longer be dealt with "from the kitchen table," the *Schalker Fan-Initiative* was set up as a registered society in February 1993 to lend the idea of "Schalke fans against racism" a more rigid structure and to create a solid financial basis as a result of being granted not-for-profit status.

The first campaigns were intended to raise awareness and demonstrate that there are Schalke fans prepared to defend their values, politically and socially, within a sports context. In the city center of Gelsenkirchen, during both demonstrations and on match days, flyers were distributed, which expressed the opposition of fans, players and coaches against all forms of discrimination. In 1992 we participated in the "Racism and Violence Against Foreigners" in the Federal Republic of Germany conference, the first nation-wide symposium concerning football fans against the political right and a series of events devoted to racism and football in particular, not to mention the support we received by players of FC Schalke 04, including Eigenrauch, Christensen, Müller and Lehmann. Two years later, on 16 April 1994, we issued the first edition of the independent fanzine *Schalke Unser*, where we tackled racism and discussed other subjects of interest and importance to supporters. Up to this day, the whole project from layout to sales is still organized independently and on an honorary basis. With 6,000 copies it has become the largest fan magazine in Germany, and it provides a country-wide voice for the Schalke fans.

Since the early years, the Fan-Initiative strove intensely to enhance communication between Polish and German fans, merely because FC Schalke's early successes were much related to the descendants of immigrants from Poland. Even today, surnames with Polish endings in the Ruhr district demonstrate the historical links with our eastern neighbors. An active exchange with the fans of Lech Poznan, for example, produced a Polish-German special edition of *Schalke Unser*. In 2005, we also organized an exchange between students from Gelsenkirchen and Krakow. The stay in Poland was particularly impressive and educational for all involved, due to the intensive workshops and the visit to the notorious Auschwitz concentration camp. A large part of the work we do involves organizing international exchange projects between supporters of various clubs. Many of the problems faced by football fans (e.g., all-seater stadia, commercialization, hooliganism) are the same in most countries, so it is important to tackle them on an international basis. An initial exchange with fans of Polish first division side Lech Poznan was quickly followed by an international fan congress in Gelsenkirchen attended by supporters from Poland (Lech Poznan), Holland (Roda JC Kerkrade) and England (Newcastle United). In recognition of our work in these projects we received an award from the German Bundestag for outstanding commitment in the civil field. At the end of January 1999 two representatives of the Fan-Initiative attended the "Networking Against Racism in European Football" conference in Vienna. A total of forty organizations from thirteen countries gathered to demonstrate their determination to fight racism and xenophobia in European sport. The delegates announced their intention to intensify their pan-European activities and founded the Football Against Racism in Europe (FARE) network, which has since organized two successful European weeks of action, both with major contributions from the Fan-Initiative. In March 1999 the Fan-Initiative organized an exhibition in Gelsenkirchen on the history of football in Germany. The exhibition was accompanied by a series of lectures on subjects such as "The German National Team Under National Socialism" and "Fans in Professional Football—What Role Do They Play? The Problems Faced by Football Fans and How to Overcome Them."

In 1996 the work involved in running the Fan-Initiative, making *Schalke Unser* and responding to inquiries from all quarters (fans, press, radio, TV) had finally become too much to manage on a spare-time basis. After many sleepless nights it eventually became clear that we had no option but "to go whole hog." In our case "going whole hog" meant opening our own shop-cum-pub, or head office, so to speak. After weeks of painting, banging in nails and laying cables the job was done and the Fan-Laden opened in all its blue-and-white glory on 17 October 1996, at Hansemannstrasse 23, close to Gelsenkirchener Hauptmarkt. This is our office, project center and a place for youth work. It is a meeting place for Schalke fans, as well as national and international guests, especially during the 2006 World Cup in Germany. Against all odds we were even able to solve the most difficult of our problems, that of how to finance the venture. Here, a big thank you goes to FC Schalke 04, who supported the initiative and many of our projects. Located in the centre of Gelsenkirchen (Musiktheater tram stop) the Fan-Laden is a venue open to all Schalke fans and a popular meeting place both before and after games. It has since played host to a wide variety of events ranging from live European and Bundesliga matches on our own big screen to concerts, readings, street festivals and theater evenings. Members also meet here once a month to plan the future activities of the Fan-Initiative.

Since the submission of our anti-racist agenda to the extraordinary meeting of the members of FC Schalke 04, the club statute duly included the following sections declaring that "the social integration of foreign fellow citizens shall be promoted" (paragraph 2) and stressed that "the exclusion from the club can take place, among other things, in response to dishonorable behavior within or outside of the club, particularly racist remarks or declaration of convictions hostile to foreigners" (paragraph 4). FC Schalke was, therefore, the first club to boast an entire paragraph devoted to anti-racist ideals in its statute. Its application was suitably highlighted with the prohibition of entry to the stadium and of membership to the club for avowed members of right-wing extremist parties. The more active the Initiative was, the clearer it became that members concentrated not only on racism, but all forms of discrimination. Considering that much of our work concerned fans and youth, more generally, we were then renamed "Schalker Fan-Initiative e.V." Except for FC Schalke 04, to emphasize and strengthen our campaign we now cooperate with the local sports community, including the Association of Schalke Fan Clubs (with its 850 registered fan clubs and approximately 70,000 organized members), the Schalke Supporters Club and the Gelsenkirchen Ultras. Our commitment to youth work is further supported by the city of Gelsenkirchen, while on the national and European levels we are a member of the Alliance of Active Football Fans (BAFF) and FARE respectively. The Schalker Fan-Initiative organized the 2004 FARE conference in the AufSchalke arena and contributed to FARE exhibitions during the European Championship in Portugal. All in all, the work of the Fan-Initiative was landed several times, for example, in 1997 with the Promotion Prize of the *Demokratiekreis Leben* in front of the German Bundestag, with the Golden Hammer of the State of North Rhine-Westphalia by the state of North Rhine-Westphalia (2000), the third prize of the *Paritätisches Jugendwerk* North Rhine-Westphalia in the year 2001 and the prize for one of the ten winning projects in the context of the competition "Grenzüberschreitungen. Equal Opportunities in Europe—An Opportunity for North Rhine-Westphalia" (for the theater project in 2007).

In 2001, the Fan-Initiative started work on its new nation-wide project "Dem Ball ist egal, wer ihn tritt" (the ball doesn't care who kicks it), which aims to produce, among other things, anti-racism education material (films, CD-ROM, etc.) for use in schools. Since 2005, it has been a stand alone project. The Fan- Initiative has the following project emphases at the moment:

- intensification of youth work outside the school context;
- observation and reaction to the extreme-right in Gelsenkirchen and its wider vicinity;
- participation in campaigns against homophobia, usually with our new partner "The Point" (a gay and lesbian center in Gelsenkirchen).

Youth work outside the school context
The most important and largest project in our youth work outside the school context was the play, *RepuBlick on Schalke*, inspired by the 2006 World Cup. The play showed that people from distinct origins celebrating together for the same purpose was clearly possible and desirable. The theater project *RepuBlick on Schalke* set the goal of uniting young people of different origins and sexual orientation and encouraging relations between otherwise opposite groups. More importantly, it underlined the capacity of the game of football as liaison of cultures. The fact that the *RepuBlick* has the ability to improve integration proved real when the Fan-Initiative was invited to the conclusive national meeting of the European Year of Equal Opportunities in Aachen on 13 November 2007, where the project was honored as one of the ten best practice projects among 317 applications. Disturbingly, racist abuse and violence in stadiums at the expense of immigrants resumed directly after the World Cup, thus demonstrating that anti-racism campaigns were still too significant to ignore.

Observation and reaction to the extreme right
How active and powerful the extreme right in Gelsenkirchen and its surrounding cities still is came to light, again, in all clarity on 10 June 2006. The National Democratic Party and the Free Forces North Rhine-Westphalia gained permission for their demonstration, "Work for Millions, Instead of Profit for Millionaires," by an express resolution of the Federal Constitutional Court, after its failure

in the first legal instances. However harmless the title sounded, the motive behind the meeting was obvious: to encourage hostility against foreigners. The
slogan and speeches were only pretending to be against capitalism and globalization. At the core, it concerned nationalism and a "healthy German community." And all this on the second day of the World Cup, the slogan of which was
"the world as guests of friends," in the city in which many Poles and Ecuadori-
ans were guests at that time. The counter-movement had organized itself in time,
so that on this day various meetings took place, such as the "for multicolored
variety, against brown stupidity" event. The Schalker Fan-Initiative was represented there together with "the Point;" however, it was particularly important to
us to be present in the streets close to the extreme-right demonstration. For this
purpose, we organized one of the counter-demonstrations with the "Alliance
Against the Right," which also purposefully reached out to football fans. An
information and help telephone line were installed in the fan shop. Over one year
later, campaigns were necessary again against right-wingers marching in our
city. Triggered by the arrest of three right-wing extremists, who had smeared
swastikas and right slogans on walls and taken part in a propaganda campaign in
the wake of the twentieth anniversary of Rudolf Hess, Hitler's former deputy,
the extreme right held demonstrations over two days in late October 2007. Not
surprisingly, perhaps, the second demonstration was planned for 30 October, the
day commemorating Germany's unification.

In June 2007 we took up the "Schalker Traces" project, which highlights the
history of the legendary Gelsenkirchener quarter, with football playing a crucial
role making reference to the club's historical premises, the Glück-Auf arena,
and to Ernst Kuzorra, Fritz Szepan and "Stan" Libuda. It was important to the
Schalker Fan-Initiative that in this context the German Jews Sally Meyer and
Julie Lichtmann were honored too. They had been the owners of the textiles
store Julius Rode & Co. at the Schalker market and were illegally expropriated,
deported and murdered by the Nazis. The well-known Schalke player Szepan
profited from the expropriation when he took over the business for a small sum.
A plaque now reminds passersby of the fate of the two citizens of Gelsenkirchen. Sadly, during autumn 2007 we heard the notorious underground song
that celebrates the existence of Auschwitz sung on public transport all the way
to the stadium. Sometimes even verbal abuse against foreign citizens can be
heard, like "we hate Turkey" or "remove the head scarf, you are in Germany."
There is certainly a good number of Schalke fans that do not share the same beliefs, but some fans feel alone, too weak or not ready enough to counter the supporters of the extreme right. Hence, the Schalker Fan-Initiative initiated the
campaign, "Our Underground Goes to the Stadium—Schalker Against Nazi
Singing," during the FARE 2007 Action Week. The message reads: "Unite and
don't stay quiet when such singing can be heard. Together we can make clear
that our foreign fellow citizens are welcome, but Nazis and racists are not! And if
civil courage is really not sufficient in your position, or you find no allies: Call
110, describe the situation and make yourself available as a witness."

Today, with approximately 400 members, the Schalker Fan-Initiative is the largest anti-racist fan club in German sports. Part of our goal is the preservation of our network while also carrying out similar activities in the coming years. We want to keep our eyes open and react fast to unpleasant situations, with old and new partners, as the world around us changes markedly. We are always aware that we must work continuously so that our stadium (for us) remains the "coolest Nazi-free zone of the world" in the future. We gladly pass on our expertise in the fight against racism and discrimination, which was so successful with Schalke, and wish to remain open to all sorts of recommendations from our current and future partners and fellow activists in Europe. All in all, the aims outlined in our statute have been met with great success. It is noteworthy that our collaboration with organizations that are similar in nature and scope—though not necessarily devoted exclusively to football or sports in that matter—has served our interests well, considering our ability to introduce football fans to delicate subjects such as racial discrimination and homophobia. In this context, our work has been expanded considerably over a number of relevant social issues. The fact that two new sections, both pertaining to anti-racism, were included in the club statute of FC Schalke 04 on December 1994 underlines our commitment to the campaign against racism in football and highlights our success too. While our work has certainly helped raise awareness, there remains one significant area that continues to hamper our endeavors every now and then is inadequate fund-raising. One other issue is our standing in the football supporters' community, as it is imperative that we maintain our status as members of an anti-racism organization while also retaining our fan identity when attending any football match.

Nigdy Wiecej[2]

The *Nigdy Wiecej* (Never Again) association is an apolitical, anti-racist organization that monitors racist incidents and publishes the *Nigdy Wiecej* magazine since 1994, which provides reliable information on the various extremist and racist groups operating in Poland and in the rest of Europe. Among other campaigns, "Let's Kick Racism out of Football" is essentially focused on eliminating all forms of discrimination from the beautiful game.

The *Nigdy Wiecej* association is one of the initiating members of Football Against Racism in Europe as well as a member of European nets United for Intercultural Action. Our group was established in 1992 in response to the growing wave of racism and anti-Semitism in post-communist Poland and aims at promoting human rights and multicultural understanding, as well as contributing to the development of a democratic civil society in Poland. *Nigdy Wiecej* is particularly concerned with the problem of educating the young against racial and ethnic prejudices. *Nigdy Wiecej* works with other organizations internationally, such as the London-based international anti-fascist magazine *Searchlight*, the European anti-racist network United for Intercultural Action, the Football Against Racism in Europe network, as well as with partner Eastern European countries. Many of the authors for the magazine *Nigdy Wiecej* are well known experts in the field of ultra-nationalism in Eastern Europe. The *Nigdy Wiecej* association also provides information directly to journalists and institutions interested in the problem of racism and xenophobia. The *Nigdy Wiecej* archives are a nearly complete representation of most racist, anti-Semitic, and neo-fascist publications produced in Poland since 1989. *Nigdy Wiecej* has been consulted by numerous programs on the national television, as well as assisted in writing many articles for the national press (e.g., *Gazeta Wyborcza*, Poland's largest circulation daily newspaper). We have provided expertise to the Parliamentary Committee on Ethnic Minorities. The goal of *Nigdy Wiecej* is to raise the awareness of the need for ethnic and religious tolerance in a democratic society. The *Nigdy Wiecej* association is also working toward the coordination of all anti-racist activities in Poland. We have collaborated with other anti-racist and anti-fascist groups as well as with minority organizations all over the country.

In 1995-1997, together with the Polish Union of Jewish Students, we organized and ran a successful campaign demanding a ban on neo-Nazi, fascist and racist organizations to be included in the new Constitution of the Polish Republic. Throughout the campaign, *Nigdy Wiecej* collaborated with Members of Parliament (MPs) from all major political parties. We briefed members of the Parliamentary Constitutional Committee, provided information to the media and mobilized public opinion by collecting signatures and sending letters to Parliament in support of our campaign. At present *Nigdy Wiecej* is focusing on two campaigns aiming at raising the level of anti-racist sensitivity among young people: "Music Against Racism" is a campaign supported by top rock artists in the country, including Kazik, Kult, Big Cyc, T. Love and many others. We have organized concerts under the title "Music Against Racism." In November 1997 a compilation record was released featuring songs with an anti-racist message. In December 1998 another anti-racist compilation was released, featuring among others Chumbawamba and Zion Train. Let's Kick Racism out of Football aims at removing racist and chauvinist attitudes prevalent among sports fans. We promote anti-racism at football grounds in cooperation with sport journalists, players and social organizations. We support anti-racist grass-roots initiatives among the fans. In April 2002 we released a CD, *Let's Kick Racism out of the Stadiums*.

Polish sports arenas, especially football stadiums, have become dangerous places full of violence and hate. This issue is being turned into a more frightening form. Waves of racism, chauvinism and xenophobia are clearly seen nowadays. The total sum of incidents referring to this matter illustrates the scale of the phenomenon. There are many league matches with fascist flags, anti-Semitic songs, and racist abuses directed at players from Africa. Racism, a growing problem in Europe, is often directed against football players and fans with a different skin color or of different ethnic origin. In many European stadiums are visible flags with the Celtic cross—the racist symbol of white power. Moreover, racist slogans and songs can be heard. In some cases these are accompanied by violence. The waving of chauvinistic flags and banners are popular ways of showing support for racist ideology. In this case Nazi fans use a special code, in which some symbols are understandable only for the initiated. Symbols which refer directly to fascist symbolism (such as the swastika) are recognizable by everyone, whereas using the numeric code, 18, 88, are obvious fascist symbols only for persons who have knowledge about this issue. In our country where there is a lack of potential victims with different colored skin, this racial hatred focuses also on persons who in some way do not match the model of a "real Pole," as promoted by racist organizations. For this reason among victims of violence there are also people from anti-fascist organizations, homosexuals, homeless persons and the handicapped. Indeed, aggression from stadiums also moves onto the streets.

The problem of racism causes anxiety in international football organizations such as FIFA and UEFA. An extraordinary FIFA congress was held in Buenos Aires in 2001, which led to the adoption of a resolution calling on national football associations to fight racism and to cooperate in this field with NGOs. Moreover, regular reports on this issue should be done by these associations for the FIFA Control Committee, just as UEFA's initiatives produced the grounds for the "Unite Against Racism" conferences in London and Barcelona. Consequently, the letter was sent to national football associations, encouraging them to create a plan, aimed at eliminating racist incidents and promoting tolerance. Furthermore, UEFA also accepted a ten-point plan against racism aimed at helping clubs and federations practically with hints for fighting racism. Referring to UEFA ethics, soccer clubs should be heavily fined for racist incidents in stadiums. What is more, UEFA supports many anti-racist projects realized by football fans. In response to racism in the football environment, some initiatives aimed at fighting this phenomenon started to appear. The longest tradition in Europe belongs to England. There, in 1993, started a campaign called Kick It Out. This action was supported by such well-known footballers as John Barnes, Tony Adams, Ruud Gullit, Gary Lineker, Ian Wright, Gary Neville and Kevin Keegan, then coach of the English national team.

The Let's Kick Racism out of Football campaign aims at

- the elimination of fascist and racist symbols from football stadiums;
- the elimination of racist shouts and slogans;
- creation a network of anti-racist fan clubs.

The campaign depends on

- cooperation with FIFA (for instance, taking part in preparing the Conference Against Racism in Buenos Aires), UEFA (the active participation in the London conference on "Unite Against Racism"), as well as with Racism in Sport Group of Council of Europe;
- networking with Football Against Racism in Europe;
- close cooperation with the Polish Football Association (i.e., our regular participation as experts on committee meetings, training of activists and soccer judges, etc.);
- regular monitoring of racist incidents in Polish stadiums;
- publishing the anti-racist magazine *Stadion* (stadium);
- organizing an anti-racist football cup under the banner "Let's Kick Racism out of Football";
- cooperation with the Polish Football Association on the appointment of the Polish Roma national team;
- cooperation with the media and participation in television and radio programs underlining the problem of racism in sport;
- arranging meetings, lectures and training sessions referring to the issue of racism in the sports environment and ways of combating this phenomenon;
- educational activities for sport fans;
- promoting international experiences in the field of eliminating racism from stadiums;
- raising petitions to the president of the Polish Football Association;
- creation and maintenance of our web page;
- support for anti-racist fan clubs.

Our achievements so far concern

- creation and launching, together with the Polish Football Association, regulations about removing fascist symbols from Polish stadiums;
- creation and publication of educational material entitled "Racist Symbols," designed for judges, football journalists and activists;
- support for our campaign "Let's Kick Racism out of Football";
- launching the "Let's Kick Racism out of Football" compact disc with songs directed against racism at the stadiums (first such CD in the world);
- anti-racist Football Cup organized annually during the musical festival Przystanek Woodstock
- regular cooperation with FC Africa (African football team composed of players playing in Polish clubs);

- football tournaments "Let's Kick Racism out of Football" taking place all over Poland;
- gathering a few thousand signatures for a petition to the president of the Polish Football Association with an appeal to resist racism in stadiums;
- organizing events during the FARE Action Week in Poland;
- cooperating, organizing and taking part in conferences in Poland and abroad concerning the problem of racism in the sports' environment;
- FARE was awarded the "Free Your Mind" prize in December 2002, aimed at raising awareness about social problems.

The problem of racism in stadiums exists and must not be ignored. Indeed, the solution needed to change this frightening situation is close cooperation of international and national sport associations, sport and fan organizations, anti-racist non-governmental organizations, educational centers and media. Experience from other countries, which began the fight against racial prejudice in football long ago, shows that the best results stem from common actions, realized by people who love sport and strongly associate with the age-old Olympian principles of fair play and respect of opponents. We believe that the "Let's Kick Racism out of Football" campaign can become an integral part of programs dedicated to the elimination of racial discrimination from our stadiums. Considering that England is widely recognized as a leader of the European campaign against racism, we hope that Poland will attain a similar position among countries in our part of the continent.

Exclusion of minorities
All in all, FARE attempts not only to fight overt forms of abuse inside stadiums, but also to tackle hidden or institutionalized forms of racism, leading to the exclusion of ethnic minorities and migrants in different levels in the administration of football. Across Europe, ethnic minorities are under-represented in stadiums, football administration and sometimes in professional football leagues. An example for open discrimination by football governing bodies is the limitation of the number of migrants in amateur football, common in Italy and Spain. In Austrian amateur football, the number of foreigners, including citizens of the European Union, is limited to three per team. During its last conference at the French Football Federation in Paris 2007, FARE discussed a more pervasive dimension of racism, embedded in the unequal football relations between Europe and Africa. These relations are a legacy of Europe's colonial past. It manifests itself in the talent drain of young Africans who are "exported" to Europe by unscrupulous agents and most often end up as illegal immigrants. FARE believes that football has a universal appeal across all communities, the impact of which cannot be underestimated. It is important to work with victims of racism and those

affected by social exclusion to aid their integration and address problems of social cohesion. It must be our goal to bring minorities closer to the game through
their integration into all levels of football—teams, stadiums, administration,
coaching and refereeing.

FACT BOX ON FARE

1996
Four football-based anti-racist projects in Sheffield, London, Bologna and
Dortmund received European Commission funding

1997
As part of the European Year Against Racism, various football projects were
sponsored by the European Commission

1999
Establishment of the Football Against Racism in Europe network and passage of
the Football Against Racism in Europe Plan of Action in Vienna

2000
Official launch of Football Against Racism in Europe in the European Parliament in Brussels before the EURO 2000 finals

2001
First Football Against Racism in Europe Action Week Against Racism and Dis-
crimination in European Football with fifty events in nine countries
Football Against Racism in Europe representatives speak at the FIFA Confer-
ence Against Racism in Buenos Aires
UEFA award their charity check of 1 million Swiss francs to Football Against
Racism in Europe
Football Against Racism in Europe becomes a member of the UEFA charity
portfolio

2002
Second Football Against Racism in Europe Action Week with one hundred
events in seventeen countries
Third Football Against Racism in Europe Action Week with more than three
hundred events in eighteen countries
Start of a two-year anti-discrimination project co-funded by the European Com-
mission
Football Against Racism in Europe receives the Free Your Mind Award at the
MTV Europe Music Awards in Barcelona

2003

The conference "Unite Against Racism" was hosted by Chelsea FC, jointly organized by UEFA, Football Against Racism in Europe and the English Football Association
Some four hundred initiatives in twenty-four countries join the fourth Football Against Racism in Europe Action Week
Football Against Racism in Europe receives the Jean Kahn Award of the European Monitoring Centre on Racism and Xenophobia

2004

Football Against Racism in Europe at UEFA EURO 2004 in Portugal
With hundreds of initiatives, including all thirty-two Champions League teams in thirty-three European countries, the fifth Football Against Racism in Europe Action Week becomes Europe's biggest antiracism campaign in football

2005

Football Against Racism in Europe networking conference in Bratislava
FARE Public Hearing at the European Parliament in Brussels

2006

FARE program in Eastern Europe funded by the Stand up Speak up campaign
FIFA and FARE establish a strategic alliance in the field of anti-discrimination
The second Unite Against Racism conference is jointly organized by UEFA, FARE and the Spanish FA hosted by FC Barcelona
European declaration on tackling racism in football becomes a formal resolution at the European Parliament in Strasbourg
FARE Program at FIFA World Cup 2006
With more than seven hundred initiatives in thirty-seven European countries—including the involvement of all thirty-two Champions League teams—the seventh FARE Action Week becomes Europe's biggest anti-racism campaign in football

2007

FARE networking conference on ethnic minorities and equality, hosted by the French Football Federation, LICRA and PSG in Paris

Notes
    1. Written by Susanne Franke.
    2. Written by Jacek Purski.

Chapter Four

Kick It Out

Danny Lynch

History

Kick It Out is football's anti-racism campaign. The brand name of the campaign—Let's Kick Racism out of Football—was established in 1993. Kick It Out works throughout the football, educational and community sectors to challenge racism and work for positive change.

The campaign is supported and funded by the game's governing bodies, including founding body the Professional Footballers' Association (PFA), the FA Premier League, the Football Foundation and The Football Association. The year 2004 marked ten years of campaigning. Internationally, Kick It Out plays a leading role in the Football Against Racism in Europe (FARE) network and has been cited as an example of good practice by the European governing body, Union of European Football Associations (UEFA), the world governing body *Fédération Internationale de Football Association* (FIFA), the Council of Europe, the European Commission, European Parliamentarians and the British Council. Our core priorities, in no particular order, are: (1) professional football—working with the professional game by offering advice and guidance on all aspects of race equality within professional football; (2) young people—using the appeal of the game to address young people within schools, colleges and youth organizations, through the development and delivery of resources and educational materials; (3) amateur football—working at grass-roots and amateur levels to tackle racial abuse and harassment in football stadia; (4) Asians in football—raising the issue of the exclusion of South Asians as professional footballers from the game; (5) ethnic minorities and sport—capacity building ethnic minority communities to engage with professional clubs, the structures of the game and access funding; and (6) European football—developing partnerships to raise the debate and tackle racism in European football.

Building bridges
Central to Kick It Out's strategy is the development of partnerships that bring together football organizations with communities to work in partnership on problems of exclusion and discrimination. At a national level the coming together of representative groups in the game with Kick It Out allows the campaign to raise issues from communities directly with those at the highest level of the football industry. At a local level Kick It Out works to bring together appropriate groupings in the different areas of our work. For example, in working to eradicate the problem of racism in the amateur game partnerships of ethnic minority football clubs, local authorities, county football associations and local leagues are formed. Similarly, in redressing the problems of racism within the professional game, partnerships between the club, local community groups, supporters representatives and local authorities are developed in order to ensure that the expertise to deliver plans of action is available. Those who have been historically excluded from the game have a key role to play through the involvement of community groups. Many of the key successes of the Kick It Out campaign, if not all, are as a result of dynamic partnerships.

Tenth anniversary
Football stars, dignitaries past and present, and representatives of community groups from across the country gathered at London's Great Eastern Hotel in January 2004 to celebrate the tenth anniversary of the Let's Kick Racism out of Football campaign. Lord Herman Ouseley, chair of Kick It Out, and Professional Footballers' Association (PFA) chief executive Gordon Taylor hosted the lunch, which was also attended by England Head Coach Sven Goran Eriksson, Sports Minister Richard Caborn, Premiership referee Uriah Rennie, Charlton manager Alan Curbishley and former England manager Graham Taylor. The campaign was launched during the 1993-1994 season by founder members the PFA and the Commission for Racial Equality (CRE). Current players such as Ashley Cole, Chris Powell, Jason Euell and Darren Moore were joined by past greats such as Cyrille Regis, Luther Blissett, Paul Elliott, Brendon Batson and many others at the event which highlighted the achievements of the campaign in challenging racism, encouraging community engagement and setting out an agenda for policy development. The campaign, which since 1997 has been run by Kick It Out with the support of the FA, Premier League, PFA and the Football Foundation, is widely cited as being the catalyst for positive changes in the game. It was an occasion to make everyone involved in the campaign proud. Not least, Gordon Taylor who said, "I wanted it to be an occasion of celebration of one of the good things happening in our game and it was wonderful to see so many people, from all areas of the game, together to mark this anniversary. It was everything I hoped it would be. There is still a long way to go with this campaign, like getting Asian footballers into the professional game and getting black players into coaching and management. They are just two steps we are hoping

to make in the next phase of the campaign." Herman Ouseley gave an impassioned speech reflecting on his experiences of observing racism in the game and citing the negative influence of sections of the media encouraging hatred on the basis of ethnic origin or status. He recalled that many people had told him he was "mad" and would make no progress in advancing change through a campaign. During the lunch, Kick It Out took the opportunity to present awards to symbolically recognize the contributions made by key groups of people over the years. An award was presented to black pioneers to recognize their achievements in the face of adversity—Cyrille Regis, Luther Blissett and Paul Elliott picked up this award. A second award was given to Chris Powell, Martin Keown and Darren Moore to acknowledge the continuing work of current players. Darren Moore's contribution in attending events on a weekly basis was singled out for particular comment. A third award was offered to recognize community and club achievement. Taj Butt of Bradford, Joss Johnson from Highfield Rangers in Leicester, Howard Holmes from Football Unites, Racism Divides in Sheffield and Martin Simons, Chairman of Charlton Athletic, shared this award. The afternoon was presented by Garth Crooks and Aasmah Mir.

Week of Action
The Kick It Out "Week of Action" is one of the most prominent anti-racism and community engagement initiatives in the country. The week has a strong community focus and celebrates the contribution made to football by black, Asian and other ethnic minorities, while continuing the call to challenge racism.

One Game, One Community
The period sees the game's biggest names stand alongside communities across the UK under the banner "One Game, One Community." During this period grass-roots clubs, schools, community groups and fans join the professional game in coming together for an extended week of symbolic activities promoting inclusion. In 2006 more than eight hundred events took place during the Week of Action, including an anti-racism match day at all ninety-two professional clubs in England and Wales. The Week of Action is the biggest series of activities of their kind in Europe.

European action
The week of action is a European wide event. On the continent our partners in the Football Against Racism in Europe (FARE) network are coordinating activities. Activities on the continent continue to grow each year, and although events in Britain are bigger than the rest of Europe together, fan groups and ethnic minorities from countries ranging from Slovakia, Germany, Austria, Italy and Spain take an active part in the week.

Black History Month
The Week of Action is held during Black History Month and has previously coincided with Ramadan, Diwali and Jewish festivals. This enables opportunities for us all to learn about and celebrate these important periods.

Schools
The involvement of schools is an important element of the Week of Action. In previous years, the week has provided an opening within the classroom for teachers to use the medium of football to teach important messages relating to anti-racism, roles and responsibilities and aspects of the citizenship curriculum. It is a time when teachers are being creative and using the appeal of the game to capture the imagination of the young people they are working with. This year the week will coincide with Black History Month, the Muslim holy month of Ramadan and the festival of Eid Al-Fitr, and the Sikh and Hindu festival of light, Diwali. This provides an opportunity to raise awareness around different religious festivals that are now celebrated across the UK. There are many ways that schools can get involved in the Week of Action. These include

- organizing a youth conference to discuss issues of racism and diversity;
- bringing in artists, poets or writers in residence to explore anti-racism themes;
- organizing an assembly to look at different faiths and religions;
- organizing a "twinning" event with another school in your area that has a different ethnic makeup than your own;
- inviting a player from your local club to attend an event;
- devising and displaying your own exhibition about black footballers who have made an important contribution to your local team;
- entering the national secondary schools' competition.

As part of the Week of Action, Kick It Out has developed a set of new teaching resources.

Your community
A key objective of the Week of Action is to engage and help build partnerships with groups excluded from the game. The involvement of ethnic minority groups in seeking to address racial exclusion is crucial. In the past community groups have found a number of innovative and effective ways to make their stand over the extended week. Many groups have used the Week of Action as a

launch pad to greater things as the week presents an opportunity to approach and build links with your local professional football club and county FA.

Here are some other ideas:

- Invite a current or former professional footballer to an event to celebrate the diversity of football in your area.
- Organize an activity around a display of the History of Black Footballers exhibition.
- Arrange for members of your local community to attend an FA coach education course.
- Organize a prize-giving ceremony for ethnic minority footballing groups to recognize community achievement.

Local authorities

Local authorities are asked to play a facilitative role in assisting community involvement in the week. Supporting groups with additional materials needed for their activities and help in making links with professional sports clubs in the area are all important things local authorities can do. Once the week is over you may also want to assist with fundraising to sustain and develop projects. If you are planning your own Black History Month project think about links that could be made with the week. We may be able to offer some resources for display during the period.

Professional clubs

Every professional club in England and Wales holds a Kick It Out match day as part of the Week of Action. Activities such as players from both home and away teams warming up in t-shirts and the distribution of badges, stickers and magazines to fans take place at clubs across the country. Many clubs go much further than this, as it is a chance to celebrate the contribution their local community makes to the game while highlighting the race and social inclusion work they are doing throughout the year. In the past, some clubs have been particularly creative in their activities. Scunthorpe United FC worked in partnership with the local council to deliver a cultural awareness day at the club. This involved over fifty schoolchildren participating in sport activity, sampling food from across the world and a presentation from the local mayor. Sunderland FC used the Week of Action to invite the Shameen Karim dancers into the Stadium of Light to entertain their fans at half-time. Norwich City FC produced their own anti-racism posters and rolled out anti-racism lessons to local schools. Outside of their anti-racism game, they organized a road show, delivering a program to over one hundred students. They also linked in with their local supporters' group and backed a local five-a-side tournament. Chelsea FC worked in some of their local schools with Zimbabwean poet Albert and local poet Crispin Thomas. Plymouth Argyle and Boston United also produced their own anti-racism banners. Blackburn Rovers FC was one of many clubs that used the Week of Action as an opportunity to showcase their community work. They worked with the Royal Commandos, who flew the Kick It Out flag into the stadium prior to kick off. Crowd choreography was also organized within the family stand that read "Rovers Against Racism." Outside of the stadium, the club organized additional activities with the local schools, including an anti-racism chant, poetry and poster competition. The winning entry of the poster competition was featured on the front cover of the match program. Arsenal FC organized a Youth Forum with Thierry Henry that was attended by local youngsters from Islington. Liverpool FC organized a mosaic, which spelled out "1 Club 4 All." They also used the event to launch their own reporting number for complaints within the stadium. Notts County FC worked with the Supporters Trust and organized a big draw artist event. They encouraged all areas of the club, including the corporate areas to display the anti-racism message. The club worked with local schools and created a fifteen-foot banner, which was paraded on the pitch during their dedicated game. All Football in the Community officers wore Kick It Out t-shirts when delivering coaching sessions at local schools. Cambridge United and Exeter City flew the flag impressively for the Nationwide Conference clubs by organizing a full series of events for the Week of Action. Cambridge United worked well with their local media to raise awareness of the week, while Exeter City organized a balloon release. Most clubs are always looking for new ideas around their Kick It Out match days. A guide to organizing such days of action has been produced for professional clubs and is available on request.

Football fans
Football fans have a proud history of challenging racism in the game. As the lifeblood of the game, fan activities are crucial to the success of the Week of Action and it will come as no surprise that the idea for the Week of Action came from a fan who wanted to become more involved in the campaign. Thousands of fans get involved in the Week of Action each year by staging their own events or working alongside their club to set out a clear message. For example, football fans can produce their own anti-racism leaflet to distribute at a match, display a banner around the ground or get fans to sign up to an anti-racism pledge. To this end, fans can apply for a Community Chest grant, which are available to groups ranging from refugee organizations to fans across the country as part of October's Week of Action. The aim of these grants is to help fund activities that raise awareness of the Week of Action and illustrate the ability that football has to help address issues of race and diversity. Projects awarded funding in the past have included drama productions, youth forums, photography projects, educational programs and anti-racism themed football tournaments. Fans may also choose to work with a club on their anti-racism game during the October period, organize a pre-match activity like a fans' anti-racism football friendly, engage minority groups in organizing the event and involve and inform online communities through forums, message boards, and so on.

Kicking it in the community
Football is played and watched by millions every week. Kick It Out works with amateur teams, youth clubs, community groups and ethnic minority communities. Many ethnic minority communities have historically felt excluded from the game. Our aim is to ensure that all communities are embraced by football and opportunities in the game are widely available to everyone. Kick It Out works with community groups to help them to use football to meet their own objectives and needs. Assistance is available for grass-roots clubs and community projects to identify funding sources for development from external agencies to support excluded communities to encourage greater involvement in the game.

Developing links with communities
Most professional clubs strive to achieve recognition as a "community" or "family" club. In doing so it is important that they develop strong links with their local communities, particularly for those that are situated in areas with significant minority ethnic populations. The majority of clubs are now undertaking a range of activities within their local communities. Our goal is to ensure that all football clubs are reaching out to every community.

Reaching out to community
Some county FA's are also increasing their efforts in reaching out to all sections of the community such as the Manchester and Birmingham FAs. Both county FAs have undertaken some good work in reaching out to their local communities. Kick It Out's work in the community has helped a number of different groups. Kick It Out can help put you in contact with the relevant organizations and offer guidance in other areas of development. Kick It Out is committed to ensuring that all communities take their rightful place as stakeholders in the football family. Identifying and unlocking funding, building contacts within existing football structures and organizing events to engage members of the community can all help to develop a club, organization or community group. But it can be difficult to know where to start when setting out to deliver this work. Among the groups Kick It Out has worked with are Black and Minority Ethnic (BME) community groups; grassroots football clubs, estate-based projects, refugee groups, Traveller communities, schools, prisons, girl's and women's groups and youth clubs. We can help groups with any enquiries or requests including the following:

- ideas for events and strategies on engaging communities;
- partnerships with football clubs;
- partnering with ethnic minority communities;
- advice on funding applications;
- delivering anti-racism workshops;
- supplying anti-racism resources to support your event;

- raising awareness of events and good practice in the media.

Funding is crucial to development. However, the processes involved in identifying the best funding pools to apply for and completing lengthy application forms can prevent groups from attaining much needed funds. The number of applications for funding received from ethnic minority groups in sport is worryingly low, despite the number of groups playing, watching and using football as a tool to deliver wider social messages. Kick It Out and funding bodies such as the Football Foundation want to address this disparity and ensure that all groups have the opportunity to develop, reach their full potential and serve communities across the country. Kick It Out understands the difficulties groups have experienced in getting funding in the past and uses this expertise to offer support and advice to groups exploring funding opportunities. The following are just a few of the funding opportunities that Kick It Out can offer help and advice on.

Junior kit scheme
The Football Foundation is currently able to provide support for junior teams (under-eighteen teams and adults with disabilities) by offering free kit and/or equipment up to the value of £400.

Small grant scheme
The small grants scheme was introduced in 2003 to encourage new activity, which aims to increase participation and provide training for volunteers to support grass-roots football. Funding is available for up to £10,000 over three years.

Community and Education Panel
The aim of the Community and Education Panel is:
    To increase participation and promote healthy and active lifestyles.
    To use football as a tool to increase education attainment, promote social inclusion and challenge social nuisance.
This scheme will fund up to £250,000 over five years for community and education projects.

Capital projects
Capital project scheme includes refurbishment or construction of changing rooms, grass and artificial pitches and clubhouses for community benefit across the country.

Barclaycard Free Kicks
Scheme to help provide teams in disadvantaged areas with equipment, kit and coaching help.

Awards for All (Sports England)
Awards for All is a National Lottery Sports Fund program delivered through Sport England.

Sports Aid
Sports Aid is an independent charity established in 1975. It has three main objectives:
> To further the education of young people through the medium of sport.
> To encourage those with social or physical disadvantages to improve their lives through sport.
> To enable those living in poverty to take advantage of the opportunities offered by sport.

Sports Aid awards grants both nationally and regionally in order to ensure that it helps as many people as possible and that its grants make a difference to the people who receive them.

Sportsmatch
The Sportsmatch scheme is funded in England by the Department for Culture, Media and Sport (DCMS) through Sport England. It has been designed to improve the quality and quantity of the sponsorship which grass-roots sport receives in Great Britain. Through the scheme, every pound of "new" money put forward by a business sponsor can be matched.

Connecting Communities Plus – Community Grants
Connecting Communities Plus is a grants program designed to support practical action to help achieve the goals set out in Improving Opportunity, Strengthening Society, the government's strategy to increase race equality and improve community cohesion. The program facilitates tailored initiatives to meet the specific needs of disadvantaged communities, rather than treating all BME communities in the same way. Connecting Communities Plus – Community Grants are aimed at locally run and managed voluntary and community organizations with an income of less than £50,000 per year, run by volunteers or one full-time or two part-time paid staff. For the first time the fund will also support local projects which are commemorating two hundred years from the passage of the 1807 Abolition of the Slave Trade Act in 2007.

Local Network Fund
The aim of the Local Network Fund is to help disadvantaged children and young people achieve their full potential by investing directly in the activities of local community and voluntary groups working for and with children and young people. Small locally managed community and voluntary groups that work with children and young people and that have constitutions and rules can apply for grants between £250 and £7,000 to help with the costs of activities or services. Most of the children and young people benefiting from the grant must be facing disadvantage or poverty.

Community Champions Fund

The Community Champions Fund supports the work of local people who can encourage others to get more involved in renewing their neighborhoods. The fund offers grants of £50 to £2,000 and is designed to increase the skills levels of individuals to enable them to act as inspirational figures, community entrepreneurs, and community mentors/leaders, in order to increase community involvement in regeneration and learning activity. An emphasis is placed on supporting individuals who have already shown leadership in stimulating community activity, or who have ideas for encouraging greater community activity. The Fund will also support small-scale community-inspired projects as part of supporting potential champions who have not previously sought funding.

Sport Relief

Sport Relief grants look to support voluntary and community groups who are using sport to:

> Increase access to sport and exercise for people who face social isolation and   exclusion.
> Help people who are experiencing difficulties in their lives to regain their confidence.

Grants of up to £10,000 are available and are distributed by local organizations.

Kick It Out is working with community groups all over the country. Groups' needs range from requiring support with events they are organizing to raising awareness of issues relevant their community to advice on funding applications to improve playing facilities. Here are a few case studies of groups that have been working with Kick It Out, using football as a tool for positive change.

Debden United

In the June 2004 local elections three British National Party (BNP) councilors were elected in Debden, Essex. The BNP had leafleted on the issue of refugees in the area alleging an unfair allocation of resources. After the campaign the area saw an increase in race hate crime with young people involved in racially aggravated nuisance activities, targeting minority shopkeepers and pensioners. The homes of the few asylum seekers that had been settled in the area were attacked. The local authority, Epping Forest council, teamed up with local youth clubs to use football activities in an attempt to bring harmony. The authority, through its community partners, received a Community Chest grant from Kick It Out for the 2004 Week of Action to set up an awareness day with a football skills workshop run by West Ham United, along with music and drama performances by youth and schoolchildren. Those interested in football were encouraged to set up a cross-community club, later named Debden United and train together to increase understanding and harmony. The team has become a focus for the community of young people from different ethnicities who are playing and training together every week. The project has made a real impact in the area attracting widespread support from other agencies. They have received funding from the Football Foundation to further the club's development and for a continuation of their aims of working and learning together.

Midland Ethic Albanian Foundation (MEAF), Birmingham
MEAF supports 5,000 Albanian-speaking refugees from Eastern Europe in Birmingham on immigration and social welfare issues. The group entered a team, Friends of Birmingham, in the Unity Cup in July 2004 in Manchester. Having enjoyed the experience they decided it would be a good way of helping the community to settle into life in the Midlands and of breaking down stereotypes of asylum seekers. As well as establishing a football team they have developed a number of educational projects working in schools to raise awareness and educate children about the reality of being a refugee. They go into schools with Birmingham City's Njazi Kuqi (younger brother of Blackburn Rovers striker Shefki Kuqi) as a volunteer. The kids are told how Albanians fled here from Slobodan Milosevic and how they are contributing to life in Birmingham. The Friends of Birmingham football team has sent players on coach education courses and is looking to sustain themselves in the Birmingham leagues. They are currently planning an application to the Football Foundation for £250k over five years after successfully applying for a Community Chest grant in 2004.

Apostolic Christian Church (Sheepfold), Enfield
Kick It Out first supported this group during the Week of Action in 2001, and later in 2003, to hold a football tournament and educational workshops for local young people. The church, led by Pastor Kyri Yiallouris, wanted to challenge the influence of drugs, ease disputes between young men from different communities and tackle anti-social behavior by offering a Saturday morning workshop followed by a football coaching session. The sessions are taken by the pastor and two parents who have taken their basic football coaching qualifications in order to get involved. The project has been enormously successful and the recipient of a small grant of £9,000 from the Football Foundation which has given the group the confidence to seek further funding to continue their positive community work.

Below is a list of other community groups that Kick It Out has worked with:
Football for All (Bedfordshire)
Toxteth Tigers
Elite Youth
Bristol—This Is Our Journey
Brent Ladies
One Game, One City
Barnsley International FC
Mandip Mudhar Memorial Foundation

The number of women involved in football, and sport in general, is growing rapidly, and recently there have been a number of encouraging stories regarding the women's game. Arsenal Ladies have been leading the way in both England and Europe, and won an unprecedented four trophies in 2007. Their squad also made up the vast majority of the England women's team that made the quarter-finals of the 2007 World Cup in China. Dame Kelly Holmes has been campaigning for more girls and young women to get involved in sport, and has launched a new more modern PE kit designed to make sport more attractive to females. Meanwhile, the Asian Football Network has started a groundbreaking new coaching course for Asian and ethnic minority women, the first of its kind in the UK. The first course had twenty-four participants from various different backgrounds, all of whom passed the course. They are now looking forward to commencing their coaching careers and completing further badges. Hampstead Women FC has now been together for over ten years, and they continue to make great strides as the only Jewish-based women's team in the country. Football coach Davinder Kaur Khangura is one of the only Asian females currently coaching football in the UK. She was brought up in a sporting family and developed a passion for the sport. Upon completing her PGCE (Teaching Qualification) she undertook several sports courses and later completed my Level 1 qualification in Football.

The Wolverhampton Wanderers striker Freddy Eastwood is currently the only high-profile member of the Gypsy community playing football in the UK. Eastwood is proud of his heritage, and explains: "My background has helped me in my career, because we're strong people, very close, and even now I'm living in Wolverhampton and my family are at every game." Sadly, Eastwood has had to put up with abuse throughout his career. "I do get picked out. I've never hidden who I am or where I come from, and because of that I get a lot of stick from other fans. I get 'pikey' shouted at me. Or I get 'Gypsy' or 'Gyppo.'" But though the Wales international may be on his own for the time being, history shows that there have been many players with similar backgrounds over the years. Raby Howell, who played for Sheffield United and Liverpool in the 1890s is thought to be the only full-blooded Romany to have played for England. He earned two caps for his country between 1895 and 1898.

Elsewhere in Europe, others of a Gypsy background have risen to the top of the game. Dragoslav Sekularac was a key player for Yugoslavia in the 1958 and 1962 World Cups. He was born into the Vasojevici community in northern Montenegro. Romanian forward Marius Lacatus, who represented his country in two World Cups, and the Yugoslavian defender Sinisa Mihajlovic, who had a long and illustrious career including spells with Lazio, Inter Milan and Roma, also both hail from a Gypsy background. In terms of current players, as well as Eastwood, there is also Jose Antonio Reyes, formerly of Arsenal, and currently playing for Atletico Madrid, who was born and raised in a well known Gypsy area in Utrera, a small town south-east of Seville in Spain. It is also hoped that the next generation of talent in this country will see the Gypsy community represented further, especially with current success stories such as Ilona Marjanska, a Polish member of the Roma community. Ilona arrived in the UK at the age of six, and the only English words she knew were "apple" and "dog." Ten years later, she was studying for her A-Levels and playing for two women's teams, Roma United and Leyton Orient Ladies.

She explained: "My family left Poland in 1996 when I was six because of the hatred against the Roma. My father was beaten and we were getting so much abuse. Britain was different. I learnt English within three months and made friends. My greatest ambition is to play professionally for Leyton Orient and England or Poland."

Education

Kick It Out has long since recognized the important role that football can play to help address issues of race, exclusion and diversity in the classroom. For a number of years, Kick It Out has been drawing on the appeal of football to help educate young people about the effects of racism on both society and individuals. Teachers are increasingly looking for innovative ways to help get messages across to young people, and the introduction of citizenship education into the national curriculum has opened up a space to assist them in bringing football into the classroom. The following are just a short sample of activities that Kick It Out is involved with. However, we are always keen to work with new partners and listen to new ideas.

Kick It Out *magazine*

One of the main resources that we can provide to schools is the *Kick It Out* magazine. The latest edition features interviews with Barcelona striker Samuel Eto'o and Chelsea ace Shaun Wright-Phillips.

Secondary schools competition

Kick It Out organizes an annual schools' competition each year as part of the Week of Action.

Football, Citizenship and Anti-Racism—A Conference for Practitioners

Kick It Out has organized two conferences in recent years at Manchester United FC to provide teachers and other professionals working in education with ideas and examples of good practice.

Work with prisons and other educational establishments

An increasing amount of educational activities are taking place with prisons, youth offending institutes, pupil referral units and youth clubs. Please contact us for further information or if you would like us to come and visit your organization.

Respect: A Playing for Success resource

Kick It Out worked closely with the Department for Education and Skills (DfES) in the production the anti-racism resource, "Respect: Together We Can

Beat Racism." The material is aimed at providing Playing for Success Centre Managers with materials with which to approach the subject of racism and to help celebrate diversity.

Working with the Nut
The Nut has provided financial support to Kick It Out for a number of years. Recent projects we are supporting them with include "The Other Side of Silence," a one-day seminar to help teachers who work within mainly white schools develop practical and sustainable strategies for valuing cultural diversity and challenging racism.

Each year, Kick It Out organizes a number of youth forums that use role models to deliver positive messages about race and ethnicity. The sessions also help to raise the aspirations and educational achievements of young people. Moving On Up Youth Forums provide young people in different areas of the country with the chance to hear and meet a number of role models, drawn from football, other sports, music and the media to help raise motivation and achievement. The aim of each session is to help instill a sense of belief in those attending and to help them understand opportunities to succeed and raise aspirations. The events also look at the effects of racism both within football (and sport more generally) and within the wider community. Each forum features three or four panelists chosen to illustrate key messages about personal motivation drawing on the dedication and work that they have put into their own profession. Events often include an element of performance such as dance, song or theater to help showcase community projects.

Events
A number of events took place as part of the 2007 Week of Action in October, including events in Liverpool and Manchester. Manchester United hosted the event in Manchester, attended by former athlete Darren Campbell, actress Shobna Gulati, Manchester United legends Paddy Crerand and Tony Whelan and former Oldham Athletic defender and PFA executive Richard Jobson. The event was hosted by the official United pitch announcer, Alan Keegan. As part of the event the young people, drawn from across Greater Manchester, got a chance to take part in a theater workshop, organized by Theatrebus, visit the Manchester United Museum and study the exhibition produced by Manchester FA, "Many Different Colours—One Beautiful Game." The Liverpool event was held at the Everton Sports Centre. Almost three hundred young people attended from schools across Merseyside. The event was organized by Kick It Out in conjunction with the Liverpool community organization, the L8 Sports Forum, with Liverpool, Everton and Tranmere football clubs supporting the activity. SKY Sports presenter Rob Palmer hosted the event and was joined by Liverpool's first black player, Howard Gayle, former Everton star Graeme Sharp, England Women's midfielder Fara Williams, Tranmere striker Calvin Zola and Great Britain Athlete, Anikya Anoura. Kick It Out's School's Resource Pack has been

put together to provide schools with ideas for work within the curriculum. The pack contains a CD with a comprehensive set of curriculum ideas for use in the classroom, which has been put together by a leading educator. The following ideas provide a useful starting point for a number of activities in the classroom that incorporate many aspects related to the teaching of citizenship. It also highlights how football can be used to explore a number of issues.

Starting out
A good starting point for any classroom work on anti-racism is to look at definitions of race, prejudice and discrimination

Race: A group of people connected by common descent.

Racism: The word "racism" comes from the word "race." Racism is the belief that people are inferior because they are of a different color or come from another part of the world. Most commonly, racism is prejudice backed up by power.

Prejudice: A judgment about something based upon ignorance; making up your mind before you have any facts.

Discrimination: When you treat someone differently because of the prejudices that you have about them.

Teachers may want to set some boundaries within the classroom when working in this area about acceptable language and they should ensure that discussions are carefully managed so that a balanced view is given. All of those involved in these activities should be encouraged to listen carefully and sensitively.

History of black footballers
An explosion of talented black footballers changed the game in Britain in the 1970s and 1980s, many from families who had arrived in Britain as immigrants after World War Two, but the history of black footballers, like that of ethnic minority communities in Britain, is much longer.

Activity: Many people would be surprised to learn that the first black professional footballer to play in England was Arthur Wharton, who made his debut in 1886, for Preston the year after football became professional.

Ask the pupils to carry out some research about the first black player to play for their local and/or their favorite club.

An interesting activity is to get the pupils to produce their own timeline on black Britain. On one side they could put notable dates related to football and on the other side notable dates relating to wider society. A blank timeline, with one or two dates to help pupils get started can be downloaded from the education section on Kick It Out's website.

Racism in football
Many black players who played in Britain, particularly during the 1970s and 1980s, faced abuse from the crowds because of the color of their skin. This abuse was in many forms and included monkey chanting and the throwing of bananas onto the pitch. Although as Rio Ferdinand acknowledges, this is less frequent du-

ring today's matches, it does still happen, particularly in Europe. There have been a number of high profile cases recently when the England team has played overseas.

Activities: The game between England and Spain in Madrid in 2005 gained huge media attention because of the racist abuse a number of England players received. Organize a class discussion about how those players would have felt and how their white teammates might also have reacted.

Ask pupils to carry out a mock interview with one of the black players who played in the game about their experiences that night.

Rio Ferdinand criticizes clubs in Europe because of their lack of security and lack of action in removing fans who participate in racist abuse. In England, strict laws are set out about how to deal with fans when this occurs. Ask pupils to research what these laws are. How have they changed over recent years? Do they think that they are strong enough and how would they change them? What would pupils do if they faced racism at school? Pupils should consider their own roles and responsibilities for ensuring their school is free from racism. It is important that pupils are empowered to believe they all have a responsibility to address this issue, whatever their color or nationality. Classes could come up with their up their own code of conduct.

Prejudice and stereotyping

Both Rio Ferdinand and Zesh Rehman talk about the lack of Asian players who play at a professional level. A number of stereotypes are often mentioned when trying to explain this absence. This includes physical makeup, diets and the belief that parents would rather their children became doctors or dentists rather than professional footballers.

Activities: It would be helpful to get pupils to carry out some general work to look at why we have stereotypes about different racial groups. It is important to point out that these are rarely based on fact. What stereotypes exist about other ethnic groups? What stereotypes do people overseas have about Britain?

Organize a classroom debate on "Asians Can't Play Football." To prepare for this debate, pupils should carry out some general research, including information about the number of Asians playing professional football. Did you know that in the 1890s the Anglo-Indian Cother brothers played for Watford?

Promoting different faiths and cultures

Rio Ferdinand believes that through initiatives such as the national anti-racism week, football help promote understanding of different faiths and cultures. Zesh Rehman is one of an increasing number of Muslims who play professional football, even during the holy month of Ramadan.

Activities: Pupils should carry out some research about the different religious festivals that are celebrated by different religions. When do they occur and what customs and festivities are practiced? How might this festival have an impact on professional footballers? Are there any professional footballers that celebrate this festival in England?

An interesting activity to help pupils think about different religious festivals would be to imagine that they are a player at the local football club. One of their teammates was from overseas and celebrated a different religious festival. The player was feeling a bit homesick, and so to cheer the player up you decide to organize a party for them at the club to celebrate the festival.

Pupils should each pick a different religious festival to plan. They will need to think about what they should serve to eat and drink, what people might wear and what customs might be practiced. Pupils could also design and produce an invitation to the party.

Role models

Rio Ferdinand lists among his role models his mum and dad, John Barnes, Paul Gascoigne and Ian Wright. He also gives details of the support that he got from the staff at Manchester United during his enforced absence from the game. Young people will have many role models from the world of films, music and sport. They will also be influenced by the behavior of their peers.

Activities: Some class discussion could take place around role models, including who do the young people look up to and respect? What qualities does this person have? What is a positive and negative role model? Is having a role model a good thing? Who chooses role models?

Pupils could write a diary entry on behalf of Rio Ferdinand during the period in which he was banned. The piece could focus on how he was going to try and keep motivated and how he was going to try and use this time in a positive way.

The work could also describe Rio's feelings when he found out about the length of the ban. To help put this into context pupils could also think about what they would do if they were banned from doing something for a long period of time.

Fans and supporters

There are still only a small number of black and Asian fans that regularly go to watch football matches in this country. In most grounds, less than 1 percent of the total crowd is made up from the black and Asian community. Campaigns like Kick It Out are working to help increase this number, and to encourage clubs to welcome black and Asian fans into the game.

Activities: Carry out a survey within the group about the number of people that go to watch football matches. Do they feel safe and welcomed? Why might people not go to games and what can be done to overcome this?

Pupils could be encouraged to develop their own campaign to encourage the community to go to watch their local team. This campaign should focus on a number of different areas, such as writing articles for their local media and developing posters and advertisements that could feature in schools, youth centers and local libraries.

Refugees and asylum-seekers
There are a number of professional footballers who are currently playing in England whose families came to Britain to seek asylum. These include Lomana Lua Lua (Portsmouth FC) and Calvin Zola (Tranmere Rovers FC).

Activities: Pupils should be encouraged to think about the reasons why people leave their own countries and the difficulties they often face settling into a new country. This process can often be made worse through the negative headlines that often appear in the tabloid press, which are based upon stereotypes and prejudice. Some interesting work can take place comparing how the different media report on this issue.

Pupils could write a letter to one of the tabloid newspapers, setting out their concern about the way that they portray refugees and asylum seekers.

Ask pupils to research some of the reasons why the family of Lua Lua might have fled their original country of residence.

There are a number of organizations that have produced a variety of resources to help organizations plan activities around anti-racism education.

Association for Citizenship Teaching (ACT)
ACT is the subject teacher's association for citizenship education. ACT aims to support all educators and organizations in the development and implementation of citizenship education. It provides members with useful networks, the latest information, and practical ideas through conferences and its quarterly journal *Teaching Citizenship*.

The Citizenship Foundation
The Citizenship Foundation provides resources for all ages, research, information, training, national mock trial and youth parliament competitions. They cover all aspects of citizenship education, including law-related, moral education, political literacy and critical thinking.

Institute for Citizenship
The Institute for Citizenship works directly with teachers and students to develop and pilot effective models of citizenship education and accessible materials for lessons.

Community Service Volunteers (CSV)
CSV provides ideas and contacts for ways of playing an active part in communities through volunteering, training, education and the media. There is a separate new website with a directory of community organizations and guidelines for good practice (www.communitypartners.org.uk).

CitizED
CitizED is a project focused on citizenship teacher education. It seeks to develop the professional knowledge of teachers through research and development in

professional learning and supports trainee teachers, newly qualified teachers, teacher mentors and others with responsibility for citizenship education.

Curriculum Online
Here you'll find multimedia resources to support teaching and learning. All resources support the curriculum taught in schools in England from Foundation to KS4. Many are free.

Institute of Race Relations
The institute has produced an award winning anti-racism educational CD-ROM called "Homebeats." The site contains information on a number of key issues and features an online quiz.

Refugee Council
The Refugee Council is the largest organization in the UK working with refugees and asylum seekers. They have produced a range of materials for use in schools.

The Holocaust Educational Trust
The Trust helps promote research and education about the Holocaust and its relevance today. They work in schools, universities and in the community, proving teacher training, an outreach program for schools, teaching aids and resource material.

1990 Trust
The 1990 Trust runs the Black Information Link (BLINK) website. This site contains a variety of information about many issues that are faced by ethnic minority communities in Britain.

A couple of other useful sites include the following.
Britkid
This website contains a game for young people about race and the effects of racism. It also contains teacher's notes and a guide on using the resources in the classroom.

BBC Learning
The BBC's learning website contains ideas, resources and lesson plans.

Channel Four
The site contains information about their current citizenship education programs.

Football poets
The site contains an interesting collection of poems based around football.

To mark the launch of his autobiography, *Black and Blue*, ex-Chelsea star and Kick It Out supporter Paul Canoville spoke to *The Voice* about the racist abuse and bigotry that he endured from the club's own supporters. The Stamford Bridge club, now one of the most cosmopolitan in Europe, today embraces players from around the world. But Canoville, who blazed a painful trail for black players at the west London club as its first black player, was not welcomed in the same way as today's heroes who include the likes of Didier Drogba, Michael Essien, Claude Makelele and Ashley Cole. He vividly remembers the first time he pulled on a Chelsea shirt recounting the moment he was told to warm-up by Chelsea manager John Neal. His runs and stretches down the side of the pitch were to be greeted by the worst possible reaction: "Nothing could have prepared me for what happened next. As I'm stretching and running, I hear a loud voice through the noise: 'Sit down you black c***! You f****** wog, f*** off!' Over and over again. Lots of different people. I hardly dared look round. They were right behind me. I snatched a glimpse. They were all wearing blue shirts and scarves—Chelsea fans, my side's fans, faces screwed with hatred and anger, all directed at me. . . . Then it came. Chanting, not just by one or two people, but what sounded like scores of people, a huge mob: 'We don't want the nigger! We don't want the nigger!" Canoville, who made his name at Hillingdon Borough before transferring to Chelsea in 1981, added: "A banana landed near me as I walked back, head bowed, to take off my training top. I felt physically sick. I was absolutely terrified. In the dressing room, dazed and confused, I sat, hunched, motionless, muttering to myself, so many thoughts racing through my head. Why all this hatred against their own player? I felt so isolated, not for the first time in my life. It had taken me completely by surprise and I was stunned." Canoville played for Chelsea for five seasons before joining Reading in 1986 for £50,000.

Racial equality standard

The Racial Equality Standard for Professional Football Clubs is a framework document setting out a series of measures to support the development of race equality policies and practices at clubs. The Racial Equality Standard is a tool that can support clubs in their journey toward racial equality. The Standard is a framework document setting out a series of measures that supports the development of racial equality practices and policies within a club environment. Professional clubs are asked to work to a series of objectives that ensure equality in all areas of their operation—from stewarding, to the recruitment of administration staff and the development of young players. The document has been developed by Kick It Out, with the support of the FA Premier League, and from source materials including Sporting Equal's "Achieving Racial Equality: A Standard for Sport."

How do clubs achieve it?
The Standard has three levels of achievement—Preliminary, Intermediate and Advanced. Each club will begin by working towards the Preliminary Level followed by Intermediate and Advanced. There are three areas of activity that cover all areas of a clubs activity—Stadium and Outreach, Policy and Planning, and Administration and Management. Within each area a number of objectives need to be met.

What is the process?
To achieve each level of the Standard, our Development Officer will work with clubs to support them in gathering evidence that address each objective at that level. This is a facilitative process that ensures that every club is supported at every step. Once the evidence is compiled, the file is submitted for consideration by an independent Accreditation Panel. The Accreditation Panel includes specialists in race and equality, organizational development and sports administration. Chaired by Lord Herman Ouseley, the other members are Jonathan Long, Director of the Centre for Leisure and Sports Research at Leeds Metropolitan University; Mike Lee, CEO of Vero communications and former Communications Director for London 2012; and Sheila Rogers, independent consultant and former CEO at the Commission for Racial Equality.

What will be the impact?
The Racial Equality Standard is a tool that can support clubs in their journey toward racial equality and help build long-term foundations for sustainable club and community development. Football has the power to engage all communities and this document will encourage clubs to expand and extend existing partnerships. As a framework it will ensure processes are in place to address the underrepresentation of ethnic minority groups within all levels of the club environment and bring with it a business advantage. There are a number of long-term benefits that can be drawn from working on the Racial Equality Standard, including (1) improvements in local perceptions, (2) better consultation and more participation from the local community in club activities and (3) increase in numbers of ethnic minority supporters and representation at all levels of the club. In terms of policy and organizational developments, it will bring advantages to employment functions including:

- better targeting of policy and marketing strategies;
- ability to attract able staff who will in time reflect the local community;
- identifying and developing good practice;
- avoiding claims of unlawful discrimination.

Racial equality practices will convey a diversity of ideas and experiences that we hope will ensure success both on and off the field.

Professional clubs working for equality

The Racial Equality Standard for Professional Football Clubs, which has been developed by Kick It Out with the support of the Premier League, sets out a series of graded measures for professional clubs. The measures encourage clubs to deliver a range of objectives that ensure equality policies are implemented in all areas of their operation, from stewarding to the recruitment of young players.

Increased understanding

Clubs achieving the standard are reporting back an increased understanding of diversity issues throughout the organization. Kick It Out believes the Standard can play its part to help to overcome issues such as representation from ethnic minorities within administration positions at clubs. All Premier League clubs are working to meet the first level of the Standard within the next year. Blackburn Rovers, Birmingham City, Everton, Fulham, Manchester City as well as Notts County became the first clubs to achieve the Preliminary Level.

Lord Herman Ouseley, Chair of Kick It Out, said, "we believe the Standard could provide the basis which would herald a new era in encouraging clubs to ensure that off-the-field-of-play equality of opportunity, inclusion and fair treatment are at the heart of what they do. This will require the determination, commitment and sustainability on the part of those people who run and manage clubs, if we are to achieve any meaningful change."

Richard Scudamore, Chief Executive of the FA Premier League, said, "we all have a responsibility and a part to play in helping to put the Standard into practice. From the Premier League our message is simple; we are committed to succeeding in this area."

The number of clubs achieving the Standard is growing. A number of clubs have achieved the Preliminary Level of the Racial Equality Standard and are now working towards the Intermediate Level. Clubs achieving the standard are reporting back an increased understanding of diversity issues throughout the organization. All Premier League clubs are working to meet the first level of the Standard within the next year.

The Racial Equality Standard can help football clubs' understanding of the strength they have in tackling social problems. The framework aims to acknowledge clubs that demonstrate (1) equality programs integrated into the club, (2) success and local impact of equality programs and (3) senior management support to community practices as well as across the business agenda. Clubs that achieve the Racial Equality Standard will have the opportunity to (1) attend an annual celebratory event, hosted by Kick It Out and the governing bodies, to congratulate club success, (2) have individual club success profiled to wider business through the annual gathering and (3) be endorsed by Lord Herman Ouseley and the governing bodies.

Case Studies
FA Premier League—Manchester City FC
Manchester City FC was the first professional club to achieve the Intermediate
Level of the Standard in September 2006. On setting out on their journey toward
race equality back in 2005, the club understood that in order to engage with the
city, they had to get themselves out into the different communities that made up
Manchester. Working with the close support of the Chief Executive, the club
organized an internal working group headed by their Social Responsibility
Manager, a unique role itself within football. They developed an action plan and
consulted with appropriate community partners and now have a successful club
brand, One City Celebrating the Cultures and Diversity of Manchester.

Coca-Cola Championship—Queens Park Rangers FC
Queens Park Rangers FC Community department proactively led on the implementation of the Standard. The department was already working with a variety
of statutory and voluntary sector agencies to deliver inclusive packages to their
local community. Colleagues within the club started from the point that in order
to make their match day environment appealing to the local community, they
had to understand and learn who this community was. They have directed significant resources into estates-based projects, as well as nurturing a sense of
sustainability through encouraging local young people to deliver activities to
their peer group, a number of which have since secured part-time coaching opportunities within the club. QPR FC was also one of the first professional clubs
to deliver a program to their local Traveller community.

Coca-Cola Championship—Blackpool FC
Working closely with the support of the Chairman, Blackpool FC have been
working towards the Preliminary Level of the Standard and have shown innova-
tion in their approach to be an all inclusive community club. Views of the junior
board and consultation from the local community are fed back to the official
club board on a regular basis. The club has a number of activities that engage
and encourage all sections of the community to experience and use the stadium
facilities, including female friendly nights at the stadium.

Coca-Cola League Two—Notts County FC
Notts County FC became the first Football League club to achieve the Preliminary Level of the Standard in September 2005. They have shown their colleagues within the industry that large resources, including finances, is not required when working toward equal opportunities. The club worked with the
Supporters' Trust as well as with a local voluntary umbrella group called Voice
East Midlands. Notts County continues to work toward implementing equality
practices and through their work in the community are able reach excluded
groups within the area. They were recently successful in a bid to Stand Up,
Speak Up for the development and launch of a poster campaign throughout the

city, encouraging participation from across all the diversity strands, as well as promoting an incident line to report potential incidents.

Professional football clubs have came together at seminars in London and Leeds to discuss their practical experiences of working on the Racial Equality Standard. Kick It Out has been working with clubs across the country on the framework document for professional clubs to help them extend and develop their racial equality work. Each seminar highlighted examples of good practice of work taking place within clubs. Both events were aimed at clubs who are already working on the Standard and those that have not yet started work but who hope to do so next season. Club representatives including club secretaries, chief executives and human resources managers attended, along with colleagues who have direct responsibility for the areas covered by the Standard. The seminars encouraged an environment where those within different clubs could discuss and share practical experiences of working on equality issues. It will also provided an opportunity to look at the ways that clubs with the Standard could help to support other clubs working toward achieving it.

Unity Cup Festival

The first Unity Cup Festival was held in Manchester four years ago. Since then the tournament has become increasingly popular with more teams participating. Refugees and asylum seekers are amongst the most reviled groups in Britain. Demonized by sections of the media, isolated by government policy and subjected to verbal and physical attacks on the streets, they face the brunt of the worst kinds of popular racism and are even despised by some sections of other settled ethnic minority communities. To help address some of these issues, Kick It Out organizes the Unity Cup Festival to engage and work with refugees, asylum seekers and other displaced communities across Britain by using the power of football to overcome exclusion, build confidence and address overt racism at refugee communities.

Football

The Unity Cup Festival is based around a national seven-a-side football tournament played over two days. The teams play against each other for the Unity Cup and Unity Shield. As the tournament is not geared toward identifying the best football talent, the main prize is the Marc Vivien Foe FairPlay Award. The award, named after the former West Ham and Manchester City midfielder who tragically died on the football field in 2003, is given to the team that has played the tournament in the best spirits.

Participants

Teams of refugees and those seeking asylum from all corners of the UK are invited to participate in the festival. To help promote integration and understanding, Kick It Out has also invited a number of mainstream football teams to participate. The annual event is aimed predominantly at young adults (the over-sixteen age group) who currently do not participate in most of the football development work undertaken by football clubs and local authorities.

Guests and VIPs
A number of guests and VIPs attend the different elements of the event to show their support and to pass on advice about how they became successful in their own fields. Guests attending previous Unity Cup Festival events include Manchester United defender Wes Brown, Coronation Street actresses Shobna Gulati and Hayley Hesmondalgh, and former footballers including Ces Podd and Tony Whelan of Bradford and Manchester United respectively.

Friendship
Over the weekend some amazing flashes of skill, moments of brilliance and gestures of great sportsmanship are witnessed, but most importantly, those attending make new friends and acquaintances while making their stand against racism and calling for equality.

Unity Cup 2005
The Unity Cup Festival final came to an exciting conclusion after a weekend of football, friendship and discussion in the Leeds sunshine. The festival, which took place in July, kicked off on Saturday afternoon with Leeds North MP, Fabian Hamilton, and West Riding County FA chief, Peter Marsden, welcoming the teams of players from displaced communities. Twenty teams from Birmingham, Cardiff, Dover, Exeter, Glasgow, Huddersfield, Hull, London, Manchester, Norwich, Sheffield, Southampton, Sunderland and Worthing joined their hosts from Leeds. A team of Roma gypsies from Slovakia flew over thanks to sponsorship from construction company, The Breyer Group. In the opening ceremony, former Bradford City pioneering black player Ces Podd, a young Somali player from Sheffield Wednesday's Youth academy, Mukhtar Mohammed, and former Leeds star Brendon Ormonsby offered words of support for the festival and drew the teams into groups. As the football got into full flow residents of Leeds were treated to some impressive football skills while refugee musicians played live music from their native countries. Keeping those unable to make it to the festival updated was Unity Radio 106.6 FM run by youngsters from Roundhay School and members of the local refugee community. Players and special guests at the festival were interviewed live on-air in between sets played by local DJs and sports bulletins. Sunday afternoon saw an exciting climax to the festival as finalists VG Foundation, a team of Angolan refugees from Manchester, and the Friends of Birmingham, an Albanian, Kosovar and Kurdish refugee team, stepped forward for a penalty shoot out following a 1-1 draw at the end of full time. VG Foundation, who had a former Benfica player in their ranks, won the shoot-out. In the Unity Shield local Leeds team, Roundhay Moles, beat Sheffield's Albanian Fire while Sunderland Samba International took the Fair Play trophy named after the late Marc Vivien Foe. Participants at the festival were

keen to offer their congratulations to the winning teams but the loudest applause went to Gilberto Gomes of Unity Cup, winners VG Foundation, and Sidiqui of Azadi from Exeter, who scored his team's only goal in the tournament over the two days. Sawd Ghiliani, who fled to Britain five years ago, seeking refuge from Iran, representing the Fair Play winners, Sunderland Samba, summed up the weekend: "We are all together, communicating with each other and building friendships through playing football." A Southampton United player who did not want to be named added, "Many British people are given false images of asylum seekers. This event may help change some people's views."

Unity Cup 2006
The Unity Cup Festival took place in Sheffield between 14 and 16 July 2006. Twenty teams of refugees and those seeking asylum from across the UK came together for a weekend of football and friendship. A weekend of friendship through football at the Unity Cup Festival in Sheffield came to an exciting climax. The national festival, organized by Kick It Out, brought twenty teams of refugees and asylum seekers together from all corners of the UK to highlight the positive contribution displaced communities are making to society and to challenge negative stereotypes. The Lord Mayor of Sheffield, Councilor Jackie Drayton, officially opened the festival on Friday evening in a ceremony that included performances by local bands, DJs and dance groups with an attendance of thousands of local people. The teams were drawn into groups at the opening with the help of Sheffield United star, Leigh Bomby, former Sheffield United strike-force, Brian Deane and Tony Agana, and local boxing star Amer "Killa" Khan. Mukhtar Mohammed, a young Somali player from the Sheffield Wednesday Academy, helped with draw. The Festival split into two on Saturday night with two separate trophies up for grabs, the Unity Cup and Unity Shield. Last year's winners VG Foundation Manchester retained their title, meeting Sheffield side Albanian Fire in the Unity Cup final. Polish Consul, attending the festival for the first time, took home the Shield after a final with Hull's Azardi ARKH. Bolton side, FC Strongbow, were voted the Marc Vivien Foe Fairplay winners and will now join Chelsea and Liverpool fans at the Community Cup Final in Cardiff next month courtesy of The FA. The vote on who would be going to Cardiff reflected how the spirit of the festival was enjoyed by all the teams, as only one vote separated the team from five others. Sheffield United Academy Director George Harrison paid testament to the teams: "There have been some fantastic players on show here over the weekend and I've been very impressed by how the teams have played the game in the right spirits. . . . The Unity Cup Festival has surpassed all of my expectations and we feel proud to have hosted this great event." The Unity Cup Festival was organized in partnership with the Sheffield-based Football Unites, Racism Divides project and is supported by Sheffield City Council, Sheffield County FA and Amicus trade union. A Bristol team featuring refugees and asylum seekers has been crowned the Unity Shield winner at a national football festival organized to help combat racism. After a tense final, the Bristol team, Polish Consul, overcame a strong Hull side with the

final decided by a penalty shoot-out. The team took home a full set of England kits, courtesy of the Football Association. The Unity Cup Festival, organized by Kick It Out, football's anti-racism campaign, brought together teams of refugees and asylum seekers from all corners of the UK to highlight the positive contribution displaced communities are making in the UK.

The weekend featured twenty teams from Birmingham, Bolton, Bristol Cardiff, Edinburgh, Hull, Leeds, London, Manchester, Newcastle, Norwich, Southampton, Stoke on Trent, Worthing and the host city Sheffield. The Marc Viven Foe Fairplay trophy, named after the former Manchester City star who tragically died on the field of play in 2003, was won by FC Strongbow from Bolton. Piara Powar, Director of Kick It Out, said, "The Unity Cup Festival is about much more than a football tournament, it is about bringing some of the most marginalized communities together through football." Sheffield United Academy Director George Harrison commented, "There have been some fantastic players on show here over the weekend and I've been very impressed by how the teams have played the game in the right spirits. The Unity Cup Festival has surpassed all of my expectations and we feel proud to have hosted this great event."

Unity Cup 2007
The Unity Cup Festival will reach more than a thousand footballers from displaced communities this year. Following the success of the annual festival, which was launched in 2003, the format has been changed to engage more displaced communities and capacity build groups across the country. This year, regional Unity Cup Festivals were held across the country to ensure that the football tournament and its message have a greater reach. Kick It Out will work with regional partners to stage the regional football festivals and provide prizes, equipment and branding for every event. To ensure that fair play is a central message at every festival, the teams collecting the biggest prices will not be the winners of the tournament, but the team that receives the Fair Play Award.

Regional Unity Cup Festivals took place in the following cities:
    Manchester—16 June
    Edinburgh—17 June
    Southampton—23 June
    Bristol—23 June
    Sunderland—24 June
    Birmingham—24 June
    Liverpool—30 June
    Sheffield—30 June

Asians in football
Hundreds of thousands of young Asians are playing and watching the game around the country every weekend. But there is a massive under-representation of

the Asian community in the professional game. The facts speak for themselves. There are only five Asian players in professional football and a recent Commission for Racial Equality (CRE) survey into professional football in 2004 revealed that in total there were only ten Asian players at Premier League club academies. Within the Asian community there continues to be a feeling that Asian players have been marginalized by the game for far too long.

Popular myths

Popular myths such as that Asians are only interested in cricket and hockey, that Asians aren't strong enough to play the game professionally and that cultural differences prevent Asian players football development are just a few of the common falsehoods that have hampered Asian players' breakthrough. In response, a number of groups have organized themselves to ensure they are providing young talented players from the Asian community with the chance to improve and progress. Teams such as London APSA and Sporting Bengal became the first Asian clubs to play in the FA Cup in 2005. Albion Sports Club from Bradford, perhaps Britain's most successful local Asian Football Club, have reached the nationwide FA Sunday Cup Final twice, and the London Asian Football League continues to grow, attracting teams from all backgrounds. These are just a few examples of how Asians are climbing the football ladder. While frustrations remain, the love for the game drives on talented young Asians in striving to achieve the goal of joining trailblazers Rehman, Chopra, Singh and Ahmed in the professional game. Under-representation in other areas of the game is also beginning to be challenged with the successes of Football League referees, Jarnail Singh and Mo Matadar. The game recognized the need to ensure that the Asian community is no longer excluded from the game following the launch of the Asians Can Play football report in 2005.

Football family commitment

Simon Johnson, the Football Association's Director of Corporate Affairs, said on behalf of the football family, "We want to create more and better coaches from the Asian communities. We want to create clear pathways for the most talented to progress. We want to ensure that, when the Clubs are scouting for players, they are doing so in such a way that they can find the very best talent from the Asian communities. Each of the bodies has a role to play in making all this happen. We know that, and we are taking the necessary action. We also want to see the active fan base at our clubs adapt to reflect the diversity of the communities in which they play." The National Asians in Football Forum are a group of individuals who are working with Asian communities and football or sports development across the UK. The group was formed with the objective of addressing the glaring under-representation of the Asian community as players, fans and administrators in the game. Following a number of meetings, Jas Bains, former chair of the National Asians in Football Forum, published the "Asians Can Play Football" report, which followed his initial report in 1996 ironically entitled, "Asians Can't Play Football." The aim of the document was to register the determination of the group to chart a new course to increase opportunities for Asians in British Football, report on progress made in developing football within community and sports projects around the UK and comment on some of the barriers that still restrict progress. The report was launched at Highbury on the 22nd September 2005 and called on the game to ensure that increased efforts are made to guarantee that Asians are no longer excluded from the game and that the overall problem of lack of representation in football is addressed throughout the sport. The group has since brought the football family together for the "Future for Asians in British Football" conference which addressed the issues facing the Asian football community and highlighted the boundaries that exist. The group has been given organizational support by Kick It Out and the Foxes Against Racism partnership in Leicester. The current Chair of the National Asians in Football Forum is Butch Fazal.

Player support

Professional footballers have been getting behind Kick It Out since its inception in 1993. As role models their words and actions can have a profound impact in promoting messages central to the campaign. A common criticism of players is that they have lost touch with their community. However, a number of players have been attending events and setting up initiatives to give something back. The Professional Footballers' Association is one of the Kick It Out's founding partners and their members have been instrumental in raising awareness of racism in football. Through attending events, speaking out about their experiences and supporting local initiatives, professional players have been adding their voices to the call for equality in the game. Jason Roberts has kick-started a foundation aiming to help enrich the lives of young people in some of London's inner cities. The Grenada born Blackburn Rovers forward was joined by an array of sporting stars, past and present, at the official launch following a successful project in North West London. The Jason Roberts Foundation will work with children and young people by providing a host of activities, including football coaching, social and life-skill training, as well as addressing issues such as social exclusion. Roberts, who is the nephew of former international footballer Cyrille Regis, has kept it a family affair by including his uncle on his qualified expert team. Even though the Premier League season is set to end, Roberts has no intention of resting during the summer; instead he plans to run a football clinic in Grenada for more than 250 children. He said, "I am fortunate enough to be able to play in the Premiership and do a job that I love. Through football, we can reach young people and get them to become the people they know they can be, both in the UK and in Grenada."

Europe

The problem of racism in European football is being described by some as "endemic." Players, fans and ethnic minority communities are abused regularly in some parts of Europe where far right activity is rife and National Football Federations are in denial of the problem. Neo-Nazi and neo-fascist groups target football grounds in Europe in the same way that the National Front and other far-right groups targeted English football stadiums as a recruitment ground. Among the worst affected clubs are Lazio and Verona in Italy, Paris Saint-Germain in France, and Real Madrid and Real Zaragoza in Spain. The problem of racism in Southern Europe was highlighted when England's black players received mass monkey chants from thousands of fans at the Bernabeu in their friendly game against Spain in November 2004. There has since been an increasing number of incidents where black players have been racially abused in Spanish football. Last season (2004-2005), Real Zaragoza were fined 600 euros by the Spanish Football Federation (RFEF) after a section of their fans directed racist abuse at Barcelona forward, Samuel Eto'o. Athletico Madrid were also fined 6,000 euros by the RFEF for the racial abuse of Espanyol's Cameroon goalkeeper Carlos Kameni in a league match. Deportivo La Coruna, Albacete, and Getafe also received fines for similar incidents in their grounds. In Italy, Messina's Ivory Coast defender Zoro threatened to halt a Serie A game in Italy this season after suffering racial abuse from visiting Inter Milan supporters. Other prominent problems in the past in Italy include when a Jewish player, Ronnie Rosenthal, was unable to play even one game for Udinese because of massive pressure from neo-fascist circles and Aaron Winter, a native of Suriname of Hindustani extraction was subject to attacks at Lazio involving cries of "Niggers and Jews Out." In Central and Eastern Europe problems of racism, and anti-Semitism in particular, are a part of everyday life. The racist abuse directed at England's black players in the Euro 2004 qualifier against Slovakia in 2002 brought the issue to the attention of the international football community. However, the problem of widespread racism in Central and Eastern European football stadiums had existed long before, with black players playing in the domestic leagues of countries including Poland, Hungary, Slovakia and Romania being subjected to mass monkey chanting and being pelted with bananas every week. To challenge the problem anti-racism campaigners, ethnic minority communities and some National Football Associations have set up anti-racism campaigns to raise awareness of the problem and encourage fans to stand against racism. Kick It Out is a leading member of the Football Against Racism in Europe (FARE) network. The FARE network dedicates itself to fight racism and xenophobia in football across Europe. Through coordinated action and common effort, at local and national levels, the network brings together all those interested in combating discrimination in football.

In February 1999, football supporters and anti-racism campaigners from across Europe came together in Vienna, Austria, alongside representatives of football associations and players' unions to develop a common strategy for combating racism and xenophobia. At that meeting, the Football Against Racism in Europe network was established. Since FARE was established the network has grown to work with groups in more than thirty-five countries with the aim of encouraging joint efforts to combat racism and discrimination and to nurture growing opposition to racism from all those involved in the game. In August 2001, FARE was presented with UEFA's Monaco Award for the 2001-2002 season, marking the start of a proactive partnership with European football's governing body. FARE has also been recognized by MTV, being awarded the prestigious Free Your Mind Award, and the European Monitoring Centre on Racism and Xenophobia, with the Jean Kahn Award. In 2004, FARE successfully organized an anti-racism program and—in partnership with Football Supporters International—fan embassies at Euro 2004 in Portugal. In the same year, UEFA renewed its partnership with FARE for three seasons.

FARE calls upon football governing bodies and clubs to:

- recognize the problem of racism in football;
- adopt, publish and enact anti-racist policy;
- make full use of football to bring people together from different communities and cultures;
- establish a partnership with all organizations committed to kicking racism out of football, in particular with supporters groups, migrants and ethnic minorities.

FARE commits itself to:

- challenging all forms of racist behavior in stadia and within clubs by making our voice(s) heard;
- including ethnic minorities and migrants within our organization and partner organizations;
- working together with all organizations willing to tackle the problem of racism in football.

Mondiali 2008

Amateur teams, particularly those from ethnic minorities, are being encouraged to join more than six thousand footballers from all corners of Europe in Italy for one of the world's largest football festivals in July. The *Mondiali Antirazzisti*, translating as "Anti-Racism World Cup," attracts hundreds of teams to a five-a-side football carnival where fans, anti-racism campaigners, youth groups, students and ex-professionals come together in a symbolic stand against racism and discrimination. The tournament operates with a group system in the early stages, then a knock-out stage involving the best sixty-four teams will take place. Not all of the pitches are used throughout the tournament therefore some will be available for friendly matches for teams not making it past the group stage. After the success of last year's tournament, the semi-finals and final will not be played, but decided on penalties. The multicultural festival will take place between 9-13 July in the northern Italian town of Montecchio, organized by Italian fan group *Progetto Ultra*, a leading member of the Football Against Racism in Europe network. The diversity of the event grows each year with teams of migrants from Ghana, Turkey, Nigeria, Pakistan and Palestine among those taking part.

Other entertainment at the *Mondiali* includes films, documentaries and performances from bands and DJs. There is also a highly popular cricket and basketball tournament that runs alongside the football. The event makes for an inexpensive weekend with cheap flights and camping facilities, restaurants and bars on hand in the sunny Italian countryside.

FARE conference 2007
European equality campaigners, fans and NGOs from over twenty countries gathered in Paris to discuss the involvement of ethnic minorities in football. The conference, organized by the Football Against Racism in Europe network, saw a call for greater representation in the game and raised specific concerns facing ethnic minorities. Among the issues raised was the lack of resources for sporting provision for many minority communities, from the lack of spaces to play, to the failure to support and encourage minorities to equip themselves through training and support. Representatives of the Brent Ladies Football Club from London questioned the FIFA International Football Association Board's global ban on wearing of the Islamic head scarf, the hijab. They explained that the recent move has created a barrier to the participation of Muslim women at their club. UEFA Director of Communications, William Gaillard, responded by saying, "Personally I can see both sides of the argument both for and against the hijab ban. It's up to the different national associations to determine their actions. It would be very complicated to unify the fifty-three associations in UEFA on this subject." The issue of the abuse of young African and South American players who are shipped to Europe in contravention of FIFA rules and humanitarian principles was a talking point. Campaigners felt that the problem of young African players, in particular, who were not offered professional contracts and were abandoned by agents and clubs and left to fend for themselves on the streets, was a practice analogous to a modern-day slave trade. Despite FIFA Article 19.4 prohibiting international transfers of minors from Africa into the EU, many clubs continue to carry on the practice or disguise the journeys made by young players. French MEP, Patrick Gaubert, called on the governing bodies of the game to address this issue as a matter of urgency. "The basic human rights of people are regularly not adhered to in football. Any player leaving Africa should only be able to do so with a contract—not without." Gaillard called on the European Commission to work with UEFA and FIFA to help address this problem: "We are told by the European Commission that sport is no different from any other business but I feel we should look at this from the prism of humanitarianism—we must protect the human rights of these young players.

"For all the time they are in Europe, playing or not, they should have a passport for life and be entitled to the same rights as us all. We are ready to work with the European Commission and the other governing bodies to ensure players are not seen as goods." French World Cup winner Christian Karambeu joined the conference to reflect on his personal experiences of prejudice. He thanked campaigners for their efforts and encouraged them to continue using the appeal of football to promote important messages. "Football has to be used as a tool to educate people and counter ills in society," said Karambeu. Ghana Director of Football, Anthony Baffoe, underlined the need for the game to recognize the contribution ethnic minorities can make to the game beyond the playing field. "It is essential to see more black ambassadors within and involved at the highest level at FIFA and UEFA. We have to create more awareness around the problems ethnic minorities are facing in football and improve the respect we are given in the game." Campaigners backed Baffoe's call from the floor and relayed to the conference that it was crucial that the game's governing bodies at the grassroots level also become more representative of the communities it governs. Baffoe went on to suggest setting up an African Professional Footballers Union to help address the issue of trafficking players by passing on advice to aspiring players from the continent and developing a mentoring program. "The establishment of an African Players Union would help to address many of the problems facing young African players who are being taken to Europe without any knowledge of the situation that is ahead of them." Delegates at the conference were united in the view that improving representation was essential ensuring that equality is at the heart of football. FARE campaigner, Dr Bella Bello Bitungu, a lecturer at Innsbruck University in Austria, conveyed the feeling of many ethnic minorities. "The only place we are equal is in the cemetery and on the football pitch." Baffoe had the final word in the closing plenary at the conference warning that to address the problems of ethnic minorities, there must be greater representation. "We have to remember that only white people alone cannot solve black problems."

Campaigners from Kick It Out welcomed FIFA's announcement to toughen up sanctions for racial abuse but have warned of the need to continue "to change hearts and minds." FIFA is to use match suspensions, point deductions and disqualification from competitions as possible punishments against acts of racism. Clubs and national associations face being deducted three points for a first offense, six for a second and relegation or expulsion from competitions for further offenses. Member associations failing to implement them face being banned from international football for two years. FIFA's move comes following a number of high profile incidents of racism this season, the latest being during the Real Zaragoza vs. Barcelona game on Saturday, 25 February, where Barcelona forward Samuel Eto'o was subjected to mass monkey chanting and had peanuts thrown at him by sections of the Zaragoza supporters. Chairman Lord Herman Ouseley said, "There are no panaceas in tackling racism but this is a significant development and will mean a harmonization of sporting sanctions. We hope it will result in an end to European FA's imposing pitiful fines for the worst types of mass racism." He continued, "Longer term the answer must lie with educational measures. We must maintain the initiative to change hearts and minds, but for now it means better protection for the victims of abuse at all levels of the game." FIFA president, Sepp Blatter, underlined the world governing bodies commitment to challenging racism in football when announcing the new procedures. "I have repeatedly stressed FIFA's and my firm personal stance against racism and discrimination." And he pledged "more severe measures to be adopted in order to kick this evil out of the beautiful game." The new penalties include:

MATCH SUSPENSIONS: Referees given power to suspend matches in which racist abuse takes place.
POINTS DEDUCTIONS: First offense to be punished by a three-point deduction, six for a second.
RELEGATION: Further offenses to be punished by relegation.
EXPULSION: Serial offenders may be expelled from league and national associations face two-year international ban.

Unite Against Racism

European football's leading administrators, former players, and anti-racism campaigners came together at a major gathering to look at racism in the game in Barcelona on 1 February 2006. The second Unite Against Racism conference, organized and promoted by UEFA, the Football Against Racism in Europe network and the Spanish Football Federation, looked at the problems of racism in Europe, highlighted examples of good work and provided an opportunity for governing bodies to work with campaigners and fan organizations. Racism in Southern, Central and Eastern Europe were a focus of the conference and the issue of homophobia was discussed for the first time at a major international football conference. In the FC Barcelona president's speech to open the conference Joan Laporta described racism as "the most serious problem facing football today." The Barcelona president went on to say, "Football is not just a sport, but a powerful means of integrating people." Delegates at the conference heard a common call from UEFA, senior Spanish political figures, action groups, nongovernmental organizations and former professional footballers. The call was for the campaign against racism to take on fresh impetus throughout Europe, with football acting as a catalyst to change and educate minds. UEFA Chief Executive Lars-Christer Olsson stated, "We have to get inside minds of racists, particularly the intelligent ones, to educate people and change their attitudes. Sport can help to bring about change—let's not just kick racism out of football but out of society as a whole." UEFA communications and public affairs director William Gaillard called upon football to use its popularity as a uniting force against racism. "Racism is a fundamental problem within society, and football can set a positive example for young people and for the future. As a fan of football, I am ashamed to see racist conduct when I watch games." Kick It Out Director, Piara Powar, co-chaired the conference, and called on national associations to play their part in spreading the anti-racist message throughout their respective countries, particularly those where such problems have surfaced. "Racism has victims—fans, professional players, ethnic communities are suffering—so it must be challenged. I hope people will go away from this conference with fresh ideas to work together for change." Former Chelsea FC and Celtic FC player Paul Elliott, now an adviser to the UK Commission for Racial Equality, said, "I have been in positions [during matches] where I have seen bananas thrown at players, and heard monkey chants. We have made tremendous progress in the fight against racism, but a tremendous amount of work still needs to be done. There has to be a policy of zero tolerance towards racism, and a sense of collective responsibility among everyone involved. Football can be a wonderful vehicle to bring everyone together, and this conference is a way of laying down a solid basis to move forward." The Spanish hosts of the conference were quick to underline that intensive work is being done in a country that is also undergoing constant social change. Spanish State Secretary for Sport Jaime Lizavesky said, "Spain is now a country with many cultures, and sport has a vital role in helping to create an inter-cultural society here."

European Resolution
Members of the European Parliament (MEPs), campaigners and representatives of European football joined the President of the European Parliament, Josep Borrell, on 14 March 2007 where a formal resolution on racism in the game was adopted. The one page document received more signatures than any other previous written resolution of the parliament with more than 420 MEPs joining the call for action. The resolution calls on all stakeholders in the game to do more to fight racism and asks for tougher sanctions for racial abuse on and off the pitch. UEFA is urged to introduce sporting sanctions, such as excluding clubs from competitions. President Borrell declared the written declaration a formal resolution of the European Parliament in Strasbourg and urged national governments and European football's authorities to tackle racism in football. "The fundamental rights of every human being cannot be abandoned during a sporting event. I call for policies of the governments, UEFA and clubs," he said. Borrell went on to stress that what happens in football can affect wider society on a global level. "Football is a mirror of society, of all the good things but also of all the bad things. Racism and xenophobia are reflected in football and they are amplified. It's a theatre scenario, seen by millions and therefore the negative scenarios are seen all over the world." UEFA Director of Communications and Public Affairs, William Gaillard, underlined the commitment of the European football's governing body and went onto to stress the importance of political support in the fight against racism. "UEFA can be a pioneer in the fight against racism but we need the help of the European Parliament so we can fight all forms of discrimination, even beyond the borders of the European Union—be it racial, religious or sexual." NGOs and fan groups from the Football Against Racism in Europe network had been lobbying MEPs across the continent over the past three months stressing the urgency of the problem. Former Chelsea, Celtic and Bari player, Paul Elliott, was in Strasbourg representing Kick It Out and the Fooball

Against Racism in Europe network and welcomed the Resolution. "As a player I faced racial abuse on the pitch in a number of different European countries. This is why I am passionate about ensuring that the next generation of players— across the continent and world—do not have to endure the same abuse I did. This resolution can help us move forward in tackling racism in the game, making football a welcoming place, wherever we chose to play or watch it," added Elliott. Kick It Out Director and FARE spokesman Piara Powar expressed that he hoped the Resolution would play a significant role in the fight against racism in the game. "Momentum to tackle the highly visible problems of racism has been growing for some time. In recent weeks we have seen the Pope declare his disgust at events in Italy and a United Nations human rights special investigator raise concerns at the levels of racism in the game. Our hope would be that the resolution could play a significant role in encouraging and endorsing action at all levels of Europe, from football administrators to national governments." The five MEPs behind the Declaration are Emine Bozkurt MEP (European Socialists Party/Netherlands), Chris Heaton-Harris MEP (European People's/UK), Cem Özdemir MEP (Greens/Germany), Alexander Nuno Alvaro MEP (Liberals and Democrats/Germany) and Claude Moraes MEP (European Socialists/UK).

Report racism
A lot of work has been done to challenge racial abuse and harassment at all levels of football, from the grass-roots through to the Premiership. However, fans, ethnic minority communities and players are still racially abused, particularly at the grass-roots level, where racist abuse is common in amateur football on our parks at the weekend. Many fans, players, clubs and leagues have adopted a policy of zero tolerance. One incident is an incident too many. Kick It Out operates a reporting line that can be used to make reports, ensure effective action is taken and help you raise issues of concern. Kick It Out staff are trained to deal with each caller and each incident sensitively and appropriately. Complainants will be asked to give us as much detail as possible, to enable us to take the best course of action and make a detailed report. Always report abuse to the appropriate authority immediately when it occurs, either to a nearby steward, the police or, in amateur football, the referee. If something needs immediate attention it should be reported directly to a steward or police officer, and in amateur football, to the referee. Always remember the police have a responsibility to act on all reports they receive, regardless of where they take place. For example, if you are assaulted while playing in a Sunday League, the police can be called. Kick It Out takes every complaint seriously. Our role is to raise the complaint with the club or governing body concerned and monitor the issue to ensure appropriate action is taken. Where the club or governing body requires additional advice in dealing with a problem, we are able to assist by providing guidance. All complainants have the choice whether they wish their report to be dealt with

in confidence. Contact details are taken from you so we can report back on how the club/governing body has responded to the complaint, or in case we require any further information. If you have chosen to make a confidential report your contact details will not be passed on.

CAMPAIGN CHRONOLOGY

Anti-racism campaigning has gone from strength to strength since the Let's Kick Racism Out of Football campaign was launched. It would be impossible to list all the achievements made in tackling issues of racism and discrimination in the game, so here are a few key landmarks for the campaign.

1993
The Let's Kick Racism Out of Football campaign is launched by the Commission for Racial Equality and Professional Footballers Association
A "ten-point plan" of measures professional football clubs should follow to challenge racism is drawn up by the campaign

1996
Jas Bains publishes "Asians Can't Play Football" report highlighting the problems British Asian footballers face trying to break into the professional game

1997
Kick It Out is funded by the Football Association, Football Foundation, FA Premier League and Professional Footballers Association to run the campaign

1998
The government's Football Task Force releases a report on racism in the game

1999
Kick It Out becomes a founding member of the Football Against Racism in Europe (FARE) network
Michael Chopra becomes the first Asian male to play for England. He scores the winner in a 2-1 victory over Argentina at Wembley for the U16's

2001
The first Kick It Out Week of Action is held in October
Kick It Out is invited to share good practice at the FIFA Conference Against Racism Conference in Argentina

2002
Kick It Out accepts the Free Your Mind award at the MTV Europe Awards on behalf of FARE

2003
The first UEFA Unite Against Racism Conference at Chelsea FC is held

The first Unity Cup Festival is held in Manchester and opened by Manchester United star Wes Brown and PFA Chief Executive Gordon Taylor

2004
Euro 2004 used to stage anti-racism activities in partnership with UEFA

The campaign celebrates its ten-year anniversary at the Great Eastern Hotel in London. Founding organization, PFA, hosts the anniversary lunch

2005
Blackburn Rovers become the first club to achieve the Preliminary Level of the Racial Equality Standard
The National Asians in Football Forum releases a report entitled "Asians Can Play Football—A Wasted Decade"
Zesh Rehman becomes the first British Asian to start a Premier League game, making his full debut for Fulham against Tottenham Hotspur

2006
Formal resolution calling on all stakeholders in the game to do more to challenge racism in football is adopted by the European Parliament in Strasbourg. A record 420 MEPs sign up to the Resolution
Manchester City become the first club to achieve the Intermediate Level of the Racial Equality Standard
World football's governing body, FIFA, amends sanctions on racism in football Article 55 now stipulates tougher sanctions across the world game at all levels
Kick It Out plays leading role in FARE and FIFA anti-racism activities at the World Cup 2006 in Germany

2007
Week of Action re-launched as One Game, One Community Week of Action, with 1,000 events taking place

2008
The Football League features five Asian professionals, and Paul Ince becomes the first black English manager to lift a trophy

Chapter Five

Football Unites, Racism Divides

Ruth Johnson

History

Football Unites, Racism Divides (FURD) was founded in 1995 by a group of Sheffield United fans who were concerned about a number of incidents of racist abuse both in and around the stadium, which is situated in a community with a large ethnic minority population. Present at the initial meeting at the Mount Pleasant Community Centre in the Sharrow district of Sheffield on 9 November 1995 were local youth workers, representatives from Sheffield United, city councilors, members of supporter organizations and young people with an interest in sports. The group met in the wake of a number of racist attacks upon Asian and Somali young people, as well as widespread anecdotal evidence of abuse of local black and Asian residents whenever Sheffield United played at home. Football Unites, Racism Divides has always sought to make a difference within the game and within its diverse local community.

In January 1996 a bid for funding from the European Commission's Cities Against Racism Project was successful, and a full-time Project Coordinator was soon appointed, with the official launch taking place at Sheffield United Football Club on 30 April 1996. In December 1996 the initial twelve months' funding from the EC was extended for a second year, with additional funding coming from the South Yorkshire Police Community Initiatives Fund, as well as in-kind help, in terms of premises, utilities costs, communication and staff supervision from the Sheffield City Council Youth Service. FURD moved into its present premises, the Stables Youth Project, in April 1997, and in September 1997, a part-time youth worker, clerical worker and resources and information worker started work. With the project in danger of running short of money in late 1997, a lifeline was provided by the Sheffield Single Regeneration Budget, which part-funded Football Unites, Racism Divides from December 1997 until March 2003.

Once the European grant ended, we were able to continue our work with a patchwork of funding sources including the Churches Commission for Racial Justice, Kick It Out, Home Office Community Relations Unit, Professional Footballers' Association, Commission for Racial Equality, The Football Asso-

ciation, Sheffield TEC, Royal Mail, Walkers Crisps, Grant Thornton Account-
ants, Heeley Development Trust, small amounts of income from the hire of our
mobile football game, "Streetkick," and from donations from individuals joining the Football Unites, Racism Divides membership scheme. In May 1999 the
Football Unites, Racism Divides Educational Trust was established with chari-
table status achieved later that year. All the work is now managed by the FURD
Educational Trust. With three-year funding being awarded by the National Lot-
teries Charities Board for the education and information work of the project
from the Department for Education and Employment to operate the FURD Millennium Volunteers program and from the European Commission to design and
maintain the Football Against Racism in Europe website, 1999 was a key year
for FURD. In July 2000 Football Unites, Racism Divides Educational Trust began working with the Shirecliffe Youth Inclusion Project, with funding from the
Home Office Positive Futures initiative, to fund coaching in the Shirecliffe and
Burngreave areas of Sheffield, a second Streetkick, and a peer mentoring program. Football Unites, Racism Divides agreed a Development Plan in February
2000, which set eight priorities for the project until 2004. These priorities were
then used for a more specific Action Plan and aimed to:

- increase the participation of ethnic minority young people
  in football as players, spectators and employees;
- significantly increase the participation and involvement of
  ethnic minority young women;
- reduce racial harassment;
- challenge racism through anti-racist education;
- develop the work of the Resources and Information Centre;
- increase the participation of volunteers in the work of
  Football Unites, Racism Divides, especially young people
  aged sixteen to twenty-four;
- develop regional, national and international initiatives;
- secure the future work of Football Unites, Racism Divides.

At the tenth Anniversary of the Let's Kick Racism out of Football campaign in
January 2004, the project received recognition for its pioneering work as a
community-based anti-racist football project, and Football Unites, Racism Divides was also highlighted as a model project in the Union of European Football
Association's (UEFA) "Unite Against Racism in European Football: UEFA
Guide to Good Practice" report. In November 2005, FURD celebrated its tenth
anniversary. Several pioneering black footballers were present, including Brandon Batson, now a consultant with the Football Association, Luther Blissett,
Gary Bennett, Ces Podd, and United's Tony Agana, Paul Ifill and Trenton Wiggan.

Politicians and influential figures within the game turned out to celebrate the project's achievements over the previous decade and to look forward to pioneering developments in the future.

Nature and scope

Football Unites, Racism Divides is an anti-racist, football-based community project, operating in the areas of social inclusion and community cohesion. It believes that football, as the world's most popular game, can help to bring together people from different backgrounds to play, watch and enjoy the game, and to break down barriers created by ignorance or prejudice. It aims to ensure that everyone who plays or watches football can do so without fear of racial abuse and harassment, in either a verbal or a physical form, and to increase the participation of people from ethnic minorities in football, as players, spectators or employees. However, its work evolves in response to community needs and current issues and is no longer restricted to just football-based work.

It has worked closely with local football clubs to help them implement anti-racist strategies and become part of the wider community; delivered football coaching to young people from a diverse range of communities and assisted them in creating their own Sunday league teams; organized regular tournaments and leagues, bringing together isolated communities, such as refugees and asylum seekers; has taken Streetkick, our portable football game, right into the heart of urban neighborhoods to involve "hard to reach" young people; used the magnetic power of football to deliver anti-racist education and youth work with young people, work that is supported by our unique anti-racist Resources and Information Centre.

FURD also delivers a volunteering scheme, which has helped hundreds of young people put something back into the community while gaining vital skills and experience. From 1999 to 2007, this went under the name of Millennium Volunteers, a government initiative to encourage sixteen to twenty-four year-olds into voluntary work. In 2008 this was replaced by the v scheme for sixteen to twenty-five year-olds, with the FURD v youth volunteering program winning three year funding. The FURD Positive Futures scheme uses sport to work with socially marginalized youngsters who could be at risk of drug misuse and crime. FURD was one of the founding members of the Football Against Racism in Europe network, a network of anti-racist groups that each year since 2001 has organized the Action Week—Europe's largest anti-racist event.

FURD is based in Sheffield and much of its work is at a local level. However, it also plays a key role in national and international anti-racist programs through the Kick It Out national campaign and the Football Against Racism in Europe network. While overt racism in football in Britain has decreased, other issues have arisen, such as a rise in Islamophobia, a widespread hostility toward refugees, asylum-seekers and new immigrants from Eastern Europe, all encoura-

ged by hostility in some parts of the media, and a big increase in the success of
the far-right British National Party, particularly in local elections. The work of
Football Unites, Racism Divides continues to evolve in response to these issues.
It is becoming increasingly concerned with tackling social exclusion and encouraging community cohesion by helping to engage young people with positive
activities to develop skills, self-esteem and mutual understanding.

Education work
Anti-racist education and training
FURD delivers tailored programs of anti-racist education, youth and community
work courses and citizenship (PHSE) for local schools, colleges, youth groups,
prisons and professionals, and for young people wishing to work in a youth and
community work setting, particularly young people who for various reasons
have been turned off more formal educational courses or settings.

Central to the work of Football Unites, Racism Divides is the use of football
as a gateway with young people, using their interest in football to enable the
youth worker or teacher to talk with them about racism, first in football and other sports, then moving on to the wider society. Sport can be a reflection of what
is occurring in society, while football is a worldwide pastime that impacts millions. Professional footballers can become role models to young people, and for
fanatical supporters the rise and fall of their football team becomes a central part
of their lives and their families' lives. Unfortunately, it is also used as an arena
to display racism. For this very reason it is important to educate people both on
and off the pitch.

The FURD education/youth worker works with schools, colleges, youth
groups and other organizations such as agencies supporting young people with
drugs and housing issues. Along with discussions with the teacher or youth
worker, the resources available enable the education/youth worker to devise
individually tailored programs of work.

The introduction of citizenship into the national curriculum in 2002 means
that many more pupils are now being taught about the diversity of national, regional, religious and ethnic identities in the UK. The anti-racism work in schools
has progressed over the years with the biggest contributing factor to this increase being the terrorist attacks on the United States on 11 September 2001.
Since then the rise of Islamophobia has been clear.

Football Unites, Racism Divides has worked with the Institute of Citizenship to help develop curriculum materials to be used in citizenship studies. Lessons dealing with the issues of identity, belonging, groups and racism have been
co-written with the help of Kick It Out's Alison Vaughan, former Education
Officer at Manchester City Football Club. Discussions took place on the Citizenship Resource Pack in its entirety and changes suggested to improve the qua-

lity of learning for young people. Elements of the pack were piloted at Firvale School, Sheffield. In 2007 the Football Unites, Racism Divides education worker developed a curriculum program alongside the Refugee Support Service, assisting young refugees in schools.

Education work in schools

The education worker, funded by the Football Foundation since 2000, has successfully continued to deliver anti-racism packages in schools, youth centers, colleges, probation teams, prisons, youth forums and neighborhood associations. For example, workshops or group work programs have been delivered at many Sheffield schools, including Fir Vale, Firth Park, Hinde House, High Storrs and Abbeydale Grange schools, Firth Park Community Centre and Norfolk Park Community Centre.

The packages have ranged from single forty-five minute presentations to group work sessions conducted over a period of several weeks. The group work combines learning in class with learning on the pitch. It is a twin package that involves participating in anti-racism lessons followed by practical football delivered by FURD football coaches. The aim of these sessions is to raise awareness of racism by utilizing young people's interest in football. Football has the ability to engage people irrespective of any barriers, be it language, race, culture or religion.

The group work sessions have had a notable impact on the young people who have participated. Their understanding of the importance of inclusion allows for progress to be made in communities, an aim that Football Unites, Racism Divides strives to further develop as a community-based project. The primary and secondary schools that have participated in the programs were selected through their request to do anti-racism work within their school, and selection was also done through our targeting of areas that were experiencing high levels of racial tensions. The education work delivered within schools has also been successful with marginalized girls. At one school, a group of predominantly Muslim girls contacted other girls in local secondary schools interested in participating in girls-only football tournaments. A learning mentor at Fir Vale Secondary School commented: "For the young people it was invigorating, inspiring and informative. It allowed the pupils to gain an insight into the diversity of their fellow peers. This link between the school and the community is crucial!"

The most successful FURD educational initiative at the secondary school level has been the Young Footballers Against Racism concept, a twin package that combines learning in class followed by football on the pitch delivered by Football Unites, Racism Divides coaches. This package can be tailored to suit the needs of the group. The pupils who are selected to do these sessions are either known for being racially intolerant, at risk of being excluded, of offending, or labeled as young people with behavioral problems. At the end of this program, the pupils who have participated will have anti-racism, basic mentoring and football skills with which to work with other young people in their schools. Such peer-led initiatives are instrumental in this fight against racism, and understanding of other cultures is imperative if we hope to live in a cohesive society. The first Young Footballers Against Racism lessons were pioneered with a group of thirteen Year 11 pupils from Abbeydale Grange Secondary School in Sheffield. Over a period of twelve weeks the group looked at issues related to peer mentoring, youth work and anti-racism. These lessons were delivered along with the learning mentor who selected the group. He was extremely pleased by the fact that the young people attended all the lessons and did so on their own time, as these classes were run after school hours.

Education work in prisons
The FURD education worker, volunteer coordinator and football coach have delivered education and football programs at Moorlands Prison, Doncaster, as part of their Diversity Week. Through the engagement and positive responses from the inmates, additional prisons in Yorkshire and Humberside have requested that FURD run a similar program in their institutions.

Education work with individuals
The education worker has supported young individuals who have experienced racism, young people who want a voice in their local communities, young refugees and young offenders who want to become peer mentors in the battle against racism.

Education work in the community
The education worker and a group of motivated young volunteers delivered a ten week anti-racism program on an estate in the north of Sheffield to targeted young people. These young people were identified by the police and the development workers as displaying racist behavior. The program took place over the summer period of July and August 2006 and ended with young people forming relationships with other young people that they would not have envisaged due to their differences in ethnicity and religion.

Education work with professionals
FURD can provide tailored training courses on request for groups of professionals. For example, FURD workers have devised an anti-racism training package which was delivered to a group of youth workers. FURD has been working continuously to combat the fear of Islam that has been propelled by people's ignorance and the media. The education and youth work team at FURD have worked actively on dispelling the myths and stereotypes associated with Islam, and in 2006 organized a conference to compliment FURD's range of activities with regard to Black History Month. The conference took place in November 2006 at Sheffield United FC and was aptly named "Creating Space—Exploring Truths and Fallacies

about Muslims." The relevant workshop concentrated on four main themes: (1) What is Islam?; (2) Islam and the media; (3) Images and perceptions; and (4) Sport and Islam. The conference targeted key organizations working with young people, probation services and the criminal justice system. The aims of the conference were to:

- raise awareness of Islam amongst educators;
- inform them about the facts of Islam in relation to the four sub-topics;
- open up a dialogue where they could explore their perceptions, stereotypes and misconceptions about Islam;
- promote a greater understanding of the Muslim way of life;
- enhance community cohesion;
- provide the tools to challenge Islamophobia.

Following the conference, resources were developed for workers engaged with young people, including fact sheets that both dispelled the myths and stereotypes of Islam and highlighted the positive contributions that Muslims have made to British society.

Resources and information work
The educational and youth work of FURD is supported by a unique anti-racist Resources and Information Centre containing an abundance of books, DVDs, posters, magazines, teaching packs and exhibitions that are free to borrow and use, an enquiry service and a website (www.furd.org) which uses the interactive potential of the Internet as a means of informal anti-racist education. It has proved invaluable in providing ideas and materials for use in anti-racist education with young people.

The idea for the Resources and Information Centre followed a meeting in Bologna between FURD workers and anti-racist projects from Bologna and Dortmund, where they saw the way the football fans' documentation center at Progetto Ultra worked. A need for the service was also identified by the number of requests for information that Football Unites, Racism Divides received in its early days when it didn't have the necessary staffing or resources to cope with the demand.

As FURD and its reputation have grown, so has the number of requests it receives for information and resources. The unique Resources and Information Centre can be accessed by anyone in person, or by telephone, post or email. The collection includes books, DVDs, videos, teaching packs, reports, magazines, CD-ROMs, exhibitions, a website and an enquiry service. Subjects covered include racism in football and other sports, racism in general and ways of tackling it, women and sport, black history, youth and community work, fan culture, hooliganism, sectarianism and football coaching materials to support our coach development program.

Exhibitions

Football Unites, Racism Divides has prepared mobile exhibitions available for hire by schools, museums, libraries, football clubs, sports centers and any other interested parties. The History of Black Footballers exhibition, for example, documents how black players have been involved in the British game, and therefore in British society, since the nineteenth century. Black players have in fact been part of the game of football since its origins as a professional sport; in the 1886-1887 season, at the dawn of the organized game, Ghanaian-born Arthur Wharton was playing in goal for Preston North End, the "Invincibles." The History of Black Footballers Exhibition, developed by Phil Vasili in association with Football Unites, Racism Divides, with support from the Professional Footballers' Association, records the achievements of black players from 1886 onward. FURD also has a free-to-hire copy of the Arthur Wharton exhibition, developed by Doncaster Museums, which looks at the life of Wharton, the first black professional footballer and his connections to South Yorkshire. Kick It Out has produced an exhibition called "Pioneers, Past Masters and Future Challenges" about racism in football and FURD has copies of it available for hire. Last, but not least, an exhibition concerning the work of Football Unites, Racism Divides is also available.

The Laurie Cunningham Project

Laurie Cunningham will probably always be best remembered as being one of West Bromwich Albion's so-called Three Degrees, along with Brendon Batson and Cyrille Regis, in the late 1970s. After attracting glowing reviews at Orient in the 1976-1977 season, Laurie Cunningham was sold to West Bromwich Albion and on 27 April 1977 became the first black player to represent England at the international level. On the occasion, Cunningham scored the only goal of the game in a 1-0 win for the England under-twenty-ones against Scotland at Bramall Lane.

For workers at FURD there is added interest in what happened after the game. Following a request from youth workers at the nearby Hub African-Caribbean Centre, Laurie Cunningham visited the pioneering youth project after the match and conversed with many of the members till late. In an ironic but appropriate twist, the Hub original youth club building is now the home of the FURD project. Friday 27 April 2007 marked the thirtieth anniversary of this landmark occasion, both as a significant milestone in the contribution of black players to the national game, but also as a memorable experience for the members and youth workers who were privileged to meet Laurie that night. As a result, the Hub, Football Unites, Racism Divides and Sheffield United FC came together to tell the wider history of black footballers in Sheffield, and an exhibition on Black Footballers in Sheffield was launched at the Legends of the Lane room at Bramall Lane in November 2007. The guest of honor was none other than Pele, the world's greatest player, who was presented with the biography of Arthur Wharton by FURD coordinator, Howard Holmes, and who voiced his support for FURD's work.

Youth work

Football Unites, Racism Divides engages in informal work with young people, from a wide variety of ethnic backgrounds, to encourage them to raise their aspirations and become good citizens. This takes place mainly through the v and Positive Futures programs.

Positive Futures

Positive Futures is a national sports-based social inclusion program, part of the government Home Office's Drug Strategy, and managed by Crime Concern. The Football Unites, Racism Divides Positive Futures program works with young people aged ten to nineteen years, particularly those who could be at risk of drug misuse and crime, and aims to move beyond sport by creating an environment where young people are able to develop both personally and socially. This "risk" could include having friends or family who take drugs, or being in an environment where drugs are common, whether at home, school, or in the neighborhood. Above all, Positive Futures is a "relationship strategy," which uses sport and other activities to build relationships with young people who are at risk of being socially marginalized. The program aims to use sport and other activities as a hook to get young people involved. It then seeks to eventually move young people beyond merely participating in these activities by creating an environment where they are able to develop in personal, social and intellectual ways.

The Positive Futures program is not a new concept to Football Unites, Racism Divides. Not surprisingly, the FURD PF scheme is not solely about football. In partnership with the Caribbean Sports Club, we have supported an under-fifteen cricket team, while many young people have been given the opportunity to participate in other sports such as snowboarding, abseiling, canoeing and climbing. We have developed a number of non-sporting activities like music and dance sessions with the aim of attracting young people with no great interest in sport and introducing more young women to the scheme. A generic youth club-type session runs weekly that provides young people with a space to meet and socialize with friends, as well as being a forum for informal learning for its users in terms of drug information, workshops regarding conflict and conflict resolution and information and resources relating to race and gender issues. FURD works closely with organizations such as the Youth Offending Service, Police and Community Safety, Connexions, local schools, Sheffield United Football Club,

Drugs Action Team and other agencies like Sheffield Black Drugs Project in order to identify and work with young people that could benefit from the Positive Futures program.

Inspiring volunteers

Youth volunteering has been a key delivery method at FURD since 1999, with over 1,000 young people, aged sixteen to twenty-four, participating in the project's Millennium Volunteers (MV) program, working up to two hundred hours in the local community.

Football Unites received Millennium Volunteers status in July 1999. The success of the project led to the initial three years' funding being extended until 2007, when MV was replaced nationally by the v youth volunteering program. Millennium Volunteers was a national initiative run by the government's Department for Education and Employment which aimed to encourage sixteen to twenty-four years olds to volunteer their time to benefit the community. The MV strapline was "build on what you're into," so young people were encouraged to turn their interests into voluntary work. Volunteers aimed to accumulate either 100 or 200 hours of voluntary work, usually within one year, in order to receive a Millennium Volunteer Certificate or Millennium Volunteer Award of Excellence. Participation in FURD MV provided young people with the opportunity to acquire new skills, work as part of a team and develop initiatives. Millennium Volunteers enabled young people to gain a sense of personal achievement, while making a valuable contribution to their local communities. FURD Millennium Volunteers were involved in a variety of voluntary work, such as anti-racist education work in schools, youth work, football coaching and banner-making. The FURD Millennium Volunteers project was launched in February 2000 by David Blunkett, Secretary of State for Education and Employment, at Sheffield United Football Club. This was attended by over 100 people representing local organizations, young people and the media.

The v scheme enables young people to choose between "taster" sessions lasting perhaps just half a day, or part-time or even full-time placements with, as the name suggests, the tasters being a way of encouraging people to get involved in further volunteering. As with MV, v's are encouraged to turn their interests into constructive and recognized voluntary activity. Volunteers are rewarded with v thank you certificates, and "v50" certificates when fifty hours of work have been completed. Further impact awards are currently being piloted.

Young volunteers at FURD are offered a wide range of volunteering opportunities which are presented at the initial recruitment meeting. They are encouraged to choose their own placements or develop completely new volunteering opportunities. FURD offers them support in this process and identifies relevant training if appropriate. Several FURD young volunteers have successfully gained football coaching qualifications, which has enabled them to coach youngsters, particularly in deprived inner-city areas. Some have then built up volunteering hours by either coaching, officiating or running a team. Others have completed the Sheffield Youth Service "Introduction to Youth Work" training course, undertaken an Open College Network accredited "Personal Boundaries" training course (such as those on placement with "Ashiana" Asian women's refuge) or completed DJing courses delivered by the Hoodz Underground rap ensemble.

The FURD young volunteers program has resulted in significant benefits to the local community, including:

- Involvement of significant numbers of local young people, the majority of whom are of ethnic minority origin, in constructive planned volunteering activity.
- A dramatic increase in the number of trained youth workers aged eighteen to twenty-four as a result of youth work training organized by Football Unites, Racism Divides staff.
- A beneficial impact upon the numbers of young people offending, with volunteers offering a positive role model to young people who may be at risk of offending.
- Assimilation of asylum seekers and refugees into the local community has been helped by both free coaching and tournaments operated by FURD coaches, including young volunteers, and the example set by asylum seekers and refugees who have become Football Unites, Racism Divides volunteers.
- Involvement in local community events, such as the annual Community Day and Sharrow Festival, where FURD young volunteers have helped organize activities including Streetkick tournaments, penalty competitions and fashion shows.

The project has developed a number of in-house training opportunities with the main aim of addressing the issue of many of our young volunteers not feeling comfortable with formal education (and/or educational establishments). A basic ten week information technology introduction course has been organized by the project, providing volunteers with the opportunity to gain a basic knowledge of word processing, spreadsheets, e-mail and the Internet.

The program has continued to build relationships and partnerships with community groups and specialist organizations which have enabled the project to access and involve people from under-represented groups such as the Bangladeshi and Chinese communities, who have traditionally been on the peripheries of most community initiatives. The project has taken steps to build capacity among young people who lacked the confidence to volunteer by introducing them to training courses, such as the Introduction to Youth Work training, Youth Developing Communities, First Aid training and sports coaching, to enable them to harness and develop their skills. For some, volunteering has provided a route to employment. The successful engagement of excluded young people has given the program credibility among other young people who have been on the sidelines, who have wanted to become involved in volunteering and the project as a whole but who saw volunteering as being "uncool." By recognizing individual capabilities and turning the traditional approach of fitting the volunteer to the role on its head by instead matching the role to the volunteer, the program has become more flexible and inclusive.

Sheffield Young People Against Conflict Group

This concerns a group of young people from across Sheffield that has been involved with the FURD project on a voluntary basis. The Sheffield Young People against Conflict group felt that something needed to be done to bring communities of young people together who, for whatever reason, were focusing on their differences, often resulting in conflict. Members of the group strongly believe that they can make a difference and bring communities together, especially groups of young people. The group aims to

- promote good relations within all the different communities in Sheffield;
- go into schools, colleges, youth centers, and community events to act as peer mediators;
- sort out issues of conflict, with a view to achieving a resolution of problems, with groups of young people;
- take an active role in promoting citizenship, in particular anti-racist work;
- tour Sheffield and South Yorkshire with the Streetkick football game and through this spread the anti-racist message and break down barriers.

The group is open to all young people who have an interest in anti-racism and conflict resolution work. The group has been able to attract young people from different communities, such as Somali, Bangladeshi, Arabic, white and Pakistani, from across the city and meet once a week at the Stables in Sharrow. Members have been trained in anti-racist and conflict resolution skills and have attended conferences and residentials in Warrington and Slough, meeting other young people who are involved in this type of work. The group has worked alongside a local theatre education worker and film-maker to produce a DVD and teaching pack—"It's Your Call"—looking at gun crime and Islamophobia and the effects on a young person's life and the community as a whole. It has also participated in a series of joint sessions with mainly white youth groups from

Barnsley and Manchester, with young people leading awareness-raising workshops, having been trained as peer educators by FURD's youth workers.

Football

The relationship between race and football takes a number of forms. It has long been the case that a number of fans have used Saturday afternoons at football matches to air their racial prejudices, but this minority of racist fans is only part of the problem. What is also important is how Black and Asian people become involved in football as players, coaches or spectators, the interest they take in football and whether in certain areas they feel excluded. It is clear, for example, that football is hugely popular among Asian boys, but Asians are rarely seen at a professional level, and they also appear to be under-represented in local amateur organized football, both at the junior and adult level. A third issue is the relationship between a professional football club and its local community; that is, whether the association is of mutual advantage or one-sided. There is also the fact that many top footballers now are black or mixed race, and this provides great potential for challenging racist attitudes among fans as most teams now include black players among their stars. Top teams can also be used as examples of how people of different ethnicities can work together in harmony to achieve success.

A major strand of Football Unites, Racism Divides' work is, of course, football. FURD is involved in a number of initiatives to encourage young people, and especially minority groups, to become actively involved in playing the game. While FURD is at the forefront of the campaign politically, we pride ourselves on tackling the problem on multiple fronts. For instance, our unique approach concentrates upon working directly with minority groups and young people in order to further involve them in the game.

Sheffield United Football Club is based at Bramall Lane, which is one of the oldest existing sports grounds in the world. At the time of the last census in 2001, the local city council ward, Sharrow, had a non-white population of about 31 percent. Much of FURD's early work was informed by a research report we commissioned, produced by Sheffield Hallam University, called "Sheffield Divided or United? A Study of 'Race' and Football." This report found that despite the ethnic diversity of the club's catchment area, only 1 percent of the crowd at a Sheffield United home game against Bolton Wanderers on 22 November 1996 were black or Asian. The research also found that 20 percent of local ethnic minority residents had suffered regular racial harassment on match days. A common reaction to this was for residents not to be seen outside before, during and after matches so as not to attract attention.

The FURD project has its origins in a small group of Sheffield United fans and youth workers, who in the early 1990s began to voice their concerns around a number of issues connected with their local football club, including racism. The project's partners have come from fans' groups, football clubs, local city council officers, youth and community groups, racial equality councils and campaigns, schools, churches, mosques and police and community safety units.

Support for local teams

Workers at FURD initially shied away from entering teams in organized leagues, wary of the amount of administration required. Then in the summer of 2000, three teenage Asian footballers came into the FURD office and announced they wanted to form a team and enter an affiliated eleven-a-side Sunday league. Football Unites, Racism Divides staff sat down with the three friends and went through what it would entail. The list was long, daunting even, but the boys' enthusiasm won the day and their team, Sharrow United, applied to join the Sheffield Regional Alliance Sunday League, Division Two for the 2000-2001 season. Sharrow soon experienced an open hostility toward Asian players by some opposing sides. Playing mainly against pub teams in the lower divisions, the speed, skill and athleticism of the young Sharrow players meant that opponents sometimes resorted to kicking, tripping and punching in a desperate attempt to compete. When the Sharrow players responded, racial abuse sometimes followed—rarely heard by the referee—from both players and spectators. Scuffles occasionally resulted and on three occasions referees abandoned the game as they lost control. It was as if the Sharrow players' refusal to take the violence and intimidation lying down, preferring instead to fight back, was both unexpected and resented. Such experiences led inevitably to disciplinary charges with members and officials of the teams being frequent visitors to the county Football Association offices. But they survived, the quality of the football played overcoming the unpleasantness, and providing genuine satisfaction that the racists had been beaten—at least at football. When the players collected their runners-up medals at the league's Presentation Night in May 2001 it was clear from the applause and comments that respect had been won. Since then, the club has not only survived but thrived, rising through the local leagues. Seven years later, in May 2008, Sharrow United established themselves as one of the best sides in Sheffield football when winning the Meadowhall Sunday League Cup at Sheffield United's Bramall Lane ground in front of over a thousand spectators. In the early years, most of the Sharrow players were Asian, but by 2008 the team included players from Africa, Iraq, Kosovo, as well as both black and white players from the Sharrow area.

As a community-based project one of FURD's key tasks is to help and support ethnic minority footballers to progress as players, coaches, referees and administrators. For any group of young people organizing themselves in order to form a team, taking part in the affiliated leagues and fulfilling all the duties required can be a daunting prospect. Moreover, the costs involved—kit, pitch hire, training venue, referees, balls, nets, washing kit, transport, league and Football

Association affiliation fees, insurance, medical supplies, coaches, as well as personal items such as boots and shin pads—can be prohibitive and enough discouragement alone to teams participating in organized leagues. Hence, when a group of players approaches Football Unites, Racism Divides for help in setting up a football team, workers go through all the factors that need to be considered, in addition to the costs involved. FURD may be able to offer short-term financial and administrative support—such as affiliation and league fees, lending a kit, locating a suitable pitch—while the team works out how to raise the necessary funds. For example, FURD has mentored several teams to successfully apply for Awards for All lottery grants. Football Unites has helped a number of teams to present their cases at Football Association disciplinary hearings, following from what they have perceived to be racist actions by opposing players, spectators or referees. In addition, FURD has negotiated with the Sheffield and Hallamshire County Football Association to allow FURD staff to sit as observers during personal hearings. More precisely, during the 2006-2007 season, Football Unites, Racism Divides supported six teams in their attempt to play in eleven-a-side affiliated Sunday football leagues: Losani Giants, a mainly Liberian team (mainly through help with applying for funding), Sharrow Athletic, most of whom are Bangladeshi, Porter United, a mainly Somali team, and the African Dream Team are now largely self-sufficient, while the under-sixteen Positive Futures side and the original FURD-backed team, Sharrow United, have benefited from more intensive support, in particular, secretarial duties.

Tournaments
Regular tournaments provide the opportunity to bring large numbers of young people from varying backgrounds together to play football. This in turn often leads to addressing a number of FURD's aims and objectives, particularly with regards to anti-racism and social cohesion, but also in terms of raising awareness among young people about social problems such as drug use, crime and safety. As well as running a number of large-scale annual events such as the Sheffield United/FURD joint Community Day, FURD also runs regular holiday tournaments for young people of different ages at venues around the city. In partnership with "Activity Sheffield," FURD Positive Futures held its first girls' football tournament at Sheffield United's Academy in 2007, aiming to attract the attention of female pupils aged ten to twelve at schools from around the Darnall and Sharrow areas of the city. Five schools took part, entering seven teams in total. The tournament was a great success, and FURD aims to make girls' tournaments a regular feature.

Work with refugees and asylum-seekers
Football Unites, Racism Divides' raison d'être is a belief in the unifying influence of football, in its power to bring people together in pursuit of a common goal, where otherwise there may be mistrust and fear. Our work with refugees and

asylum-seekers is designed to offer the chance to play in an organized tournament or league, and also to help players and teams to become involved in affiliated football, as individuals or clubs. This contributes to improving the sense of inclusion felt by the people concerned and can have effects such as helping to improve people's English, confidence, employability and general well being, with many refugees and asylum-seekers engaging in voluntary work such as helping to run teams or coaching children.

After several tournaments and coaching sessions aimed at asylum seekers during 2002, FURD made a breakthrough after teaming up with County Football Association development officer Brian Peck, together with financial support from Sheffield First for Safety and contacts through the Refugee Housing Association. This partnership initiative resulted in seventeen seven-a-side teams attending the All Nations tournament in Sheffield. This was followed by the All Nations Summer League, in which eight teams competed each week at the Sheffield United Academy. The teams included players from Afghanistan, Iraq, Albania, Yemen, Sierra Leone, Somalia, Nigeria, Chile, Iran and Jamaica. FURD has developed effective methods of working in partnership with local and national refugee agencies to organize football events for refugees and asylum-seekers, and increase their participation in local affiliated leagues. Most of the coaching staff at Football Unites are refugees themselves and this has been of great benefit in making and maintaining contact with a wide range of displaced communities in Sheffield.

Since then, the All Nations tournament has become an annual event. The 2008 tournament attracted twelve teams and was won by the Galeed Giants, a team consisting mainly but not exclusively of Liberian players. The tournament is an opportunity for keen footballers to gain support and advice about getting involved in football on a more organized level, as well as for people from different backgrounds to meet together through a shared love of football.

In July 2006, Football Unites hosted the national Unity Cup Festival, organized in partnership with Kick It Out, which brought twenty teams of refugees and asylum-seekers together from all corners of the United Kingdom to highlight the positive contribution displaced communities are making to society and to challenge negative stereotypes. The Lord Mayor of Sheffield, Councilor Jackie Drayton, officially opened the festival in a ceremony on Devonshire Green in Sheffield city center that included performances by local bands, DJs and dance groups, as well as Streetkick, with an attendance of hundreds of local people. The teams were drawn into groups at the opening ceremony with the help of Sheffield United star Leigh Bromby, former Sheffield United strike-force Brian Deane and Tony Agana, local boxing star Amer "Killa" Khan and Mukhtar Mohammed, a young Somali player referred by FURD coaches to the Sheffield Wednesday Academy. The 2005 winners VG Foundation from Manchester retained their title, beating Sheffield side Albanian Fire in the final, played at the Sheffield United Academy. Sheffield United Academy Director, George Harrison, was impressed by the quality of the football and stressed that "the Unity Cup Festival has surpassed all of my expectations and we feel proud to have hosted this great event." The festival was organized with the support of the Sheffield and Hallamshire County Football Association, Sheffield City Council and Amicus trade union.

Streetkick

Streetkick is a mobile, inflatable mini-football pitch that can be packed into a trailer and moved from one location to another. Since its humble beginnings in the autumn of 1998, the Streetkick game has grown to become one of FURD's most high-profile areas of work. Nowadays, the game has visually changed dramatically. The original wooden-paneled game, built by FURD volunteer Kevin Titterton, was replaced by a larger inflatable one in the summer of 2003, thanks to Sport Relief funding. This new Streetkick excels in terms of practicality, mobility and how it has been received by young people. There are many things about Streetkick that have changed during the game's lifespan. However, the one thing that remains the same, the "immovable goalpost," is the underlying aim behind its creation, namely anti-racism, or more specifically,

- targeting areas with relatively high numbers of Black and Ethnic Minority (BEM) young people, where these youngsters may lack opportunities to take part in organized football;
- targeting areas with known racial problems and/or areas with low numbers of BEM young people in order to raise racial awareness;
- bringing young people from different racial, cultural and religious backgrounds together in positive ways so to break down barriers.

Streetkick has adopted a number of interventions, and both mixed and themed events have taken place with the aim of encouraging young people to integrate. Anti-racist and educational materials have also been developed, displayed and distributed during events, and anti-racist banners are attached to the pitch perimeter. Music is also used at some events to attract young people and create a good atmosphere, and announcements and commentaries can also play a part when a public address (PA) system is used. Streetkick events have informed young participants of contributions made by black players to the national game, while a diverse range of staff and volunteers from differing communities have been used with the aim of creating positive role models that young participants can relate to. On the whole, Streetkick is an excellent method of reaching significant numbers of young people with information about the anti-racist campaign in football and it has achieved a good geographical spread around the city.

This has included events at Sheffield College sites and being present at many of Sheffield's large-scale events, such as the Sheffield Show, May Fest, Sharrow Festival and Sheffield United's open days. A number of Streetkick events have also been held outside the city, predominantly in Barnsley and Rotherham. Volunteer involvement has been a major contribution to its success: many have taken lead roles in the planning, organizing and running both high profile events such as the Sheffield Show and May Fest and also short-term projects like the work at Barnsley and Sheffield College.

A measure of its success is that FURD has been invited to run Streetkick events at the European Championship finals in Portugal in 2004 and Austria and Switzerland in 2008 and at the World Cup finals in Germany in 2006. The international dimension of our work will be discussed later in this chapter.

Football coaching and talent identification
Ever since its early years, Football Unites, Racism Divides has organized coaching sessions, delivered by Football Association qualified coaches, in some of the most disadvantaged areas of Sheffield. All this coaching continues to be either free or low cost, thus removing one of the key barriers to participation among ethnic minority young people, and the coaching staff are an ethnically diverse team, which helps to provide role models and inspiration to young people. The most significant development in FURD's coaching program has been the use of Sheffield United Academy all-weather facilities, where the majority of the coaching has been based since it opened in 2003. The academy, in the Shirecliffe area of Sheffield, is ideally situated in a number of ways, including its proximity to the multiracial Burngreave neighborhood. The facilities, described as "awesome" by Sharrow United players, are a far cry from the muddy parks and open spaces used for coaching in FURD's early years, when the first task of every session for the coaches was to clear away litter and dog dirt. Up to 150 young people attend the Sunday afternoon under-fourteen and over-fourteen sessions.

A group of up to twenty-five players, aged between fourteen and seventeen, are coached together three days a week as part of the project's Positive Futures program. This intensity of coaching time has led to the youngsters' dramatic improvement, both as players and young citizens, and an under-eighteen team made up from the Positive Futures group entered the Sheffield and District under-eighteen league in the 2007-2008 season after a year in the under-sixteen Junior Sunday League.

Football Unites also operates weekly sessions at local schools in Sharrow and is involved in a number of joint initiatives with the project's education worker in both primary and secondary schools across Sheffield. Additionally, sessions are run on request and in partnership with other community organizations at various locations including open spaces on housing estates and in local parks, with extra sessions usually being held during school holidays.

One of FURD's coaches is Chilean Luis Silva, who played professionally in Argentina, Chile and Peru, before escaping from Pinochet's torture squads, eventually arriving in Sheffield in 1975 as a political refugee. Luis's major role at FURD is in talent identification, and players considered up to the standard required are referred to both Sheffield United and Sheffield Wednesday Academy coaching staff. As word spreads of the coaches' links with local clubs, more young people are attracted to the FURD coaching schemes as a result.

This link with professional clubs is now paying off, as several FURD trainees have been signed up by United and other clubs. Liban Abdi has become one of the first Somali professional footballers in the country and scored the winning goal in his debut for Sheffield United's first team in a friendly game against Hungarian side Ferencvaros in March 2008. In July 2008 he joined Ferencvaros on a season's loan.

Also in March 2008, FURD graduate and Sheffield United professional Aymen Tahar made his international debut for the Algeria under-twenties in a 1-0 win over Tunisia. Abdi, Tahar and Kyle Walker were all playing for United's Reserves and under-eighteen sides in the 2007-2008 season. Across the city, another Somali player referred by FURD, Mukhtar Mohammed, made his first team debut for Sheffield Wednesday in a pre-season friendly match in August 2008. Warren Burrell also signed as a professional with Mansfield Town at the end of the 2007-2008 season, making his first team debut in the last game of the season. Warren said of his involvement with FURD, "I went to a youth club in Sheffield and there were some coaching sessions going on which I was encouraged to join. . . . Luis Silva from Football Unites, Racism Divides was leading the coaching and I went along. It was the best thing I've ever done. . . . I knew that Luis meant business and I found out that he'd got really good links with the local league clubs like Sheffield United. . . . Teams come to him looking for talent and that came across pretty quickly. He's really well respected. . . . Luis taught me about discipline and he's got a way about him that lads respect. If you mess about you're out and that's how it is at league clubs." We are following the development of these players with interest.

FURD has also undertaken a number of initiatives to encourage ethnic minority young women to participate in football, as players, coaches and fans. This has proved to be one of the more difficult areas of our work, with evidence that while some girls have family or cultural issues to contend with that make it difficult to get involved, many girls are put off playing by the attitudes of boys, or the perception that boys will make fun of them. However, progress is being made and in 2008 a group of young women, mostly Asian, was meeting every Sunday in an indoor, enclosed venue for free, fun football coaching with qualified female coaches. We hope this will enable the women involved to gain skills and confidence in a supportive environment which they can then use to encourage more young women to get involved.

Football Unites, Racism Divides also sponsors people to gain Football Association coaching qualifications, often as part of a volunteer's placement. Opportunities are available to gain voluntary coaching experience under the direction of FURD's coaches, and paid coaching opportunities sometimes arise. This has helped to increase the number of coaches from ethnic minorities who in turn can act as role models to help inspire and raise the aspirations of young people in the community.

Football Unites, Racism Divides has identified the lack of local, safe, all-weather facilities as a major obstacle to ethnic minority young people progressing further in football. We are working in partnership with community groups, schools, Sheffield City Council and Sheffield Futures to consult, plan and secure funding to radically improve this situation as quickly as possible.

Work with professional clubs

Football Unites, Racism Divides has worked closely with Sheffield United and Sheffield Wednesday to advise them on measures such as introducing equal opportunities policies and race equality standards, attracting more ethnic minority fans and dealing with racist incidents. Sheffield United's Bramall Lane stadium now plays host to an annual Community Day, a joint event run by Sheffield United and Football Unites, Racism Divides, to welcome the local community to the ground.

The support of professional clubs is key to the successful campaigning against racism in football, and the proximity of the Football Unites project to the Bramall Lane ground, added to the racist attacks and harassment associated with football fans identified at the birth of the organization, has led to a concentration on developing strategies with Sheffield United Football Club. The "Sheffield Divided or United?" report published in 1997 showed that over 80 percent of the Sheffield United supporters questioned favored strong action being taken against racists within the crowd, such as ejection from the ground and the canceling of season tickets. It is essential that clubs and supporters act together in tackling racism within their club, particularly since a poll running since 2003 on the FURD website has consistently returned about 84 percent of votes in favor of firm action.

Locally, FURD has always had a constructive relationship with Sheffield United Football Club (the Blades), whose Bramall Lane stadium is a short walk from FURD's office. For example, it has been a member of the Blades Partnership, made up of representatives from Sheffield United Football Club, Sharrow Community Forum, Sheffield College, Asian Welfare Association 96 and the Federation of Stadium Communities. Its combined efforts brought in £1.8 million in grants, as well as help in securing planning permission for the Blades Enterprise Centre and the Community Hall, both new developments at the stadium.

The Blades Enterprise Centre has set targets for the number of local and ethnic minority small businesses that it needs to attract as clients and the Community Hall for use by local residents is now situated underneath the corner of the Kop and John Street stand. The Blades Partnership has developed plans to ensure that local people receive the relevant training required for the jobs that will come with the ground development. The Blades Partnership has gained a national reputation as a model for other clubs and their communities to follow and the 2000 conference of the Federation of Stadium Communities was held at Bramall Lane. One of the early means by which Sheffield United was able to contribute to the achievement of the project's objectives was the ticket distribution scheme in conjunction with FURD. The initiative enabled hundreds of local Black and Asian young people to experience a live professional football match, leading to an increase in self-confidence and security among those attending. FURD has also distributed free tickets for Sheffield Wednesday games. Further examples of work undertaken with Sheffield United include:

- the adoption of a club equal opportunities policy in 1999;
- regular articles in the club's match day program;
- anti-racist messages flashed up on the electronic scoreboard during every home game;
- subsidized use of the Academy facilities for coaching sessions;
- junior players recommended to Academy staff;
- membership of the Blades Partnership group;
- representatives from Sheffield United as trustees of the Football Unites, Racism Divides Educational Trust;
- "Football Unites, Racism Divides" is displayed on a pitchside hoarding at every match.

In 2008 Sheffield United became the first club in the Championship to attain the preliminary level of the Kick It Out Racial Equality Standard. A number of initiatives have also been undertaken in cooperation with Sheffield Wednesday FC, including:

- membership in the Owls Against Racism Group;
- joint events with Show Racism the Red Card and Sheffield Wednesday;
- collaborative work between Sheffield Wednesday's Study Support Centre and the FURD education worker;
- representatives from Sheffield Wednesday acting as trustees of the Football Unites, Racism Divides Educational Trust.

Anti-Racism Week of Action

Since 2001, FARE has been coordinating a Europe-wide Anti-Racism Action Week in Football each year in October. Every professional club in England and Wales, as well as many amateur clubs and schools, youth clubs and other organizations now take part in anti-racist activities during the week.

FURD works closely with Sheffield United to plan events at a home match during Action Week. This usually involves distributing anti-racist magazines, posters and stickers to fans before the game, and sometimes youngsters from FURD's coaching schemes are able to take part in an exhibition game on the pitch at half-time.

FURD held its biggest-ever Week of Action event at the game between Sheffield United and Chelsea on 28 October 2006, while United were in the Premiership. "The match against Chelsea provided the perfect opportunity of a packed stadium, plus Sky TV coverage, to do something a bit special," said FURD coordinator Howard Holmes. Some twenty-five Football Unites, Racism Divides volunteers worked for three hours to lay out 6,000 cards, which spelled out a giant "Kick It Out" message, as the players shook hands before the game. FURD worked with the club and Show Racism the Red Card to produce a team poster against racism, 4,500 copies of which were handed out to fans, along with Kick It Out's "One Game, One Community" leaflet and poster. Moreover, "Blades United Against Racism" and "Kick It Out" messages were flashed every ten minutes on the giant scoreboard and twelve young players from the Football Unites, Racism Divides sessions at the Sheffield United Academy took part in a coaching demonstration on the pitch at half-time.

Community Day

The annual Community Day has become one of the most high profile joint ventures between FURD and Sheffield United. Its roots go back to July 1998, when Football Unites, Racism Divides and Sheffield Youth Service staff took two teams to play in the Anti-Racist World Cup, held in Montefiorino, Italy. Both the Somali Blades and Sharrow United (then known as the Abbeydale Asian Youth Project) won all their games, before meeting in the final. After a goalless draw, the teams decided to forego a penalty shoot-out and share the winner's title. Back home in Sharrow, then FURD youth worker Tom Collins had the bright idea of replaying the final at Bramall Lane. Once the club agreed, the concept of Community Day was born, involving small-sided games in four quarters of the pitch, Streetkick, plus stalls, displays, exhibitions, food and entertainment in the John Street conference suites. The Somali Blades beat Sharrow United 2-0 to win the first Community Cup in May 1999.

The Community Day has since become a popular annual event, usually held on a Sunday afternoon shortly after the end of the season. Thousands of people from all across the region's diverse communities turn up for a family day out to celebrate their love of football. Hundreds of young people from local schools and youth groups revel in the chance to play in a series of football tournaments held on the famous Bramall Lane pitch, watched by the crowds of onlookers on the sidelines and in the stands. Those children not involved in the tournaments have the chance to play on Streetkick. Youngsters can enjoy themselves on the bouncy castle and inflatable slide and other entertainment often includes a clown, cheerleaders, DJs, rap crews and dancing displays and boxing exhibitions. Local community groups set up stalls and exhibitions and some specially chosen food stalls provide a taste of something different. The henna painting, hair braiding, beauty therapy, face painting, nail art and the Indian head massage are all extremely popular.

The greatest success of the Community Day is the sheer diversity of the people attending. Attendees of the Community Day feature unusually high proportions of female and ethnic minority groups. While many football clubs are finding it very difficult to engage themselves with local communities, the ongoing partnership of Football Unites, Racism Divides with Sheffield United Football Club has helped the Bramall Lane outfit to become far more involved and especially aware of the needs of the local community.

The Community Day has been praised by the national anti-racist campaign Kick It Out, as a model of good practice that should be shared with other clubs. FURD has undertaken the task of disseminating knowledge, skills and experience to other professional clubs throughout the United Kingdom as part of their "Stand Up, Speak Up" award. Inspired by our joint success in combating racism, Barnsley Football Club held their first Community Day in 2007, having worked closely with FURD and Kick It Out staff to develop their own model. Nottingham County and Bradford City are other clubs in our region to have held Community Days.

In 2008, Sheffield United set up the United Initiative, the club's community arm, with the aim of building links between the club and the community. This has the potential of further improving the relationship between FURD and the club with more scope for joint working. Early examples of this are that the club took a much bigger role in planning and running the 2008 Community Day, and the United Initiative will be the major sponsors of Sharrow United for the 2008-2009 and 2009-2010 seasons. Additionally, FURD coach Keith Ward has been appointed to the post of coordinator of the new Kickz program, set up by Sheffield United in consultation with local partners including FURD to provide sporting and other positive activities for young people in the area. Keith has been involved with FURD from the age of fifteen, starting out as one of our first volunteers.

International work
Football Unites, Racism Divides started out life as a purely community-based initiative. However, two factors soon led the project to adopt a wider profile. One was FURD's key involvement in telling the story of Arthur Wharton, the world's first black professional footballer, including raising the funds for a headstone to be placed on Wharton's unmarked grave in May 2007; the second reason was the cross-fertilization of ideas and experiences with other anti-racist initiatives in Europe, in particular *Progetto Ultra* in Bologna and the Dortmund Fan Project. FURD based their Streetkick game on the Dortmund version that toured Sheffield, Huddersfield and Leeds in 1997, and the inspiration for the Resources and Information Centre was the *Archivio del Tifo* run by *Progetto Ultra*.

Football Against Racism in Europe (FARE)
In early 1999, Football Unites, Racism Divides was one of a handful of other like-minded groups and campaigners across Europe that formed the Football Against Racism in Europe (FARE) network. The network has since grown to include hundreds of member groups affiliated with it, from grass-roots fan groups to political campaigns throughout the length and breadth of the continent. This loose network of independent organizations seeks to coordinate anti-racist activities in football across Europe. One way in which it achieves this is through its annual Action Week against racism and discrimination in football. Launched back in the 2001-2002 season with activities in nine countries, the Action Week boasted over a thousand simultaneous events in almost every European country by 2007, becoming Europe's largest anti-racist event. Particularly encouraging is the involvement of previously absent countries such as Spain, France and those in Eastern Europe. FURD helps coordinate this huge annual event, and also organizes its own activities as part of it. Football Against Racism in Europe works tirelessly with football clubs and authorities to ensure that they recognize the problem of racism in football; adopts, publishes and enforces an anti-racist policy; uses the power of football to unite people from different communities and cultures; and establishes partnerships with organizations committed to ridding the game of racism, in particular, supporters' groups, migrants and ethnic minorities.

In February 2002, Football Unites, Racism Divides hosted an international conference, "Building the Network," at Bramall Lane, Sheffield United's football ground. Over eighty delegates attended the event, representing forty-six different organizations from across Europe. The event was designed to share good practice of practical action. Many of the individuals present were from grass-roots organizations and the conference proved a key stepping stone in the development of the Football Against Racism in Europe network. The Sheffield conference has since been used as the template for further FARE grass-roots conferences, such as the "Networking against racism and discrimination in European

Football—The Role of Fans, Football Clubs and Ethnic Minorities" conference held in Germany in 2004, as well as the FARE grass-roots conference in Slovakia held in 2005.

FURD has also been heavily involved in designing and updating the FARE website (www.farenet.org), which has English, French, German and Italian versions and contains news about FARE members' activities as well as about racism in football.

Anti-Racist World Cup

FURD has been a regular participant in the *Mondiali Antirazzisti*, or Anti-Racist World Cup, which was held in the town of Montecchio, near Parma, in northern Italy from 2000 to 2006, following three years at Montefiorino. Over 160 young people from Sheffield have taken part: the largest single party, 41 people in total, being in July 2003. In 2005, 192 teams from all over Europe took part in the friendly competition, with over 5,000 people attending the event. The tournament is spread over four days with mini-football leagues leading to a knockout competition on the last day.

In 2002, FURD entered a women's team for the first time, which played in a mixed league. The FURD Women All-Stars won the *Coppa Multiculti*, or Multicultural Cup, awarded for being the most multicultural team and upholding the ethos of the event, described by the organizers as the most prestigious award of the tournament. FURD's Somali Blades team reached the final in both 1998 and 2001.

Many of the participating organizations, FURD included, set up displays and information stalls, which gives the event a real "festival" feel. During the evening the event comes alive with live bands, many of whom have an anti-racist/anti-fascist slant, plus DJs, displays and exhibitions. All of the young people from Football Unites, Racism Divides who have visited the *Mondiali* have found it really enjoyable and rewarding, for different reasons. For some young people it has been the social aspect; the fact that they had the opportunity to mix, converse and share stories and ideas with other young people from around Europe. For others it is the feeling of unity; the feeling that so many people are gathered together to fight a common cause, racism, along with the opportunity to increase awareness of anti-racist practice around Europe. Ever since 2007 the *Mondiali* has been held in Casalecchio, near Bologna.

World Cup and European Championship work

A team of Football Unites, Racism Divides workers toured Portugal during Euro 2004 as part of the UEFA-funded FARE program of activities, helping to keep fans entertained and peacefully interacting with each other by staging Streetkick tournaments in host cities. The game also provided an opportunity to distribute FARE information on anti-racism in football. Teams made up of different nationalities played street football in a relaxed atmosphere before the "real" football matches they'd come to see. For many supporters it was the perfect opportunity to kill some time during the long wait for the big matches. The impact of the inflatable game was such that FURD was invited to stage Streetkick events in Germany during the 2006 World Cup finals and in Austria and Switzerland during Euro 2008. The Streetkick tours clearly demonstrated the unique power of football in bringing together people in a celebratory atmosphere through a common love of the game.

Football Between Communities
Football Unites coach Desbon Bushiri has been instrumental in spreading the FURD ethos to the Democratic Republic of Congo in Africa. With the help of a grant from FIFA in 2007 he set up the Football Inter-Communautaire (FIC, or Football Between Communities) project to establish a program of positive activities for young people in the Sud Kivu province, Territory of Barka-Fizi, situated in the Eastern of DR Congo, an area severely affected by civil war and conflict. In this area, more than 50 percent of young people between the ages of six and twenty years old are orphans from war, conflict and disease such as HIV and Malaria, and 70 percent of young people are without access to education.

FIC's aim is to gather young people from all ethnic origins who share their opposition toward racism, war and division and to help them express aspirations for peace, tolerance and reconciliation, building solidarity, links and understanding among different communities through sporting activities. In order to achieve this aim, FIC believes that it is important to use sporting activities with schools, local football teams and across communities. There is a need to spread the message across the region by building a stronger mechanism of networking and partnership. This will benefit young people in school, out of school, on the street, and in displaced and refugee places.

Recognition
Football Unites, Racism Divides's work in breaking down barriers in Sheffield received civic recognition when in April 2007, a party of staff, young people, volunteers and friends of Football Unites, Racism Divides were guests of the Lord Mayor, Councilor Jackie Drayton, at a reception at Sheffield Town Hall in recognition of the contribution Football Unites, Racism Divides has made to social inclusion and community cohesion in the city. "I wish to congratulate everyone at Football Unites, Racism Divides on their hard work and commitment to overcoming the prejudices and fears which threaten to divide us," said the Lord Mayor, adding, "it's really great that you have been able to use the power of football to increase social inclusion, both in Sheffield and the wider world."

This followed a report by OFSTED, the government's Office for Standards in Education, on Sheffield Futures, the company delivering youth services in Sheffield, which praised the work of Football Unites, Racism Divides. The report, published on 12 December 2006, stressed that "Sheffield Futures continues to support the exemplary work of Football Unites, Racism Divides, where effective youth work is delivered through a varied program of football coaching, peer education and youth volunteering."

At the national Kick It Out campaign's tenth anniversary ceremony in 2004, FURD also received an award for its pioneering work as a community-based anti-racist football project. FURD has also been quoted as a model project in a number of reports, including the UEFA guide to good practice to tackling racism in football, published in 2003.

Future challenges

The nature of our work means we are constantly being faced with challenges, whether in relation to securing funding, or in adapting our work to a changing society and challenging new manifestations of ignorance and prejudice that that brings with it. However, the experience we've built up makes us confident that we have already made a difference, and we are determined to carry on finding ways to help people harness their desires to work together to make our communities better, stronger, safer and fairer places.

A Critical View

Set in 1995, the main aims of Football Unites, Racism Divides focused upon (1) ensuring that people who play or watch football can do so without fear of racial abuse and harassment, in either a verbal or physical form; and (2) increasing the participation of people from ethnic minorities in football, as either players, spectators or employees.

With regard to our first objective, significant improvements have been made in this area. Racist abuse does still occur at football matches, but less frequently, and when it does, it usually comes from a tiny minority. Laws and policies have been tightened to make explicit the non-acceptability of racism. Clubs and football's governing bodies have now got behind the campaign and more sanctions are available to deal with it when it does occur. There are still a few problems concerning the difficulties of apprehending or identifying culprits when they're part of a large crowd, especially as it is often stewards rather than police who are the first officials to be informed and they sometimes appear unwilling to deal with the offenders when part of a crowd. An important part of our work has been working with clubs and the local county Football Association to ensure that they have anti-racist policies in place and that they are understood and adhered to when an incident is reported. Through our partnerships with national and international groups such as Kick It Out and FARE, we have also been able to influence football authorities like UEFA (for example, in 2002 UEFA adopted the ten-point plan of action originally developed by Kick It Out in 1993). This role as a kind of pressure group has also enabled us to influence government legislation. For example, in 1997 the new Labour government set up a Football Task Force "to tackle the problems of the game." In March 1998, the Task Force submitted the "Eliminating Racism from Football" report to the Minister for Sport. FURD made a submission to the Task Force and was cited in the report as a case study as "one of the most successful partnership initiatives." The report produced numerous recommendations for the government, local authorities, football clubs and football governing bodies, many of which have now been taken up. One of these was the amending of the Football (Offences and Disorder) Act which had since 1991 made racist chanting at football matches a criminal offense only if offenders were chanting in unison and not individually. This was amended in 2001 to make chanting by one individual an offense. Some recent reports of racist incidents illustrate the changing nature of our communities, of the international nature of top football teams at the current time, and of racism. For example, when Sheffield United fielded a Chinese player, Sun Jihai, there were chants and songs from a minority of United fans alluding to his nationality and supposed customs of Chinese people. There has been some debate about whether this constitutes racism or harmless humor, and it seems unlikely that such songs would have been sung by so many people at or about an African Caribbean player, as most fans now understand that this would be seen as racist and may lead to punishment. Recently, Middlesborough's Egyptian player, Mido, was subject to Islamophobic chants such as "Mido, he's got a bomb." Some people have defended the abuse, saying it was a joke based on the fact that he looks like Richard Reid, the convicted shoe bomber, rather than being racist. The main defense in both these cases has been that the chants weren't racist, not that racist chants should be allowed. These two examples illustrate the changing nature of racism in our society and why our work needs to develop to keep pace with it.

Concerning our second goal, FURD has helped to set up and run several teams competing in local leagues which consist mainly of teams from communities under-represented in organized football. This includes Asians, Somalis and other Africans and players from new communities locally who may have arrived as asylum-seekers. Our coaching sessions and tournaments are also particularly aimed at young players from under-represented communities and have successfully attracted a diverse clientele, with the low cost and anti-racist name and reputation of FURD undoubtedly helping to do so. Several players from our coaching schemes, including two Somalis and an Algerian, have now signed for local professional clubs. FURD has worked consistently with local clubs, particularly Sheffield United, to ensure the club is seen by the local community as safe and welcoming. One of FURD's strategies for encouraging more ethnic minority fans to attend matches was the distribution of free match tickets donated by Sheffield United. This scheme ran for several seasons with numbers of tickets available varying from six to one hundred and fifty. Anecdotally, on the whole, people who have taken up this ticket offer have enjoyed the experience and haven't experienced racism. This has contradicted some people's expectations of the football stadium being a hostile environment. The 1996 survey mentioned earlier in this chapter found 1 percent of the fans at a Sheffield United home match were from ethnic minorities. A comparable survey hasn't been carried out since, but looking around at a match, it is clear that the proportion has increased somewhat, although it is still way below the proportion of the local population. On a national level, an annual survey of Premiership fans is carried out. To summarize, the 1997 survey found 98.8 percent of fans were white, and by 2007-2008 it was 94 percent. As with any statistical survey it's not necessarily 100 percent accurate and the methodology used has changed a bit over the years—earlier attempts surveyed season ticket holders by post. The 2006-2007 survey included an email survey for the first time which probably increased the number of younger fans taking part, and more effort has been made in recent years to include people who attend matches but don't have season tickets. Generally these figures are fairly encouraging as the percentage of ethnic minority fans attending matches is moving closer to that of the ethnic minority population as a whole, although it is still well below being proportionate. Other factors such as high ticket prices mitigate against football match attendance being a truly democratic experience as ethnic minorities are over-represented at the poorer end of society.

FURD being publicized as a model of good practice has inspired numerous other schemes, which are now being founded on similar principles. This is important as there is a limit to what FURD can achieve, as much of its work is at a local level. That its principles are now being applied in other parts of the country and by other organizations can only be a good thing. Yet our success has never been effortless. One regular challenge we face is in securing funding. While this has gotten easier in some respects as our profile has increased and the political climate has been relatively sympathetic, we cannot assume this will continue to be the case. Our funding has always come from a patchwork of different sponsors for different aspects of our work and it is always for a limited period of time, making planning and stability difficult to achieve. There is often a balance to be struck between setting our own agenda and working to the agendas of potential sponsors. Issues around race have been very prominent in British society over the lifetime of FURD as the society has become more diverse. In particular, contentious issues concerning many people include levels of immigration, including people seeking asylum, and the ability of the country and its services to cope with it and a fear of terrorist attacks by Muslim extremists and the apparent lack of integration between different communities. These fears are being reflected in the increasing political success of the far-right British National Party. A calm and balanced response to these issues has not been encouraged by the irresponsible and sensationalist reporting by some major newspapers. While the campaign against racism in football has been relatively successful, and no doubt helped by the success of many black players, there is no room for complacency as the tensions being expressed in the wider society may at any time spill over into football. Many of the fears people have are the result of ignorance—people may believe something they read in the paper if they don't have the personal experiences to counter it. This is where our education, youth work and coaching can help, as they encourage those people to learn about those from other cultures and provide opportunities for people to interact with others they wouldn't otherwise meet, whether through football or other positive activity.

MILESTONES

1995: Attacks on local Asian and Somali people in the vicinity of Sheffield United's ground, particularly on match days.

November 1995: Football Unites, Racism Divides partnership set up including fans, Sheffield United and community groups.

January 1996: Successful bid for funding from the European Cities Anti-Racism Project.

April 1996: Project coordinator appointed and Football Unites, Racism Divides officially launched at Sheffield United FC.

May 1997: Publication of "Sheffield Divided or United? A Study of 'Race' and Football," research report commissioned by Football Unites, Racism Divides.

May 1997: Headstone on Arthur Wharton's previously unmarked grave unveiled after FURD set up an appeal fund.

September 1997: European funding enables Football Unites to appoint a part-time youth worker, resources and information worker, and an administrative worker.

November 1997: Football Unites, Racism Divides Resources and Information Centre officially opened.

January 1998: Football Unites, Racism Divides website launched.

July 1998: FURD takes two teams to the Anti-Racist World Cup in Italy for the first time and has taken a party regularly ever since. Football Unites, Racism

Divides teams, the Somali Blades and Abbeydale Youth Project, meet and draw in the final.

September 1998: Publication of the book *The First Black Footballer: Arthur Wharton 1865-1930*, by Phil Vasili, research funded by Football Unites, Racism Divides.

October 1998: "History of Black Footballers Exhibition" launched at Manchester United's Museum.

November 1998: Somali Blades win the Philip Lawrence Award for good citizenship.

November 1998: Streetkick mobile football game unveiled at Sheffield United's Open Day.

February 1999: Football Against Racism in Europe founded by supporters' groups from thirteen countries. FURD is a founding member and partner.

May 1999: Football Unites, Racism Divides Educational Trust established.

May 1999: First Community Day held by FURD and Sheffield United at Bramall Lane with Somali Blades playing the Abbeydale Youth Project in a replay of the Anti-Racist World Cup final. Community Day becomes an established part of the calendar with days being held every year since.

July 1999: FURD begins delivering Sheffield Futures' Millennium Volunteers scheme funded by the Department for Education and Employment.

February 2000: David Blunkett attends launch of Football Unites, Racism Divides Millennium Volunteers project at Bramall Lane.

2000: FURD begins working with the Shirecliffe Youth Inclusion Project, funded by the Home Office Positive Futures initiative, to provide coaching, a second Streetkick game and a peer mentoring program.

August 2000: Sharrow United, sponsored by Football Unites, Racism Divides, becomes the first mainly Asian team in Sheffield local eleven-a-side league football.

April 2001: *United Colors of Football* fanzine, issue 2, launched by FURD and Kick It Out as part of the first Europe-wide anti-racist Week of Action in football.

April 2001: FURD launches website for the Football Against Racism in Europe network.

May 2001: Sharrow United win promotion in their first season in the Regional Alliance Sunday League Division 2.

October 2001: John Barnes is among the inspirational speakers at "Moving on Up," a Football Unites, Racism Divides–run conference aimed at raising young people's aspirations.

February 2002: Eighty delegates from fourteen countries attend the Football Against Racism in Europe conference.

May 2002: Sharrow United wins promotion again, this time to the Regional Alliance Premier League.

July 2002: FURD enters a women's team in the Anti-Racist World Cup for the first time and the team wins the Coppa Multiculti.

October 2002: National and Europe-wide Anti-Racist Action Week sees all ninety-two league clubs take part. The week has since become an established annual event.

November 2002: Football Against Racism in Europe wins the MTV Free Your Mind human rights award.

July-August 2003: Unity Cup, national tournament for refugees and asylum-seekers, is held in Manchester, with Sheffield teams taking part, and a seven-a-side summer league starts for refugees and asylum-seekers in Sheffield.

September 2003: Football Unites backs a new Somali under-eighteen team, Surud United, who enter the eleven-a-side Sheffield and District DB Sports Under-18 League.

January 2004: The national Kick It Out campaign marks its tenth anniversary at a star-studded ceremony. Football Unites, Racism Divides receives a special award for its pioneering work as a community-based anti-racist football project.

April 2004: Sharrow United win the Sheffield Regional Alliance Sunday League Cup.

June 2004: Streetkick tours Portugal helping promote a friendly atmosphere among fans during Euro 2004.

July 2004: A break-in, theft and fire at the FURD office disrupt work and cause the project to move to temporary premises for six months.

September 2004: Sharrow United joins the Meadowhall Sunday League, and the African Dream Team enters a team in the Regional Alliance League.

April 2005: Football Unites wins contract from the Home Office to deliver a Positive Futures program in Sharrow and Burngreave, initially for one year until March 2006.

May 2005: FURD delivers its first anti-racist training package to youth workers.

November 2005: Football Unites, Racism Divides marks its tenth anniversary with a gala evening at Bramall Lane.

June 2006: FURD's Streetkick tours the World Cup finals in Germany.

July 2006: FURD hosts the national Unity Cup tournament for refugees and asylum-seekers in Sheffield.

September 2006: FURD Positive Futures enters an under-sixteen team in the Sheffield and District Junior Sunday League.

October 2006: Six thousand cards are laid out on seats at Bramall Lane by FURD volunteers, which were held up by fans to spell the message "Kick It Out" before the Sheffield United v. Chelsea Premiership fixture.

November 2006: FURD and Sheffield Futures organize "Creating Space," a conference about Islamophobia.

December 2006: An Ofsted inspection report on Sheffield Futures, the company delivering youth services in Sheffield, praises the "exemplary" work of Football Unites.

April 2007: Sharrow United wins promotion to the First Division of the Meadowhall Sheffield Sunday Football League.

April 2007: FURD staff and volunteers attend a civic reception at the Lord Mayor's Parlour in recognition of FURD's work in the community.

July 2007: FURD volunteers feature in Prime Minister Gordon Brown's book *Britain's Everyday Heroes*.

November 2007: Pele meets FURD staff and backs the campaign.

December 2007: FURD coach Desbon Bushiri establishes the Football Between Communities project in the Democratic Republic of Congo.

March 2008: FURD volunteer Abdi Hussein wins Community Champion award for voluntary work at Football Without Frontiers conference in Belfast.

March 2008: FURD trainee, Liban Abdi, who is of Somali origin, makes his debut for the Sheffield United first team, scoring the winning goal in a 1-0 friendly game against Ferencvaros in Hungary.

April 2008: African Dream Team wins Division Three of Meadowhall Sunday League, after winning twenty of their twenty-two matches.

April 2008: "From Sharrow to Soweto" event at Sheffield United's Tunnel Bar raises £500 for the Football Between Communities project.

May 2008: Sharrow United wins the Meadowhall Sunday League Cup, the final being played at Sheffield United FC.

June 2008: FURD takes Streetkick to the Euro 2008 finals in Austria and Switzerland.

Chapter Six

Show Racism the Red Card

Ged Grebby

History

Show Racism the Red Card is an anti-racist charity that was established in January 1996 with the aim of using professional footballers as anti-racist role models. Although racism is on the decline in professional football, it is unfortunately on the increase in British and indeed European society. The aim of our campaign is to combat racism through anti-racist education and professional footballers are showing the way in terms of making a stand and fighting racism. The campaign has been able to involve hundreds of top footballers and managers, and has harnessed the high profile of these role models to combat racism. Show Racism the Red Card is now present in United Kingdom, Norway, Sweden, Finland, Denmark and Ireland. The campaigns in each country have education through sport as a common goal but draw on different local resources to get the message across. So in Ireland, the involvement of the Gaelic Players Association and Irish Rugby Union Players Association is of great importance to us.

While racism in sport has been a major problem in many countries it is not so manifest in Ireland and we want to keep it that way. Racism is a problem of society and it has been the case that in countries such as Italy, England and elsewhere, racism found its reflection in the football stadium. Racism has only declined in English football because of a series of very strong anti-racism campaigns within the sport over the years, yet it still remains a problem for society. The Show Racism the Red Card video reveals this as a problem where professionals such as Chris Hughton were subject to a torrent of abuse every match they played in the 1980s, while Shaka Hislop notes that it was an experience where he was perceived as "just another black person" that led to him being active in the Show Racism the Red Card campaign. "I was putting petrol in my car at the garage and these kids started shouting racist abuse. Then after a bit one of them realized who I was and told his friends. Then they came over looking for autographs. That really hurt," said Shaka. In the 1970s and 1980s players experienced it in the stadium while in the 1990s and today they experience it outside the ground. On the video many players reveal that they are subject to racism outside the game because of the work inside the game has had an impact, but the video revealingly shows that there is a lot of work to do in society. Young people talk about the isolation they feel when they are suffering racism in the amateur leagues where there is not the protection surrounding a professional in the premier league. Through playing together, working together and being educated together we can grow with enough understanding to Show Racism the Red Card. Racist chants on the terraces at football matches have been an issue in football for many years and football grounds have been a favorite place for fascist groups to recruit new members. Kevin Keegan remembers walking into a football ground once and being handed a leaflet with a picture of an ape on it, which said, "Would you like these people to have your job?" This was a leaflet probably produced by a fascist group, like the National Front or the British National Party, who were targeting that ground and who were using racist ideas to promote their party.

This year has seen our tenth anniversary and we celebrated it in style at the Hilton in Newcastle, thanks to the financial support of Coutts Bank. One hundred and seventy-five guests joined us to mark the occasion and it was a great way of saying thank you to all the organizations and individuals that have made our campaign so successful.

Show Racism the Red Card activities

Since our last Annual Review was printed in July 2005 we have been through an extremely busy period for our organization. Back then we had a staff team of five workers in the North East and two in Scotland, whereas today we have grown to six workers in the North East of England, three in Scotland and one in Wales. In addition, we have been working with five ex-professional footballers in Scotland, who are helping us to deliver anti-racist education and football training. The scope of the work we are undertaking has grown to such an extent that we are unable to cover all aspects of the work in this Annual Review without it looking like an encyclopedia. While our organization has grown and the impact we have made has been greater, the need for our resources and campaigning is also on the increase. Racism has been on the increase in the United Kingdom and we are trying to address some of the key growth areas, Islamophobia being the main one. Our main Show Racism the Red Card video was updated in October 2005 and we were privileged that Frederic Kanoute was able to share some of his experiences as a Muslim playing in top-flight football. The DVD has proven extremely popular and has been a great addition to our resources. The fact that more than 3,500 schools in Scotland have a copy of our video, while some 2,000 schools in Wales have a copy of our DVD, has been a huge achievement for Show Racism the Red Card. Demand for all of our resources remains high, reflecting their accessibility and popularity.

One of the reasons we did not produce an Annual Review in 2006 was due to the fact that we wanted to put our limited resources into printing England World Cup posters and producing a high quality magazine. In the end we printed and distributed 300,000 England posters in 2006, bringing our total number of posters and magazines distributed in one year to over 1,000,000. The brand new magazine was twice the size of previous magazines at sixty-four pages and this allowed us to cover more issues and interviews than ever before. It has proven to be a great asset to our public work and profile. We have expanded our work at schools in the last two years and this has given us a great bonus to our educational work. The campaign harnesses the high profile of professional footballers to combat racism in society, but it is not just the current footballers that are role models to young people. The ex-players we work with are able to have a great impact and the football training has been a great way of making our campaign an exciting addition to the school curriculum wherever we have been. The direct work in schools also allows us to assess how good our resources are and what improvements and additional resources are required. All of the above advances in our work have been made possible thanks to an increase in funding and we now have more sponsors than ever before. Although we are continually striving to improve on what we do, we also need to restate that our original "big idea" in December 1995 to "use our contacts in professional football to produce anti-racist materials directly accessible to young people," remains the key to our organization's development today. In the last ten years the status of professional footballers as role models has, if anything, increased.

Summary of our main areas of work:
Development of anti-racist educational resources

DVD
The DVD has been a great addition to our resources, having on it not only our main video, but also two of our previous videos. The DVD has also allowed us to display some of the winning videos from the school competition, and the animations from the young prize winners have become a feature of our public events. The main video from our DVD has been shown several times on the Community Channel.

A Safe Place
The *A Safe Place* video, which combats racist myths against asylum-seekers, has proven to be an invaluable addition to our resources. The "coaching with a conscience" scheme in Scotland is built around using this video, and the report by Gerry Britton shows that this video has been a great way of turning negative attitudes toward asylum-seekers around. Of the children who took part in the workshop and football training, 92 percent felt that their awareness of issues relating to racism had been increased through their involvement. The *A Safe Place* video has been shown on Teachers TV a number of times.

Scottish video
In Scotland we have also produced a Scottish version of the main video with a Scottish education pack. Thanks to the Scottish Executive, this resource was sent to every school in Scotland.

Websites and downloadable resources
Tommy Breslin has been working on improving our website and set up a new Scottish website. The websites are the easiest way to update our resources and we are looking at ways to improve them. For example, Zoobia Aslam has been working on downloadable anti-racist worksheets. The idea of these worksheets is to challenge growing forms of racism with reference to Islamophobia, discrimination against Travellers and racist behavior toward migrant workers from Eastern Europe.

Guides on how to use our campaign and resources
We have also been working on best practice guides, designed to increase the number of organizations working with our campaign and improve the way we work with other bodies. Sarah Soyei has produced a guide for councils and a separate guide for football clubs. The aim is to increase the number of partnership councils and football clubs working with our charity over the next five years.

Ireland
We have had reports of racism in sport in Ireland over the last several years. In July 2005, Shelbourne player Joseph Ndo was subject to a torrent of racist abuse when he played at Steaua Bucharest in the Champions League second round qualifier. Racism is becoming a big issue in Ireland so much so that a survey by the Irish government's anti-racism campaign, Know Racism, revealed that one in five Irish people have witnessed racism. In a previous event organized by Show Racism the Red Card, Irish Independent journalist Karl McGinty spoke to the young person next to him. Though immensely happy in school, she told of the sickening catalog of abuse she endures daily from complete strangers and which, she confessed, "makes life miserable for blacks." Amnesty International revealed the issue of bullying by use of mobile phones: "The kids in school send me text messages on my mobile phone saying 'you black nigger bastard.' I am afraid to look at my messages." Racism breeds through fear and ignorance and not knowing or understanding those from different backgrounds. Integration in society happens through school, work and college along with active involvement in extra-curricular activities. The Know Racism report revealed that 36 percent of Irish people have no contact with non-Irish nationals in Ireland, and this goes some way to explain the level of racism in Ireland. Through our partnership of those involved in education and sport we hope to promote integration and stamp out racism. We hope that our partnership of Gaelic games, rugby and soccer, and those involved in education open the way for more participation and integration of Irish and non-Irish.

Scotland

Show Racism the Red Card in Scotland has gone from strength to strength with the help of our Scottish Advisory Committee and the Scottish Executive. The Scottish Advisory Committee is made up of representatives from the Scottish Football Association, the Education Institute of Scotland, Unison and the Scottish Professional Footballers' Association. The Scottish Executive has increased our funding year after year and backed our business plan 2006-2009 to the tune of £275,000. They have also been extremely flexible with our organization and allowed us extra funding when initiatives have presented themselves such as, for example, the coaching with a conscience scheme. Thanks to this funding we were able to increase our staff by taking two more full-time staff members in June 2006: Tommy Breslin, the administrative worker and Zoobia Aslam, the campaign worker. In July, however, we suffered a setback when Roddy McNulty left our staff. The development of our campaign in Scotland owes a lot to both Roddy and Imran Alam and we thank them both and wish them all the best in their respective careers.

Wales

The Welsh Advisory Committee has been running well throughout 2006 and we have secured funding from all the major partners in Wales: the Football Association of Wales, the Sports Council for Wales, the Welsh Assembly and Unison. The Football Association of Wales Trust has also provided us with office space and administrative support for our new coordinator for Wales, Sunil Patel. Sunil started with us in October 2006 and has hit the ground running, organizing a whole series of events and initiatives. As you can see from Sunil's report we are now running the schools competition Wales with the support of the Welsh Assembly, who paid for every school in the country to get our DVD and education pack. We are currently working on a three year business plan for Wales and hope to see a real transformation of our work in this country. My thanks go to all the Welsh Advisory Committee members for their time and support and in particular, Dawn Hayes, the secretary and Unison, her trade union.

The school's competition

The schools competition is a great way of engaging young people in our campaign, and the work produced by the young people (posters, poetry, short stories, videos, songs, etc.) has been a fantastic addition to our resources. The Football Clubs again gave us great prizes for the competition in 2006 and we had a great turnout of players to hand over the prizes, including for the third year in a row Thierry Henry. We have secured funding for the competition from the Hilton Foundation, the National Union of Teachers, the Education Institute of Scotland and the Scottish Executive, and the competition is a major priority for our campaign. We will again be having the Scottish prize-giving ceremony at Hampden and are aiming to have our first-ever prize giving ceremony in Wales at the Millennium Stadium. The winning entries will also be made into display stands, which will tour libraries, schools, football clubs and other public venues in 2007.

These stands have proven very popular in Scotland and we will now be producing around fifty stands with this year's winning work.

Events at football clubs and posters
Another priority for 2007 is to increase the number of football clubs working with our campaign. The posters of first team squads holding up our red cards have proven very popular over the years and since 1997 we have printed and distributed over six million posters. These posters advertise our educational resources, schools competition and website. Groups in several other European countries have also taken up this idea from us, as it is a simple way of getting the football clubs and players to identify themselves as being anti-racist. This year we have done posters with a number of new clubs including Plymouth Argyle, Colchester United and Dagenham and Redbridge FC and we aim to build on this in 2007-2008. The event at football clubs with the players present remains one of the highlights of our campaign and as you can see from events reports, we held twenty-four of these in England and Wales in 2006. The impact of these events both in terms of the press and publicity they receive and the direct impact on the people who attend has been fantastic and we aim to increase the number of events in 2007 to fifty.

North East schools work
The direct work in schools in the North East of England has now been running since June 2004 and has made a major impact on our work. In this time we have run sessions with 13,407 pupils. These pupils have received both football training from Gary Bennett and anti-racist education from Kieron Brady and Gary Bennett. At the time of writing our last Annual Review we had two partnership councils funding this work—Sunderland and South Tyneside—but this has now increased to four with Newcastle and North Tyneside Councils becoming partners in this work. The development of this work has allowed us to increase our contacts with a whole range of organizations in the region and consequently improve the way we operate as an organization. In August 2006 we had our first ever Community Day organized in conjunction with Walker Football Club. The first Community Day took place in order to address the rise of racism against asylum-seekers in parts of Newcastle and was a great success with over 2,000 people attending during the day. We are looking to using the model of this day to see if we can do similar events with community football clubs in 2007.

Partnership councils
One of the key aspects of our educational work is establishing links with local councils. In Scotland and the North East of England we have a number of excellent partnerships with councils and we intend to deliver the best service that we can.

Volunteers and secondees

Volunteers remain very important to our campaign and they are involved at every level of our organization from the management committee to our schools work. We have had too many volunteers to thank them all individually, but they have been a great asset to our work, allowing us to reach a far greater audience than our staffing alone would allow. In Scotland and Wales the work has developed on a sound footing thanks to the advisory committees and the invaluable time and support the individual members have put into the work. The organizations that make up these committees have also been great in delivering either funding or funding in kind. In London we have managed to intervene in a number of conferences and events thanks to our dedicated team of volunteers. Special thanks go to Kim Burns, Ben North, Steve Grebby and Colleen Harris. We also have a partnership agreement with Newcastle City Council to harness the skills of their design team. We would like to thank Judith Hinnitt, Pat Dale, Paul Burgess, Lee Dobson and Margaret Baird at Newcastle City Council. We have also managed to build up a team of entertainers who are volunteers and include Elliot Joseph, our poet in residence; Richard Braithwaite, who does football skills; Ian Solomon and a group of London rappers and Amer Sheikh and his rappers from Thornhill School in Sunderland.

Some preliminary conclusions

Year 2006 was quite productive for Show Racism the Red Card and we are now on a far stronger footing in terms of staffing and finance at the start of 2007. We aim to increase both the quality of our educational resources and our impact geographically this year. In England and Wales we have set ourselves five main targets to help do this:

- Increase the number of football clubs working with our campaign.
- Increase the partnership local authorities.
- Improve the schools competition and increase the number of schools taking part in 2007.
- Continue to improve our direct work in schools and increase the scope of this work.
- Update our educational resources and continue to strive to increase orders.

In Scotland a sixth major target is to build upon the Fortnight of Action successes. Within each of these targets we have a whole range of improvements we can make to try and make 2007 and 2008 more successful years for our campaign. The growth of racism in society, particularly around Islamophobia, is of concern to all anti-racists and our organization will endeavor to increase resources, partnerships and efforts in tackling racism through anti-racist education.

Campaign work in Wales[1]

Since becoming the coordinator for Wales in October 2006, our work in Wales has seen great support from various groups, organizations and from the people of Wales. I am proud to be part of the campaign and look forward to developing the work throughout Wales in the year ahead. With the support I have received from our Wales Advisory Committee, the campaign in Wales has made great strides in the past few months and will continue to gather momentum in the coming months ahead. We have produced posters with the three Welsh football teams playing in the English leagues and printed 20,000 posters between them. The posters have started to be distributed free to the people of Wales and the clubs have distributed them directly to their supporters carrying our anti-racist message. In conjunction with the Football Association of Wales, our campaign will also be working with the clubs from the Welsh Premier League arranging events around the grounds. We will also be working with grassroots football organizations in Wales and Black and Minority Ethnic (BME) organizations with the aim of reaching all areas of the game. The campaign also recognizes the importance of other sports in Wales such as rugby and will be producing posters with Welsh rugby clubs in the months ahead; we will also look to work with other areas such as women's football.

Events

My first Show Racism the Red Card anti-racism event was at Cardiff City which was attended by schoolchildren from two local schools. It was great to see children at such a young age quiz the players with testing questions on their experiences of racism and then listening to the answers with interest. The events are an integral part of our work and we will be holding regular events with clubs around Wales in the year ahead.

Schools competition 2007

Our annual schools competition will be the most successful yet with the backing we have had in Wales from the Education Minister Jane Davidson. The National Assembly has helped promote the competition in Wales by sending out our DVD and education pack to nearly 2,000 schools throughout Wales. Our launch of the competition was held at the National Assembly for Wales in December 2006 and highlighted the backing we are getting from organizations in Wales which included the teaching unions, sporting authorities and local councils. The launch was also attended by Wales International Rugby players from Cardiff Blues Rugby club and showed our commitment to work with other areas in sports.

Website

The website gets updated regularly with the campaign in Wales and our supporters are kept aware of the developments on a regular basis.

Working with other groups
There has been great interest from other groups in Wales and we will be looking to build relationships that will enable us to promote our anti-racism message through a variety of ways. An example was when I was approached by a student at one of the top universities in the United Kingdom who wanted to promote our message through the university football teams; we arranged an event prior to kick-off and an article was published in the student paper that got distributed free to over 23,000 students.

The way ahead
The campaign in Wales has a long way to go in reaching its goal, but it will continue to grow in the times ahead. We will be looking to form and build partnerships with organizations around Wales, in particular the football clubs, local councils, sporting authorities and the national assembly for Wales. We will be looking for support that will enable the campaign to make an impact on Wales in the long term. The coming years will concern:

- more schools than ever entering our schools competition;
- regular events held at clubs throughout Wales;
- campaign work with grass-roots football organizations;
- other areas in sport being covered by the campaign;
- more activities than ever in Wales during the Football Against Racism in Europe's "Week of Action";
- joint events with other organizations.

Resources
Show Racism the Red Card has developed structurally and expanded its range of resources. The organization has continued to be fortunate enough to receive much publicity due to the work undertaken and events held and by using professional footballers to promote our message. There is no doubt that this high media profile constantly motivates people to find out about Show Racism the Red Card, its resources and activities. The North East office has continued to manage a high volume of orders and enquiries, distribution of free resources and participation in or providing materials for other organizations' events. During the period April 2005 to March 2006, Show Racism the Red Card's North East office received a total of 837 orders for resources. An impressive 253 of these orders have been for multiple resources, either multiple copies of a particular resource or offer (such as the 200 magazines offer) or for a combination of our resources. Through direct sales of our resources we have generated an income of £94,449.

We handle hundreds of requests each year for information, free materials or assistance with external events. Show Racism the Red Card has always tried, wherever possible, to provide free materials for distribution at stalls, at other organizations' events and to those who contact us for information about the campaign, whether for a school or college project, interest in being a volunteer or simply curiosity. The distribution of free materials is a great way to involve people in the campaign and publicize our other, saleable, resources. The numbers of resources distributed from the North East office were significant in terms of t-shirts, education packs, posters, magazines and the *A Safe Place* pack and lesser for button badges, carrier bags and stickers. The posters, in particular, have proved extremely popular. In England and Wales, we printed nearly 360,000 posters with some forty different football teams, three rugby teams and the Newcastle Eagles basketball team.

Competition 2006

The competition in England and Wales was not promoted as extensively this year. This was because we did not have the people-power to run a competition of the size of last year's without other areas of our work suffering. The competition was promoted on our website; however, a flyer advertising it was not produced and enquiries about the competition from formerly participating schools were referred to the website. That said, we had some great entries submitted and retained interest from many schools who have taken part before. We have also managed to forge links and strengthen existing ties to partnership councils, who have run a local level competition in their schools; these councils are Milton Keynes Council, Nottinghamshire County Council, Bury CLAS and Derby City Council.

An impressive 162 schools took part in England and Wales this year and successful prize-giving ceremonies were organized at Charlton Athletic FC and Newcastle Civic Centre for the winners in the South and North of England respectively. Winners again received framed certificates, signed shirts and balls, match tickets and Show Racism the Red Card goody bags. My thanks to the football clubs who donated prizes, all who took part, the teachers who organized participation in their school, and those at the partnership councils, Charlton Athletic FC and Newcastle City Council who helped to organize the competition in their areas and make such memorable prize-giving events. Reports on these events are available in the Event Reports section of this Review. The organization for the schools competition 2007 has gone extremely well so far. Schools are currently registering with us for this, and since the project worker role has changed to that of campaign worker, now responsible for event organization, the school competition and posters only, since October 2006, I have been able to devote more time to the competition and aim to have school participation up to 2005 levels by the end of registration in February. It is our aim to have organized a prize-giving ceremony in early May at a nationally renowned venue.

North East Community Education Scheme[2]

We have been running a program of community anti-racist education in the North East of England since June 2004. This work is delivered by our staff team of ex-Sunderland stars Gary Bennett and Kieron Brady and aided by a team of volunteers. Gary Bennett was one of the first black footballers in the North East; he played for the Black Cats for eleven years and was their captain for five, before moving on to become the manager of Darlington FC for two years. Kieron was said to be a truly exciting natural talent before injury sadly caused his early retirement from football when he was only twenty-one years old. Gary runs football training sessions with the young people, which are always extremely popular; even those who say that they hate playing football are converted by the end of the session due to Gary's natural enthusiasm and skill in involving everybody. Kieron delivers the classroom workshops; he is unable to participate in the football training due to an injury, which forced his early retirement from professional football. We have discovered that the football training and presence of ex-professional players add an extra dimension to the work and increase the enjoyment and participation of the young people.

While the main focus of our work is delivering anti-racism workshops to young people in schools and youth groups across the North East, we have been working in the community on other more high profile events. Among other things since April 2005 we have organized:

- Stalls at several community events throughout North East England;
- events at premier and football league clubs in the North East;
- an anti-racist community day entitled "Walker United" in conjunction with Walker United Football Club and other local community organizations;
- a teacher training conference entitled "Teaching in a Diverse City" in conjunction with Newcastle University and other smaller teacher training events;
- a "Gold Standard for Race Equality" scheme in conjunction with South Tyneside Council;
- the production of a guide to working with Show Racism the Red Card's resources for councils and football clubs;
- a schools anti-racist football tournament.

Since the start of the project we have run workshops with over 10,000 young people in the North East. We have visited fifty-three primary schools, eighteen secondary schools and seventeen youth groups, and had stalls at thirty-two conferences, festivals and other events.

We deliver anti-racist workshops around the Show Racism the Red Card DVD and we also run workshops aimed at dispelling the myths surrounding asylum-seekers and refugees using the *A Safe Place* video. These workshops are extremely important in today's climate where newspapers and politicians help to feed the misunderstandings and resentment that many people have toward asylum-seekers and refugees. It is not surprising that many of the young people we meet are very confused about the issue. Previously we only delivered the A Safe Place workshop to secondary schools. However, the success of the scheme in Glasgow, where they have been delivering this workshop to ten and eleven year olds with great success has inspired us to open the workshop to these ages in the North East. It will also be a good way to follow up the original workshop and build upon the work that we have already done. We have often been asked whether girls and those not interested in football engage with our resources. In order to answer this question we have started to ask the child's gender on the feedback form. We have collected feedback for 300 young people and so far there is no indication of any difference in the levels of enjoyment or participation between the sexes, and 99 percent of both boys and girls asked have said that they enjoyed the session overall.

Show Racism the Red Card Gold Standard for Schools
In a partnership meeting representatives from South Tyneside council mentioned the difficulty they were having in getting schools to work with them to report racial incidents, release staff for training and devise and put into use relevant race equality policies, so we came up with the idea of working together to put in place a Gold Standard for schools who are prepared to commit themselves to the task of reducing racism and increasing equality. We are working with local councils to produce a guide to advise schools of the criteria they need to meet and how they can evidence this work. We will be piloting the scheme in 2007.

Partnership working and information sharing
By working in partnership with other organizations we are able to offer a much more in depth and valuable experience to the young people we work with. In the current format, on our own, we spend a maximum of two hours in the classroom with each class. When working in partnership teachers become involved in the organization of the day and have more ownership of the event, and we can ensure that each group works around the issues for a whole day.
During 2006 we worked in partnership with the following organizations.

Community Connections–CSV. This project finds volunteering positions and supports volunteers from an asylum-seeking background. They had already realized the potential these volunteers could have in dispelling racist myths and had taken a group of volunteers to work in a school in South Tyneside. After discussing the issues at some length we realized the best outcomes would be achieved by working in partnership, as CSV were already equipped to recruit and support the volunteers while we had the access to schools and were equipped to educate the young people around the issue. We visited our first school in partnership on 1 December 2006 and worked with 160 young people over an entire day. Show Racism the Red Card provided two workshops while volunteers from CSV provided four more. The volunteers worked across the curriculum, telling their stories and providing workshops in drama, home economics, geography and history, and the day was a great success. We then visited St. Bedes in Peterlee together, working with ninety young people over the course of the afternoon, and we hope to work in partnership regularly throughout 2007.

Nu-Mcs. London anti-racist rappers Ian Solomon and Serocee came up and worked with us to deliver two workshops in South Tyneside and Sunderland. They taught the young people how to rap, alongside delivering an anti-racism and anti-gangster lesson. It was an excellent workshop. The young people were completely engaged and thoroughly enjoyed the session. Some 67 percent of those who took part described the workshop as excellent and the other 33 percent as very good. We are currently looking at ways to build upon the initial success of this partnership and to work together on a larger scale in the new school year.

The Word. An anti-racist hip-hop group who was set up in Thornhill School in Sunderland has run several large-scale community events in which we have taken part. Gary and Kieron helped to comprise a panel taking questions on racism from the audience. We provided them with resources to distribute and invited them to participate in our events, and we hope to extend this partnership in the future.

L'Afrique a Newcastle. We worked with the festival organizers to deliver a series of workshops in Newcastle as part of the week-long festival. We are currently developing a partnership with Newcastle Football Development Service to visit schools together in 2007.

Justice First. We worked together to deliver a week-long program of work in Stockton on Tees. The posters that the young people produced during these workshops were made into a booklet to be given out at a charity football match that was held as part of the FARE Week of Action on 22 October 2006.

Sharing Good Practice

Our work in the North East and partnerships with local councils has attracted interest from all over the UK; Glasgow, Edinburgh and Nottingham Councils have already begun their own projects and QPR, Carlisle and Milton Keynes's have expressed an interest in developing football-in-the-community schemes in their areas.

We have also developed guides advising organizations of the ways in which they can best engage with Show Racism the Red Card's resources. There are two guides; one for football teams and one for councils in which we will be able to share the experience that we have had in the North East so that they can set up similar schemes in their own areas. To our great pleasure, the model of the schools work developed here has been successfully adopted and used to run workshops in Glasgow where ex-"Old Firm" players have been delivering "A Safe Place" Workshops in conjunction with football training. Representatives from Notts County football club have been to observe workshops and receive advice on how to set up a similar scheme in their area and Gary and Kieron have visited Carlisle United to share good practice with them.

Looking Forward
The project has been extremely successful in its first two and a half years, and we are ever looking to expand and improve the work. In 2007 we are:

- aiming to run a series of workshops in conjunction with Newcastle Football Development Service;
- planning to build upon the success of Walker United to work in conjunction with other grass-roots football clubs to work in partnership to hold further community events in 2007. We are also on the steering committee for a large music-based community event in partnership with UNI-SON and other local groups, which will be held in Sunderland in the summer;
- looking to hold anti-racist football schools, which will be run by ex-professional footballers and contain a strong element of anti-racist education;
- aiming to build upon the Gold Standard for Race Equality Scheme;
- planning to run annual regional anti-racist football tournaments;
- planning to run regular events at all of the high profile sporting clubs in the North East;
- planning to work in partnership with other organizations working in the field of anti-racism and myth busting around asylum issues. We have already set up events to be delivered in partnership with Save the Children, the Word, North East Refugee Service and Community Service Volunteers;
- planning to run monitoring events with young people;
- going to distribute the guides that we have produced to councils and football clubs and meet with them to help set

up anti-racism education schemes in their areas.

Education
Coaching with a Conscience
The Coaching with a Conscience campaign was instigated by Show Racism the Red Card, in association with the Scottish Professional Footballer's Association and the Scottish Refugee Council. The idea behind the project was to run a pilot scheme in schools in the Glasgow area, whereby schoolchildren would take part in "A Safe Place" workshop and be coached by former top "Old Firm" footballers in a fun football session.

Recent studies have highlighted that for children in Glasgow who are black or of ethnic origin, "racism is a feature of daily life." Show Racism the Red Card is an anti-racist charity that aims to raise awareness among young people about the dangers of, and issues surrounding, racism in society. We make use of the powerful position of professional footballers as role models to deliver our anti-racist message. At each school visited during the campaign, the children would watch the Show Racism the Red Card educational video and engage in activities and discussions designed to raise awareness of issues relating to asylum-seekers, refugees and racism in our contemporary society. The children would also take part in a fun football coaching session with ex-"Old Firm" players Gerry Britton and Derek Ferguson who would also spread our important message to the children in a relaxed and informal environment.

Our campaign embraced seventeen schools in the Glasgow area, and both primary and secondary schools were visited. Five schools were chosen to take part in an evaluation of the project. A variety of schools were included in terms of numbers belonging to black or ethnic minority groups, primary or secondary schools and the number of asylum-seeking children on the school roll. Before taking part in the workshop every child was asked to fill out a questionnaire detailing their preconceptions surrounding refugees and asylum-seekers. A similar questionnaire completed after the workshop attempted to evaluate whether the children's attitudes had been altered by taking part in the sessions. The teachers involved in each school were also asked to detail their opinions on the effectiveness of the process.

Glasgow: January-March 2006
The questionnaires attempted to establish the inherent attitudes in the school pupils with regard to refugees, asylum-seekers and racism in general. To measure the success of our project, four specific lines of questioning were followed.

> 1. Should refugees and asylum-seekers be allowed to live in Scotland?

2. Why do refugees and asylum-seekers come to live in Scotland?
3. What words best describe refugees and asylum-seekers?
4. Has involvement in the workshop increased awareness of these issues?

Responses
1. Should refugees and asylum-seekers be allowed to live in Scotland?

School visited	Yes	No	If no, similar attitude after workshop?	If no, altered attitude after workshop?
Shawlands Academy	79%	21%	40%	60%
Govan High	78%	22%	40%	60%
St. Philomena's Primary	54%	46%	0%	100%
Holy Cross Primary	23%	76%	31%	69%
St. David's Primary	91%	9%	33%	67%
All pupils	65%	35%	29%	71%

From all the pupils who responded negatively prior to the workshop, 71 percent displayed a different outlook when asked this question after taking part. One pupil from St. Philomena's who had initially stated his dissent at the influx of refugees and asylum-seekers to Scotland, when asked after the session his opinion, replied that they should be allowed to live in Scotland "as they are only looking for a safe place." A pupil from Holy Cross stated in response to this question that "they shouldn't be allowed to live in Scotland, because they take over our shops and raid our bins and sometimes we see them stealing other people's things." After the workshop her reply was altered significantly: "yes, they should be allowed to live here as their own country might be having a war and they don't want to die." Another child from Holy Cross answered that they shouldn't be allowed "because they come here to steal, annoy and bully. They should stay in their own country." The same child when asked after the workshop replied, "Yes, they should. I have changed my mind because they are just the same as us. It is fair."

2. Why do refugees and asylum-seekers come to live in Scotland?

School visited	Yes	No	If no, similar attitude after workshop?	If no, altered attitude after workshop?
Shawlands Academy	91%	9%	33%	67%
Govan High	95%	5%	50%	50%
St. Philomena's Primary	73%	27%	0%	100%
Holy Cross Primary	79%	21%	25%	75%
St. David's Primary	93%	7%	0%	100%
All pupils	86%	14%	22%	78%

We can see, therefore, that of the pupils who responded in a negative manner to this question prior to the workshop, 78 percent of these pupils gave a positive reply after their involvement with the project. A pupil from St. David's Primary gave a telling example of the ignorance that some children have with respect to people from other races. When asked the above question, his reply was that our government "had brought them over to be slaves." After the workshop his answer to the same question was that "the asylum-seekers are here so they do not get hurt. They are scared because there are wars in their countries." Another example of a child not understanding a situation was when a pupil from Holy Cross stated that asylum-seekers and refugees were in Scotland "because their countries are too hot." After the workshop the same question brought the response that "they are looking for a safe place." A personal view from a pupil at Shawlands Academy was that "they come to Scotland to get money and houses here." Following her involvement in the workshop, her response to the same question was that "they come to Scotland because it is too dangerous to live in their country."

3. What words best describe refugees and asylum-seekers?

School visited	Positive	Negative	If negative, similar attitude after workshop?	If negative, altered attitude after workshop?
Shawlands Academy	71%	29%	39%	61%
Govan High	89%	11%	50%	50%
St. Philomena's Primary	36%	64%	0%	100%
Holy Cross Primary	29%	71%	21%	79%
St. David's Primary	83%	17%	12%	88%
All pupils	62%	38%	24%	76%

Of the pupils who responded negatively before the workshop, 76 percent gave a positive response when asked a similar question after the session. In response to this question before the workshop, a pupil from St. David's could only come up with one word, namely, "colored." After the session the same child's response was "frightened, scared, upset, petrified and miserable." For this child the focus was no longer on the person's skin color but on the underlying reasons for their arrival in our country. A pupil from St. Philomena's five-word description was "uneducated, poor, dumb, criminals and cheeky." After the session the reply was "frightened, lonely, sad, smart and young." A child from Holy Cross had written her five words to be "nasty, stealing, homeless, hungry and jobless." After taking part in the workshop these had altered to "homeless, jobless, hungry, scared and desperate." A Shawlands Academy pupil's description changed from "scary" to "helpless" following their involvement in the workshop. Another pupil from Shawlands whose description was "cheeky, scary and weird," altered to "scared, lonely and ashamed." "Creepy and weird" became "lost and isolated" for another pupil from Shawlands following their workshop.

4. Has involvement in the workshop increased awareness of these issues?

School visited	Yes	No
Shawlands Academy	76%	24%
Govan High	89%	11%
St. Philomena's Primary	100%	0%
Holy Cross Primary	93%	7%
St. David's Primary	98%	2%
All pupils	92%	8%

It can be evidenced that the vast majority of the children who took part in the workshop, 92 percent, felt that their awareness of issues relating to racism has been increased through their involvement. One child from St. David's, when stating his increased knowledge, asserted that he "didn't know that refugees and asylum-seekers could be white people as well."

The next step

The evaluation process has merely underlined the extent to which the campaign has achieved its aims of raising the awareness and understanding of Glasgow's schoolchildren in these vitally important areas. The workshops reached out to 900 pupils but, as stated previously, there are 80,000 schoolchildren in Glasgow so the current campaign has merely scratched the surface in terms of the possible numbers that could be involved.

The use of professional football in raising awareness cannot be underestimated. A recent study applauded the value of Show Racism the Red Card's work, in both the quality of the information dispersed and the manner in which it is transmitted to the participants involved. Children are particularly receptive to their role models' promptings on contemporary issues, and the workshop being run in conjunction with the fun coaching session created an engaging atmosphere where old attitudes could be questioned and new ideas firmly implanted in inquiring minds.

The evaluation has showed the unrivalled success of the workshop in altering racist attitudes and raising awareness, but there is still a great deal of work to be done as our society continues to diversify. Show Racism the Red Card is the ideal vehicle to continue to educate and inform Scotland's young people about the dangers of and issues surrounding racism.

Resources for schools

Show Racism the Red Card has produced a series of excellent educational resources. These include videos, DVDs and education packs.

England—schools competition 2008

This is the eighth successive year that we have run an anti-racist schools competition and we have found them to be an extremely useful way of engaging young peoples' interest in anti-racism. The prize-giving ceremony for the 2007 competition took place at the new Wembley Stadium. All prize winners from England attended and received their prizes which included an England shirt, ball and cap, signed shirts, match tickets and a framed certificate. Show Racism the Red Card will organize a similarly prestigious prize-giving event for the winners of the 2008 competition.

Anti-racist schools competition 2007

Show Racism the Red Card is an anti-racist charity, which specializes in producing educational resources. These include videos, a DVD, magazines, posters and education packs. The aim of our project is to combat racism through the use of footballers as anti-racist role models. We are fortunate to have the backing of many top managers and players. This is the seventh successive year that we have run an anti-racist schools competition and we have found them to be an extremely useful way of encouraging young peoples' interest in anti-racism. The Show Racism the Red Card video/DVD is twenty minutes long and conveys a powerful anti-racist message through the medium of professional football. It covers new ground in anti-racist education and is suitable for a broad range of age groups. The video/DVD features interviews with some of the most popular footballers currently in the game and is accompanied by a new education pack with ideas and activities suitable for a broad age range, from primary to secondary schools.

Schools visits—England and Wales
Show Racism the Red Card delivers anti-racism workshops in schools and youth groups in the North East. This program has run since 2004 and is a great success. We have already worked with over 10,000 young people in the region. Our aim is to combine football training run by ex-Sunderland Captain Gary Bennett with anti-racist education delivered by ex-Sunderland footballer Kieron Brady. The program will include films featuring footballers as anti-racist role models, quizzes, group work, role-play and discussion. We also have resources and prizes to distribute to the young people. We have two films, *Show Racism the Red Card*, which tackles the general issues surrounding racism, and *A Safe Place*, which is targeted at secondary schoolchildren and confronts the specific issue of racism against asylum-seekers.

Our aims are as follows:

- to familiarize young people with a range of facts and skills that will enable them to challenge racism;
- to increase young people's understanding of issues of diversity and identity, their rights and responsibilities;
- to promote young people's involvement as active and responsible citizens in a growing multiracial society.

Moving forward
After ten years in the field, we have again taken our organization forward on a number of fronts. The work in Scotland has broken all our original targets and the profile of the campaign is massive. This has led our funding from the Scottish Executive to increase from £25,000 to £64,000 each year. Our schools' work in Sunderland has had such a great impact that South Tyneside Council reserved our services for the next three years. The increase in our workload and resources has been made possible by an increase in our funding. Our overall funding has increased from £180,571 in 2004 to £323,634, thus reflecting our progress over the past few years.

Results in Scotland's fight against racism
When we established our office in October 2003, our aim was to reach every young person in Scotland with our educational resources over a three-year period. Thanks to the support of a vast array of individuals and organizations, Show Racism the Red Card campaigns have been quite successful. During the 2004-2005 football season in Scotland, for example, Show Racism the Red Card campaign had as many twists and turns as the Scottish Premier League itself, beginning with our first-ever nationwide Week of Action involving all forty-two professional clubs in October, ending with a mass "red card" action by the Tartan Army at Hampden in June.

Show Racism the Red Card held anti-racist presentations at seven out of the twelve Scottish Premier League clubs that season, from Inverness Football Club in the north to Kilmarnock Football Club in the south. Dundee United Football Club even held two events, with the help of the ArabTrust. The events were attended by over 1,200 local schoolchildren, and local authorities were a welcome addition, not only in terms of their input on the day, but also fostering ongoing anti-racist partnerships between clubs, councils and Show Racism the Red Card. We were also involved in scores of other local events, sending posters, speakers and resources along to make our contribution to a growing number of equality days at schools, youth initiatives and grass-roots sporting organizations. The joint Educational Institute of Scotland/Show Racism the Red Card schools' competition was the educational highlight of the events calendar, and this year was no disappointment with a record 262 entries. The Hampden prize-giving ceremony was once again worthy of the excellent standard of work produced by the schoolchildren, as were the prizes donated by the Scottish Premier League clubs and sponsors.

Football remains one of the most powerful mediums for breaking down the barriers that lead to racist attitudes and behavior. Once again, Scotland's footballers gave their wholehearted backing to the Show Racism the Red Card campaign this season, attending events and doing interviews for the anti-racism cause. Under the Show Racism the Red Card umbrella, a concerted effort has been established to drive racism out of stadiums in Scotland. The goal is to create a fans' culture where racist behavior is neither accepted nor tolerated at any stadium in Scotland. Much progress has been made in the drive to increase BME representation at all levels of Scottish football. With the support of our partners, we will begin implementing strategies so a level playing-field can be established for all in the beautiful game. The 2004-2005 season saw a marked reduction in the number of complaints Show Racism the Red Card received for incidents of racist abuse in the professional game. The problem has not been eradicated yet, but thanks to the support of fans, clubs, authorities and football players, we are moving closer to the necessary zero tolerance approach to racism in Scottish football stadiums. The Show Racism the Red Card Week of Action sees anti-racist action at all forty-two professional clubs in Scotland. Clubs and fans also engage with several local BME organizations on a local level which have proven to be the catalyst for ongoing anti-racist initiatives. One of the major developments during the 2004-2005 season was the more proactive support Show Racism the Red Card received from fans' organizations worldwide. Particular mention goes to Dundee United, Raith Rovers and Ayr United Supporters Trusts that made excellent contributions locally. Other supporters' groups indicated they will be setting up similar programs in the coming year. Finally, nearly all Scottish Premier League and Scottish Football League first division sides gave the campaign a great boost by selling "Racism Bands" in their club shops. This campaign, a partnership between Revolutionary Young Enterprise, Graeme High School, Falkirk and Show Racism the Red Card Scotland, sent out a strong anti-racist message to both young people and football fans and also raised considerable funds for Show Racism the Red Card's ongoing campaign against racism in football and society.

For the successful completion of the activities mentioned above we thank our major sponsors in Scotland, namely the Scottish Executive, One Scotland Many Cultures, the Educational Institute of Scotland, the Scottish Refugee Council, the Scottish Professional Footballers Association, the Scottish Football Association and all other unions, councils, organizations and individuals who have backed the campaign.

Show Racism the Red Card in Ireland

Show Racism the Red Card has established an excellent profile in Ireland over the last few years as a result of consistent hard work which has helped establish contacts in the media, trade unions, players' organizations and, most importantly, schools. The launch of the competition took place just before Ireland's game against Switzerland in October with a photo-call involving Chris Hughton and other players. At the same time we circulated to all 750 second level schools in the country a pack including the Show Racism the Red Card CD-ROM, and a poster and leaflet outlining competition prizes and rules. The fantastic prizes on offer were no doubt one of the contributing factors in 1,200 entries to the art competition being received from 75 schools. But this overwhelming response also indicates the willingness of people to engage with and come to a real understanding of the issues surrounding racism in Ireland.

Our initiative demonstrates that teachers and students in schools are willing to tackle the current problems with racism in Ireland. Unfortunately, the government has a different agenda, having recently closed its Know Racism anti-racism awareness campaign. A survey commissioned by the Know Racism campaign illustrates why the government should be allocating more resources into education against racism. The survey of 1,200 adults chosen at random from all sections of the population found the following:

- Only 36 percent of all Irish adults had direct contact with anyone from an ethnic minority group.
- When asked about full employment, 31 percent believed minorities are taking jobs away from Irish people.
- Forty-one percent believed asylum-seekers are coming to Ireland for economic gain due to poor circumstances in their own countries but are not intending to work here.
- Fifty-four percent believed asylum-seekers are abusing the system.
- Forty-eight percent of Irish people believed Ireland is already or likely to become racist, but 20 percent disagreed with this view.

Anti-racism education could, if given the resources, make an impact on this figure, given that a large number, 66 percent, believes anyone should be able to live in Ireland as long as they pay their taxes.

The profiles of Irish international players who are supporting our campaign are a great lever in making anti-racism education accessible to young people. To date, Kenny Cunningham (captain, Ireland and Birmingham Football Club), Chris Hughton (coach), Curtis Fleming (Crystal Palace Football Club), John O'Shea (Manchester United Football Club), Gary Breen (Sunderland Football Club), Stephen Carr (Tottenham Hotspurs Football Club), Matt Holland (Charlton Football Club) and Clinton Morrison (Birmingham Football Club) have attended various events in Dublin supporting Show Racism the Red Card in Ireland. We plan to enlarge our partnership to include the Rugby Players' Association and the Gaelic Players' Association alongside our existing partners in the Association of Secondary Teachers in Ireland, the Teachers' Union of Ireland and the Professional Footballers' Association of Ireland. Although Irish players in the English and Scottish Premier Leagues are so well known that the existing Show Racism the Red Card resources are useful, we see a need for Irish-specific anti-racism education resources. We aim to produce an Irish-orientated CD-ROM for use in schools, organizations working with young people and a wide variety of training environments.

Show Racism the Red Card survey report
In 2003 we conducted, once again, a survey of users of our resources to help us establish a clear picture of how they are being used and the users' reactions to the resources. The results outlined herein were compiled by Mike Burrows from the University of Illinois.

From the 3,200 surveys distributed we have received 352, a marked improvement on the response rate of the year before. This positive figure has been reciprocated by the optimistic nature of feedback from our users. The responses have shown that Show Racism the Red Card continues to have its main impact within the education system. Encouragingly, our user base is ever expanding as organizations and institutions learn of our user-friendly, effective resources. This development has been aided by the publicity and recognition we have been able to put forward through a wide range of promotion material. When asked "How useful did you find the resources that you ordered?" the responses confirmed that the materials produced by Show Racism the Red Card continue to be of the highest quality. Equally useful was our magazine, which we encouraged people to order in conjunction with the video, CD-ROM and education pack in the hope that the resources would complement each other. We have also been able to realize a lot about our organization through the descriptive comments related to what users would like to see us produce as well as general thoughts and feelings about Show Racism the Red Card.

One of the main points that pervaded the responses focused on the video becoming dated. We are aware that the appeal of footballers can change very quickly and we are therefore in the process of putting together a new video that will feature current superstars. Secondly, teachers in particular have expressed a concern about the effectiveness of the video for girls who may not be too receptive to the idea of footballers as role models. Many of our responses came from Scotland where there was a demand for more attention to be paid to Scottish players and issues. The implementation of our new Scottish-based worker will help to address these concerns. We believe that feedback shows our resources are most effective when used in conjunction with each other. We will therefore continue to promote our combination package containing the video, CD-ROM and education pack. In addition we are keen to promote the magazine as it serves not just as support to the other resources, but we have been informed that schools have sent these magazines home. This can enable our message to reach others, including parents, which we see as crucial. Finally, it seems the recent and successful release of our video to combat racism against asylum-seekers entitled *North of England Refugee World Cup 2002* could not have come at a better time. Of the 352 surveys returned, an overwhelming 309 respondents said that a video on asylum issues would be useful; around 90 percent of this figure said it would be very useful. This is an issue that requires immediate attention. To add to this, there is a demand for materials that oppose abuse toward Travellers and Show Racism the Red Card strongly agrees with this notion. We could look to formulate ideas to address this most prevalent of issues in the near future.

Annual Review 2008
Campaign work in Wales
A lot has happened since our last Annual Review, including Cardiff City reaching the FA Cup final, Swansea City getting promoted and Wales winning the Grand Slam in Rugby. It's been as good a period for Welsh sport as it has been for

our campaign in Wales. We've had tremendous support from clubs in Wales, including players from other sports helping to promote our message by attending our events and workshops at stadiums and schools. We also produced our first-ever poster with a cricket team as Glamorgan players helped "show racism the red card" and distributed 3,000 posters to fans ahead of games in Cardiff and Colwyn Bay. Our work has expanded into other areas, such as delivering work-shops in schools, youth clubs and football academies with the assistance of ex-West Ham and Fulham footballer Leroy Rosenior. The workshops have seen a great response from teachers and pupils with the majority of youngsters recog-nizing Leroy and engrossed during the workshops. The campaign in Wales has recently taken on our first information and support worker, Jason Webber, who will help us toward our next goal, which is to sustain the campaign for the com-ing years.

As well as providing administrative support, Jason will also look to strengthen our work in other areas such as volunteer recruitment and partnership work with Sports Development Officers such as Football Development, 5 x 60 and Dragon Sport Officers, along with voluntary sector organizations. Through media channels such as newspapers, radio and television, the campaign has started to establish itself throughout many parts of Wales. We've had good newspaper coverage of our football club events, schools competition and work-shops in schools and youth clubs. Radio interviews have been aired on the Wave Radio, Red Dragon and on Champion 103, and we've also featured on Welsh language football program *Sgorio*. We have produced over 50,000 anti-racist posters with sporting clubs such as Cardiff City, Wales under-nineteen women's team and Glamorgan Cricket club that have been distributed through schools, councils and sports clubs.

Football club events
Since the last review, our football club events have taken us into the Welsh Premier League as well as our regular events with Cardiff City, Wrexham and Swansea City. The New Saints (TNS) became the first WPL club to host an event as we delivered our workshop to their youth academy players with the help of first team players who answered questions on racism from the young-sters. Our next club was Porthmadog FC and this event attracted well over one hundred schoolchildren from local schools as well as S4C football program *Sgorio* which featured the event during a live broadcast. Swansea City players Jason Scotland and Dennis Lawrence visited a local school to talk to youngsters about their experiences of racism in football and in society as we started to take this format into schools. Penydarren Park the home of Merthyr Tydfil FC was another venue we visited as first team players were joined by Leroy Rosenior who briefly managed the club, to talk to pupils from a nearby school, who also watched our campaign DVD. The new season will see us continue working with the football clubs and we will also be working with other sports such as rugby clubs to promote our message. In response to incidents of racism at football matches,

we contacted two clubs involved and this led to immediate action by the clubs to promote their stance that racism will not be tolerated at their grounds. We will continue to monitor incidents in the coming season and will work with the clubs as soon as any incidents arise.

Anti-racism educational workshops—schools
Our workshops have been delivered to schools in Wrexham, Merthyr, Cardiff and Vale of Glamorgan to approximately 800 young people. Recent workshops in the Vale of Glamorgan has seen us deliver football coaching alongside class-room-based workshops; the coaching has been delivered by our football coach, Leroy Rosenior. The Vale of Glamorgan Council became the first in Wales to give us funding toward our anti-racist workshops, and we visited ten schools and six youth clubs in the area. We are hopeful that other councils will see the benefits of these workshops and will support them so that we can deliver them in other parts of Wales. We will expand the workshops so that they are delivered to junior football clubs and football academies; this will be done with the assistance of volunteers who will be recruited in the coming months. The Show Racism the Red Card schools competition has been running for eight years and the number of schools entering from Wales has continued to increase over the past two competitions. We have seen more than one hundred schools from eighteen of the twenty-two local authorities in Wales involved, and this year saw an increase of 24 percent from the previous year. It's been a great response and the standard of entries has been excellent; entries have also been in Welsh, and we will continue, where possible, to promote our work bilingual with production of our materials and resources. Our prize-giving ceremonies were held at the Millennium Stadium in Cardiff and the prizes have included category winners meeting the Wales football squad players arranged by the Football Association in Wales. The competition in Wales will see more schools being involved in future competitions and we have already received orders for the new DVD/education packs that are being released later this year.

Fortnight of Action
Every October sees the FARE Fortnight of Action, and for the past two seasons, the Fortnight in Wales has seen all the Welsh Premier League clubs taking a united stance against racism. Match programs and club websites promoted a message to fans as well as players warming up with Show Racism the Red Card t-shirts and holding up red cards. Other clubs such as Cardiff City and Merthyr Tydfil FC also took similar action and our football coaches Dave Bennett and Leroy Rosenior visited schools and youth clubs to deliver workshops.

Working to promote football inclusion of BME groups
The last eighteen months has seen us work with under-represented groups and toward involving them in all areas of the game. We are currently working with a group of asylum-seekers and refugees to form a club that can enter the football

league in Wales. Having secured kit for the players, we are now looking to arrange courses in first aid and coaching to help progress the work. We will look to build on this work and engage with other sports departments and to promote participation among the BME communities.

Campaign work in Scotland[3]

The campaign in Scotland has had its most successful period to date. From over 100 members of the Scottish Parliament participating in a Red Card action at the Scottish Parliament to delivering anti-racist workshops to over 4,000 pupils, our message has been spread far and wide. But there remains a lot to be done. Statistics show that racism in Scotland is on the increase. We hear daily reports of people being verbally and physically abused all over Scotland. Anecdotal evidence suggests that racism still rears its ugly head in the junior, amateur and youth leagues. Gone are the days when racism is based only on color. Racism toward migrant workers, asylum-seekers, refugees, the Irish and English communities is also occurring on a daily basis. Show Racism the Red Card will endeavor to tackle racism in all its guises. But we all have a role to play by challenging racist attitudes on our streets and in our workplace. Only then can we truly say that "We're a' Jock Tamson's Bairns." On a very sad note the campaign lost two of its most ardent supporters with the passing away of Phil O'Donnell of Motherwell and Tommy Burns of Celtic. Phil had attended many Red Card events and appeared on our educational video, and we met with Tommy recently when we were filming at Celtic for our new educational DVD. Both will be sadly missed but we have happy memories of two outstanding individuals and true gentlemen who helped spread our anti-racist message.

Educational workshops

In partnership with Inverclyde, North Ayrshire, East Ayrshire and Falkirk Councils we have delivered anti-racist workshops and football coaching sessions to over 4,200 pupils in 140 schools. The campaign relies heavily on the role model status of footballers to deliver our anti-racist message. We currently have Derek Ferguson, Jim Duffy, Brian Irvine, Gary MacKay and Michael Weir delivering our workshops in schools and communities.

Islamophobia and new Scottish education pack

Educating to challenge racist attitudes and exclusion remains the key to combating racism in the long term. Our educational strategies and projects aim to keep apace with the changing faces of racism in Scottish society. There will be a concerted effort to tackle the rise in Islamophobia and our new educational resource tackling this issue will be key to this. A new DVD and education pack for Scotland will also be available toward the end of the year. The film will include interviews with Barry Ferguson, Jean Claude Darcheville, Stephen McManus, Robbie

Neilson, Craig Levein, Simon Ford, Abdessalam Benjelloun, Thierry Henry, Ryan Giggs, Rio Ferdinand, Julie Fleeting and Gordon Smith.

Community-based events
A further sixty-three organizations participated during the fortnight. As a result over 500 actions took place as part of the Fortnight of Action. Many grass-roots teams in Ayrshire, Glasgow and Edinburgh held center circle Red Card displays prior to kick-off. These actions are particularly popular and create a sense of unity from the grass-roots through to the professional levels. An increased number of schools were involved in actions, taking the form of anti-racist workshops, fun runs and football tournaments. The Dar Al-Falaah Community Education Association, the Sudanese Community and others celebrated the religious festivals of Ramadam and Eid Ul Fitr. Govanhill Community Development Trust and the Active Life Club both organized anti-racist and multicultural days for the whole family at the Larkfield Centre in Govanhill, Glasgow. These days were attended by over 1,000 local people. The celebrations tackled racism and sought to bring people of different faiths, beliefs and cultural backgrounds together. Anecdotal evidence indicates that there are many more organizations taking action during this period making good use of our grant scheme. Many groups, schools and others have SRTRC resources that are utilized to educate young people about the dangers of racism during the fortnight. As October is Black History Month, non-SRTRC initiatives are also very evident throughout this time.

The Fortnight of Action as a catalyst
A major aim of the Fortnight of Action is to encourage anti-racist actions, events and initiatives to take place throughout the year. Many organizations begin their actions during October and run follow-up events during the year. There are other organizations including schools and community groups that look to the Fortnight of Action for ideas and inspirations. Days of action were undertaken by the Scottish Hockey Union and the Scottish Junior Football Association following the model developed by the Scottish Premier League and Scottish Football League events. The 2007 Fortnight of Action built on the success of the three previous years with an unprecedented estimated 500 actions taking place across Scotland. The grant scheme strongly encourages community groups to get involved. The Weekend of Action generates positive media publicity and reaches people of many different ages and socio-economic groupings; it is the highest profile event of the SRTRC calendar.

Schools art competition 2007-2008
This year's competition was focused around a central theme, "Welcoming New Scots: Challenging Racism, Celebrating Diversity." Over 8,000 pupils took part from 135 schools. The judging panel this year was made up of Yvonne Strachan (Scottish Government, Head of Equality), Mark Fernandes (The Educational Institute of Scotland), Jim Duffy (Red Card coach, former footballer/manager,

media pundit) and Dan Gerrard (Spartans FC). All entries were of a very high standard and the judges had a difficult task picking the winners. Over 280 schoolchildren, from as far afield as the Isle of Harris and Wick, attended the gala prize-giving ceremony held at Hampden Park. Prizes included signed footballs, signed football shirts, match day tickets, VIP days and prize money up to £1000 for their school. The football prizes were kindly donated once again by clubs throughout Scotland. Players in attendance included Gary Caldwell (Celtic), Mark Hately (Rangers), Robbie Neilson (Hearts FC) and Rob Jones (Hibernian FC) and they were joined by new Scotland manager George Burley and Scottish FA Chief Executive Gordon Smith.

Anti-racist club events
Events were held at seventeen clubs including Aberdeen, Dundee FC, Dundee United, Dunfermline, Falkirk, Heart of Midlothian, Hibernian, Kilmarnock, Livingston, Motherwell, Partick Thistle, Rangers and St. Johnstone. These involve one-hour anti-racist workshops with local schoolchildren, Red Card representatives and first team players from the club.

Campaign work in England[4]
Since the 2006 Annual Review was published, the role of campaign worker has been established. The specific areas of responsibility for this role are the organization and management of education events at football clubs, the organization of the Anti-Racist School Competition and development of partnership councils working with SRTRC on the competition. We are pleased to report that since January 2007 great progress has been made in these areas of the Show Racism the Red Card campaign. SRTRC is now working with an increasing number of football clubs around England and is reaching many more young people directly with the anti-racism message at our educational events. The School Competition has also been greatly improved and since the last Annual Review two fantastic prize-giving ceremonies have been organized for the 2007 and 2008 competitions respectively.

Education events at football clubs
A major part of the campaign worker role in England is to increase the number of education events at football clubs. The target for events at football clubs during 2007 was forty events, which we managed to attain, an increase of fifteen events on the highest total taking place in any previous year. The events are one of the pivotal parts of the campaign, combining education of young people on the subject of racism, football club and player involvement in the campaign, press interest in the campaign and in many instances, partnership work with local authorities. As you can see the map overleaf, from January 2007 to May 2008, we have covered the length and breadth of England, staff teams clocking up approximately 21,345 miles to work with more football clubs than ever before

in the history of the campaign. Show Racism the Red Card has aimed to run quality educational events at football clubs and, in doing so, affords young people the opportunity to view SRTRC resources and question players on their experiences in society and football. We also try to further develop relationships with footballers, football clubs, other sports stars, other potential role models, local authorities, councils and other organizations to encourage them to become active with Show Racism the Red Card. It is important for us to continue to try and develop relationships with football clubs who have not hosted events before, and when we have worked with a club, to maintain that relationship. In the first half of 2008 SRTRC has been fortunate enough to hold events at all of the football clubs who hosted events during the period January to May 2007. We have also been able to work with four clubs who have not hosted events before in the first four months of 2008 and we will continue to strive to ensure the events are of a high educational standard and expand the range of clubs we work with throughout the remainder of the year. SRTRC has managed to work with more local authorities at the education events, which is helping us to forge more partnerships for other areas of our work, such as the competition and introducing resources to new regions. In the period January 2007 to May 2008, forty-five councilors and council representatives have taken part in the panels at the education events as well as three Members of Parliament. An increasing number of football clubs are also now hosting full day events with Show Racism the Red Card which presents the young people who attend with a range of workshops on anti-racism themes. This also allows us to work with other organizations that are invited to host a workshop. A typical full-day event at a football club will see four rotating workshops and typically one will be run by SRTRC, one by the football club (such as a ground tour or workshop run by the study support center) and two workshops run by external organizations. In the afternoon all groups re-convene for a SRTRC event with players from the club. Show Racism the Red Card aims to introduce the idea of full-day events to more football clubs around England. This type of event adds real educational value for the young people who attend and makes the experience of attending a SRTRC event all the more memorable for them. Space is limited in this Annual Review to detail reports of all of the events undertaken, but these reports are available on our website. I would like to thank all of the staff and volunteers who have worked on these events and all of the football clubs who have hosted them for their time, support and efforts, as well as the schools who have attended and local authorities and other organizations who have taken part and helped support the events.

Anti-Racist School Competition

One of the most valuable projects the campaign undertakes each year is the School Competition, which has been greatly improved in 2007 and 2008 to ensure a more effectively organized competition. As well as being rewarding, the competition also produces one of the highest profile events SRTRC organizes, in the prize-giving ceremony. The aims of the competition are to engage young people in thinking about the issues of racism and producing their own work, to increase the number of schools working with our campaign's resources and to make use of the winning entries as part of our campaign resources. We think that over the last two years we have been able to meet these aims. It has been possible for Show Racism the Red Card to give more staff time to the organization of the competition in 2007 and 2008 competitions through the campaign worker role, which has allowed us to effectively promote the competition nationally. In England, SRTRC was able to produce 40,000 flyers advertising the competition each year and one of the competition's sponsors, the National Union of Teachers, was able to circulate 30,000 copies of the flyer for us to every school in England. The competition was also promoted through our magazine, website, a calendar at the start of 2008, which used winning pieces of artwork from the 2007 competitions in England, Scotland and Wales. All of the entries in the 2007 competition in England were used as a touring exhibition in England to promote the competition, which visited public buildings around England, such as libraries and town halls. All of this promotion has meant that in 2007, 610 schools registered to participate in the competition, both independently and through partnership councils running competitions in their localities, which then send on their entries to the National SRTRC Competition. In 2008, 569 schools registered to participate in the same ways. Both registration figures are a huge improvement on the registrations of 2006, which was 181 schools. The competition has allowed the campaign to establish new partnerships with councils. In 2008 seven councils ran competitions in their areas, an increase of two councils over 2007's total. Through the continued promotion of the competition and our resources we aim to continue to engage with councils in this way, as it produces some brilliant work and ensures a strong anti-racist message is delivered to young people in each of the partnership areas. We have produced a full report on each of the last two competitions, which is available by contacting me at the office. Full reports on the prize-giving ceremonies are also available from the office or on our website. We could not have wished for two more prestigious venues than Wembley Stadium (2007) and The Emirate Stadium (2008), and over the two years twenty-one players, former players and SRTRC Honorary Patrons attended the prize-giving ceremonies to present prizes to sixty-seven winning pupils of all ages, from all over England.

International work
Every year we continue to work closely with European partner organizations to carry the anti-racist message across Europe.

Ireland
Show Racism the Red Card in Ireland is carried out under the public awareness program, Know Racism. Our grants have enabled us to employ a worker to develop anti-racism education in schools. Schools and colleges in Dublin, Kildare,

Limerick and Cork are visited and seminars are held using the video and discussing with young people the issue of racism in football and society as a whole.

Over one hundred letters were sent to various schools and colleges in the aforementioned cities. All letters contained information about Show Racism the Red Card. Well over half the schools and colleges contacted responded enthusiastically. The school seminars last about an hour, starting with an introduction of the video and followed by discussion. The initiative kicked off in Limerick. We visited four schools over two days involving assemblies of 50 to 100 pupils in each. The first school visit was to Colaiste Mhichil CBS. The room was packed with pupils eager for the seminar to begin. The group varied from twelve to fifteen years of age, and they participated well, were attentive and very enthusiastic. The feedback was very encouraging. Some of the answers to the questions posed were exceptional for the age of the students. The visits proved that this initiative is long overdue and it is imperative that we continue to highlight our message at a grass-roots level.

Show Racism the Red Card has since visited schools in Dublin, Cork and Kildare, where the response has been phenomenal. Pupils were waiting at the school gates of one school. The seminar was received with enthusiasm. After the seminars each pupil is given a fact sheet. It is four pages long, colorful and informative. During and after the sessions Show Racism the Red Card workers distribute the posters we have produced including the Irish national team and clubs such as Celtic, Arsenal and Liverpool bearing the "Show Racism the Red Card" slogan. Enamel Show Racism the Red Card badges are also snapped up by youngsters. The school usually agrees future visits and buys the video and CD-ROM packs. The importance of anti-racist education in Ireland has been highlighted over the past weeks with the murder of a Chinese immigrant and a separate incident of a gun-wielding father entering a refugee camp just north of Dublin. The role of some politicians has been equally horrifying with one Cork TD calling refugees "scroungers, freeloaders" and demanding that the doors be shut. Policy in practice has been equally crude, with the Gardai (police) arresting a Nigerian man on his way to be married to an Irish girl. To continue the important work against racism we will be launching another poster of the Ireland team bearing the "Show Racism the Red Card" slogan. The Professional Footballers' Association of Ireland featured our launch on their website.

Norway

The Norwegian Show Racism the Red Card is proud of its link to Show Racism the Red Card in England. Year 2001 found us building further on the experiences of Show Racism the Red Card and trying out the school competitions that have been such a success in England. Our first school competition was in collaboration with Premier club Lyn. Combined with school visits together with top players of Lyn, the school competition against racism was a huge success in Oslo and has since spread to several other cities in Norway. In the autumn of 2001 both Valerenga Football Club and Fredrikstad Football Club held similar school competitions, and the latter had a big event as the contributions of the young people were exhibited in the town hall of Fredrikstad for a week in April 2002. Another Premier club, Molde Football Club, had its first competition in collaboration with the supporter team Tornekrattet in May 2002. We also visited several football tournaments for young people and special football schools and raised awareness about racism and discrimination.

When the Norwegian football league kicked off on 16 April 2001 we had an event at every single premier arena. Thus, at three minutes to 6 pm, the top 154 players in the country showed racism the red card. The campaign was rapidly spreading and the top three women's clubs also got involved. The national team held the same event at two world cup qualifiers, while more and more clubs in the lower divisions became part of the campaign, too. That same year between 150 and 200 top players showed racism the red card every single week during the season. The volunteers from Norwegian People's Aid handed out new small red cards with team photos and statistics, where the players are shown holding up the red cards. The cards of individual players rapidly became collector's items among the young. In 2001 we also made buttons of red cards against racism, new t-shirts and caps with the red card. We have also started collaborations with supporter clubs and the national supporter alliance. We have produced special supporter flags with huge red cards against racism, and the supporter clubs are raising awareness among their members on racism and on behavior that will not be tolerated.

In 2002 we reduced the number of events at the stadiums. By having such an event every time year after year we feared that our campaign would lose its power and effect and, therefore, most Premier teams held Show Racism the Red Card events during six of the home matches. However, we increased activities involving children together with top players. We translated the English Red Card video into Norwegian and added clips and interviews from local top players. Given that 2002 was the last year of the Norwegian Show Racism the Red Card as a project, our biggest challenge was to secure some kind of continuation of the campaign for the next few years. The Norwegian Show Racism the Red Card is based on the collaboration between Norwegian People's Aid and the Norwegian Players' Union.

Germany

The cooperation with Show Racism the Red Card was, and still is, a great possibility for BAFF to enlarge and enforce our work. We used the Show Racism the Red Card video in every town where the exhibition "Target Stadium, Racism and Discrimination in Football" was shown. Over 13,000 people in Berlin, Hamburg, Bochum, Dresden and Kiel watched the video while visiting our exhibition in 2001. Many school classes attended, too, with many teachers receiving a video to prepare before their visit. Material such as folders, magazines and pins of Show Racism the Red Card were not only very useful to the exhibition, but also on the information days we took part in, especially on 1 May in Berlin, the German trades unions' event. In Germany the work against racism in football is just beginning, so the material of Show Racism the Red Card is a good opportunity to develop their work and get closer to fans and institutions, thus the significance of close collaboration between Show Racism the Red Card and our German partners of BAFF.

FARE

The development of the Football Against Racism in Europe project over the recent years has been very encouraging. Unfortunately, at the same time we have witnessed an increase in racist, xenophobic, anti-Semitic and homophobic incidents in some national football leagues and in competitions at a European level. In 2001, Football Against Racism in Europe developed trusted partnerships with the most influential football governing bodies, namely, FIFA and UEFA. Football Against Racism in Europe was invited by FIFA to contribute to the drafting of the FIFA resolution against racism, which was adopted by the FIFA Extraordinary Congress in Buenos Aires on 7 July 2001. Europe's football governing body, UEFA, decided to honor the commitment of Football Against Racism in Europe in the fight against racism by nominating it for the 2001 charity award. When Football Unites, Racism Divides hosted the Football Against Racism in Europe conference at Bramall Lane on February 2002 and in cooperation with Sheffield United Football Club, Show Racism the Red Card facilitated the "Football as a Gateway—Using Football as an Educational Resource in Campaigning Against Racism" workshop.

An overview

In terms of our work in schools, we have recorded a change in the attitude of pupils; however, in the game of football it is always difficult to quantify changes in racist conduct, given the complexity in evaluating the factors that may account for the changing behavior of spectators, club officials, managers and players. Members of Show Racism the Red Card believe that racism in football has decreased considerably, much because of their successful campaigning against racism, their collaboration with local authorities and overall achievements in education. Still, the change of attitude in society and the success of players from a distinct ethnic background should be disregarded. In addition, the fact that British football is played in all-seater stadiums has contributed much to the elimination of racism from the popular game, since all-seater stadiums effectively facilitate the detection, and therefore the ejection, of racist offenders.

Notes

1. Based on a report by Sunil Patel.
2. Based on a report by Sarah Soyei.
3. Based on a report by Billy Singh.
4. Based on a report by Gavin Sutherland.

Chapter Seven

Anti-Racism in Football

Christos Kassimeris

While racism is a political term deeply rooted in European history, ascribing a proper definition to it has hardly ever been a straightforward task, for the term nowadays encompasses several forms of discrimination that elude the more traditional—stereotypical, rather—discriminatory conduct along ethno-centric lines. In her *Race and Racism* (1943), Ruth Benedict stated that racism is best understood in terms of a dogma stipulating that "one ethnic group is condemned by nature to congenital inferiority and another group is destined to congenital superiority."[1] The need to define racism accurately notwithstanding, it is widely agreed that this unsettling phenomenon should be eradicated with effect. It suffices to say that the novel forms of discrimination witnessed time and again across Europe necessitate equally novel remedies that go beyond the mere purpose of raising awareness. In the case of football, for example, anti-racist campaigns cover a wide range of initiatives, in an attempt to combat racial discrimination on all fronts, by either making good use of the game's immense popularity to communicate appropriate messages that condemn racist conduct or utilizing its very qualities in conjunction with analogous cultural manifestations, such as education. On the whole, combating racial discrimination in society (the game of football included) dictates that a vigorous approach be adopted so as to anticipate its complete elimination with a certain degree of confidence.

Race and racism

There is little doubt that the core values epitomizing the European Union's very motto, "United in Diversity," will cease to hearten integration enthusiasts before long, given the all-expanding properties of racism—a phenomenon that may unreservedly subscribe to the essence of human condition, distinctiveness. Laying siege to diversity, therefore, is a phenomenon of multiple shapes and forms. Despite the obvious merits encapsulating the sheer notion of individuality, xenophobia today is almost perceived as a necessary evil that defends national identity and the innermost cultural characteristics that differentiate one ethnic group from another. Xenophobia in Europe is closely related to the menacing fascist movements that stigmatized the continent during the first half of the twentieth century. Drawing from notions pertaining to European romanticism and associated utopian ideals, though in a much perverted sense, fascist ideology endeavors the construction of an organic society ingrained with a distinct "sense of belonging," much like a guiding principle, if you will, designed in such fashion so as to recruit (include) or dismiss (exclude) people along nationalistic principles.

It is important to note, nevertheless, that despite the obvious differences between fascism and nationalism, proponents of neo-fascism and neo-nationalism alike are nowadays intermingled. At the same time as the European Union endeavors to promote further integration, the sheer opposition of overtly nationalistic movements resisting cultural diversity continues to frustrate Eurocrats. As a matter of fact, a report produced on behalf of the European Monitoring Centre on Racism and Xenophobia clearly indicates that

> neo-fascists and neo-nationalists still have close ideological affinities, though they have been—until now—represented by oppositional factions among the political classes in Europe. Neo-nationalism is a reaction towards globalisation and post-industrialism. Its political strategies and perspectives are understood to be alternatives to the development of the EU as a political project transcending the idea of the nation-state. Until the end of the 1990s, the project of a European Union was designed in terms of supranational economies and cultures as well as in terms of developing democracy and loyalty in the contexts of sub-national regions. In opposition to this, neo-nationalists are reviving the nation-state as the systemic basis for social collaboration and political responsibilities, defined to be national interests. The nation-state's borders are again understood to be the most important boundaries to be upheld in order to prevent further economic and social decay.[2]

All in all, neo-fascists and neo-nationalists would probably agree that the nation-state needs ostracize all things foreign to maintain its cultural uniqueness. Along similar lines, neo-racism too is the end result of a long process of transformation that European societies have undergone in the past, as the classical notion of racism has recently been expanded over new forms of discrimination to include anti-Semitism, anti-Ziganism and anti-Muslimism. Interestingly, the second half of the twentieth century also highlights the origins of what today is a broad consensus across European societies that has come to form a common front against discrimination. Yet it appears that the "relationship between anti-racism and racism is not clear. There is antiracism in some countries without an open racist activity, and there are many areas in Europe with widespread racist activities, but where no direct antiracism confronts these racist or xenophobic phenomena."[3]

This is precisely the subject matter of the present chapter, since anti-racism—and, for that matter, the objectives of related campaigns—is occasionally misinterpreted, as much as it is often mistakenly charged for further engendering racism.

Writing in the early 1990s, more or less the same period of time when the first anti-racism organizations devoted to ridding football of racism came to life, John Solomos made the following observation:

> Today some of the most strident voices in the mass media and academic discourse are raised not against racism but against one of the favourite targets of the new right, namely anti-racism. Sections of the media are almost daily concerned with aspects of the work of either local authorities or of agencies such as the Commission for Racial Equality. Additionally it has become an important focus of concern for the various right-wing think tanks, who see anti-racism as an intrusion on individual freedom and a threat to the interests of the white majority.[4]

Unsurprisingly, the same author commented on Russell Lewis's *Anti-Racism: A Mania Exposed* (1988), describing it as "one of the most strident attacks on the work of what he sees as anti-racist fanatics. It was published amid much publicity, with a preface by Enoch Powell, and has been taken up by the new right as a fundamental critique of anti-racist politics. . . . Indeed, for Lewis, the main harm to race relations results not from racism but from the lunatic outrages done in the name of anti-racism and the failure of the black minorities to respect the way of life and customs of the white majority."[5] What is beyond doubt, says Solomos, is that compromising the work of anti-racism organizations, as well as attacking the black communities in Britain for apparently disregarding the rights of the majority population, was merely intended to distract the attention of the public and accuse anti-racists and blacks for characterizing Britain as racist.

To enhance our knowledge regarding the nature and scope of anti-racism campaigns, it is imperative that we address the issue of racism more fully. To this end, Robert Miles stresses that "the idea of 'race' first appeared in the English language in the early seventeenth century and began to be used in European and North American scientific writing in the late eighteenth century in order to name and explain certain phenotypical differences between human beings. By the mid-nineteenth century, the dominant theory of 'race' asserted that the world's population is constituted by a number of distinct 'races,' each of which has a biologically determined capacity for cultural development."[6] What was once perceived as scientific racism dictated that the human species could well be classified into separate biological categories that not only highlighted the sort of cultural diversity that characterizes humans, it also identified the potential (or even the lack of it) for spawning culture, thus making it explicitly clear that not all "races" were equal. Instead, "races" were *hierarchically* positioned on an axis of disgrace, ranging from superior to inferior, their cultural and biological supremacy and/or weakness constituting the main criterion intended for this shocking classification. Not surprisingly, perhaps, such "arguments gained considerable credibility. In part, this was because they were advanced by people who practised as scientists in a period when science was, for the first time, widely regarded as proficient in revealing the truth about the world."[7] What is far more disturbing is that "scientific racism was not simply the product of conservative, backward-looking reactionaries but . . . was espoused by men who were by and large politically liberal, scientifically minded and believed in progress and modernity."[8] Other than failing to appreciate the magnitude of the human species' diversity, the perilous oversimplification of "race," as a scientific term, accounts for the growth of the slave trade and the ill-treatment of creatures that differed little from their masters, barring their skin color.

In a similar context, colonialism too was facilitated to a great extent by similar notions of cultural superiority, as promoted by the same imperial powers that fervently sought to justify their expansionist plans. From a Marxist perspective, the "modernization" of less advanced nations became synonymous with exploitation, as the dignity of the indigenous population of pretty much every colony was sacrificed in order to better serve the interests of capitalism. Sadly, contemporary expressions of racial discrimination have hardly changed since then, although skin color is nowadays nothing more but an aspect of a seemingly multifaceted phenomenon. The concept of *interior racism*, for instance, is usually overlooked, even though it pertains to a process whereby peasants and proletarians across Europe were "civilized" by the ruling classes. As a matter of fact, it becomes apparent that when considering "class formation and reproduction within European nation states, the bourgeoisie has always sought to legitimate its position of domination over other classes. For example, during the early nineteenth century, an ideology of "breeding" justified political and economic privilege by representing class differences in terms of somatic or genetic characteristics."[9] Likewise, Jewish and Irish people have also been discriminated against, yet skin color played no part in the kind of degradation that these communities have suffered. There is no question that the Holocaust, in particular, commands our attention for it continues to serve as a macabre reminder of the immense pain that man is capable of inflicting upon his own species. Aristotle once described man as a "political animal" that never fails to organize society in like manner. Centuries later societies differed little for the powerless animals remained firmly under the influence of formidable rulers, more often than not separated by distinctly identifiable features that the elite manipulated almost effortlessly so as to maintain its grip on power.

For these reasons, the study of racism is, obviously, a rather complex task for it entails a series of interrelated yet obscure issues such the concept of "race" itself, the causes of racial discrimination and, of course, the consequences of this phenomenon upon society. In European terms, from an exclusively economic viewpoint, racial segregation reached its height in the aftermath of the Second

World War as the devastated nation-states across the continent sought to revitalize their economies and increase productivity as they welcomed the first, admittedly, large waves of immigrants that reached Europe as the all-important workforce. In retrospection, while colonialism provided the much-sought-after pool of resources and labor, the post-war period provided the platform that would later, unintentionally, facilitate a reformed process of social exclusion based on nationality, religion and social class. It was within this societal context that the study of "race" and, shortly thereafter, racism, really developed. It goes without saying that the "role of colonial history in determining popular conceptions of colour, race and ethnicity in European societies"[10] gained much prominence in the academia. According to Miles,

> The idea of "race" evolved in such a way that its object became the supposed existence of biological types of human being. When, during the first half of the twentieth century, scientific knowledge demonstrated conclusively that the world's population could not be legitimately categorised in this way, the idea of "race" no longer had a "real" object. What remained was the common-sense idea that "races" existed, an idea sustained by the unquestionable reality of somatic and cultural differences between people. If social scientists retain the idea of "race" as an analytical concept to refer to the social reproduction and consequences of this belief, it necessarily implicitly carries the meaning of its use in the everyday world.[11]

Needless to say, the present author has the same opinion but feels obliged, nonetheless, to ascertain that certain somatic and cultural characteristics may, indeed, prove decisive within the realm of sport insofar as an athlete's success or failure is concerned. Chapter 2 has already addressed this matter extensively, regarding the playing positions of a footballer on the pitch and the relevant views of some managers. Hence, it is worthy of note that "race" still plays an important role in assessing a football player's skills, though in a fundamentally dogmatic manner that persists in denying certain players the right to equal opportunities.

Racism and anti-racism

Solomos and Back, in their *Racism and Society*, produce a compelling account of racism in society through a rather meticulous assessment of the theoretical background of all pertinent terms and key historical evidence, while also examining the impact of anti-racism campaigns in combating racial discrimination. With regard to the latter issue, the two authors argue that

> anti-racist movements and ideas have tended to attract less attention than racism, but they cannot easily be ignored in the current socio-political environment. Part of the reason for this may be the result of

a political preoccupation with the history of racism and the role of racist ideas and movements in contemporary societies. It is also the case that in much of the recent social science and popular literature on this issue there is what Miles has called "a one-sided emphasis on racism and associated practices." Whatever the reason for this relative absence of an analysis of the role and limits of anti-racism, it is clearly the case that any rounded account of the role of racism in contemporary societies needs to examine in some detail the complex web of issues that underlie contemporary debates about anti-racism.[12]

Certainly, an account of the role (and relative success or failure) of anti-racism organizations in the campaign against racial discrimination is surely invaluable, yet their contribution this far cannot be measured, not just because racism continues to disturb European societies. Rather, anti-racism organizations have not gathered as much support as anticipated perhaps from the outset of their campaigns merely because few relevant policies are in effect at national level, despite the persistent struggle of the European Union to secure a racism-free environment the continent over. Support for extreme right-wing parties and like movements, eager to exploit issues related to migration so as to manipulate the rise of xenophobia for the purpose of advancing inherently nationalistic agendas, has recently reached upsetting levels—even though their electoral success is currently considered marginal.

Yet the main obstacle that such organizations need to overcome is the lack of a common and coherent ideology encapsulating their aims and beliefs. More precisely, the "diversity of understandings of what is meant by the notion of anti-racism symbolises the absence of a common theoretical language and the paucity of historical studies about the role of anti-racist ideologies and movements."[13] Some even argue that "by being too tied to the 'anti,' anti-racisms have generally neglected thinking through the goal of building a more just and fair society for all"[14]—an unforgiving remark that definitely (assuming it is accurate) compromises the seemingly evenhanded strategies employed by these organizations, not to mention that it blemishes both their record and campaign. On the other hand, it is also quite possible that the objectives set by anti-racism organizations are occasionally sacrificed merely "because funds may be available for one type of activity rather than another,"[15] at the same time as the activities of these groups may become central to political debates that, ultimately, succeed in undermining their overall efforts. Regardless of the likely impact of the omnipresent political forces, it is also probable that the agendas of policymakers and anti-racism organizations seldom coincide, given the very nature of the phenomenon concerned. Actually, there appears to be an intricate correlation between the two parties, taking into account the fact that

> groups with close relationships to centres of power benefit from funding and may find some of their priorities taken up by decision-makers. This may, however, be at the expense of their credibility with

the grass-roots sections of the anti-racist movement who may suspect that their concerns are being diluted. This question of co-option is important for anti-racists because of the centrality of their claims to legitimately represent their constituency. . . . These problems are not outweighed by the scope of opportunities presented to anti-racists by the European Parliament and the European Commission. The opportunities also contain the danger that the anti-racist agenda could be co-opted by these powerful organisations and that groups could become dependent on European funding and lose touch with their grass-roots support, which is a crucial resource.[16]

Evidently, anti-racism organizations depend much on local, national and even supranational authorities for funding and are, therefore, susceptible to external pressure. What's more, the notion of anti-racism has acquired several different interpretations, Bonnett argues, to an extent that it has now come to describe every "thought and/or practice that seeks to confront, eradicate and/or ameliorate racism."[17]

It is worthy of note that the term "anti-racism" was more widely employed by academics and relevant agencies in the 1960s, despite the prevalence of racism in modern societies; nevertheless, Bonnett states that "the concept of racism was conceived by those who opposed it, by *anti*-racists. Strictly speaking, any attempt to portray *anti*-racism before this time, *before* the concept of racism existed, is anachronistic" (original emphasis).[18] What the reader must appreciate, therefore, is that anti-racism and racism are intrinsically interwoven—one simply cannot exist without the other. Central to this argument, however, are debates surrounding the notion of "race" itself. Solomos and Back are adamant when stating that "it is widely accepted that 'races' as such do not exist,"[19] just as Miles argues that "there are no 'races' and therefore no 'race relations.' There is only a belief that there are such things, a belief which is used by some social groups to construct an Other (and therefore the Self) in thought as a prelude to exclusion and domination, and by other social groups to define Self (and so to construct an Other) as a means of resisting that exclusion. Hence, if it is used at all, the idea of 'race' should be used only to refer descriptively to such uses of the idea of 'race.'"[20] All the same, other scholars such as Paul Gilroy do not support this standpoint in its entirety. While Gilroy, too, argues that "there is, of course, only one human race," he maintains that "for Miles this observation is entangled with a demolition of the sociology of 'race relations' and becomes the trigger for an intensive critique of all attempts to use the concept 'race' in either description or analysis. It is as if the recognition of the limited value of 'race' as an analytical tool provided, in itself, a coherent theory of contemporary racisms. Miles writes on occasions as if he believes that banishing the concept of 'race' is a means to abolish racism."[21] Regardless of the preceding perceptions, Bonnett concludes in the first chapter of his book—suitably named *Roots of Resistance: The Antecedents and Ambivalences of Anti-Racism*—that the sources of anti-racism "run deep into history and stretch right across the globe" and that "racism and anti-racism are not necessarily two discrete warring discourses, good versus evil."[22] The latter remark raises a very provocative point, as Bonnett himself acknowledges, which obviously suggests that anti-racism need not be regarded as the opposite of racism, nor perhaps as its effect, despite what the prefix "anti" typically signifies.

Anti-racism and football

Before any analysis delving into the role of anti-racism in football, the reader needs first be reminded of the complex nature of racial discrimination within the game as a whole. What the previous chapters have revealed makes reference to an intricate phenomenon that concerns race relations (a) among players, managers, fans and officials of all sorts; (b) at clubs, national teams and relevant governing bodies; (c) at local, national and supranational levels, as far as football competitions are concerned; and (d) in different manifestations, ranging from racist chants to fascist salutes and from offensive banners to banana missiles. Back, Crabbe and Solomos identified seven different forms and expressions of racial discrimination in football that are categorized as racist verbal abuse in grounds occurs in intermittent outbursts; racist activity that is unevenly developed within the ground; racist verbal abuse that takes a variety of expressive forms or ritual styles; racism that is often expressed rhetorically through humor and play; racist abuse that can take on player-specific forms; verbal racist abuse in and around football grounds that rarely escalates into physical violence; and racist abuse that is perpetrated by fans of all ages.[23] What illustrates the intricacy of racism in football is best described in terms of "fans who racially abuse the black players who play for their opponents, yet cheer those who play for their own side,"[24] even though "the 'acceptance' of black players and spectators by certain white fans can be contingent upon them demonstrating allegiance to the 'right' club or team."[25] Evidently, racial discrimination in football concerns a phenomenon full of twists and turns that necessitates an equally versatile approach or else the sheer prospect of its eradication will, in due course, evade all pertinent actors.

The archetype of overt racist conduct in football is almost certainly closely associated to spectators employing foul language in football grounds. Football fans engaging in racist chanting, however, does not quite entail the presence of conscious racists in football—an indisputable fact that definitely questions the treatment and punishment of perpetrators, not to mention the validity and application of relevant legislative measures. Garland and Rowe seem to concur, arguing that

> the notion that individuals act differently when part of a mass of people continues to be referred to by those who argue that the expression of racism within a football crowd is fundamentally different and dis-

tinct from such behaviour elsewhere. Prohibiting the expression of racism in football grounds will not—of itself—serve to change the attitudes of spectators, and it is difficult not to agree that many of those who make monkey chants or shout out their opposition to the "black bastard" centre-forward are probably not active racists or supporters of the NF or BNP. Nonetheless, the idea that such expressions should be tolerated as "heat of the moment" aberrations of no great significance can be rejected. Given that minority ethnic groups are put off from attending matches because they dread such incidents, it is in nobody's interest, except perhaps some of the far-right groups referred to earlier in the chapter, to smugly accept racist abuse as part and parcel of the game.[26]

With the notable exception of monkey chanting, nevertheless, most other forms of racist conduct in football stadiums are almost identical to those witnessed in other segments of society. Sadly, this difficult-to-confront piece of evidence only serves to emphasize that racism in football is nothing more than a socially transmitted disease that society must remedy; therefore, implying that football's premier governing bodies need not address the issue single-handedly or, perhaps, not even at all. The following account is telling.

Following on from the problem of concentrating on countering racist behaviour instead of beliefs is the issue of displacement of racism away from football stadia and into other fields. If racist behaviour does not occur within grounds but is simply transferred to the street, the factory or other areas where it continues to be expressed relatively unhindered, then little has been gained except that football clubs and the industries that share a stake in the game's success can congratulate themselves on their efforts and forget about the problem. This is not an argument for tolerating racism within grounds, though, as we reject the idea that football matches provide an isolated "safety valve" via which unpleasant and objectionable attitudes can be exorcised. It does raise the question, however, of what is really gained from a zero tolerance strategy if it only serves to relocate racism from one arena to another. A more fundamental approach to challenging racism on social, political and economic levels is preferable, a challenge to racism which does not assume that the problem is solely about the reprehensible behaviour of an extreme deviant minority but which recognises the subtle, contradictory and pervasive nature of a diversity of racisms.[27]

All the same, the compelling urge to eliminate racist conduct from football presupposes the authenticity of those allegations, suggesting that the popular game is infested with prejudice. Against this background, the semiotics of football fan culture cannot be overlooked. The festive atmosphere of football matches exempted, abusing the players and fans of opposing clubs alike is, irrefutably, the main feature of football culture the world over.

The physique of black footballers, whether those playing their football for "us" or "them," has always been attributed "racialized" features that either complement their physical qualities or designate their "natural" shortcomings respectively. The black players that defend the values of "our club" are, more often than not, portrayed in a much celebrated manner by bestowing them with nicknames emphasizing their athletic competence. Those unfortunate enough to play for the opposition are habitually ridiculed in hope of affecting their overall performance during the match and not, perhaps, with the intention of expressing instinctively racist beliefs. In this respect, the task of confronting "racist" fans becomes increasingly difficult for anti-racism organizations. Furthermore, football culture dictates that while racism in the game is more or less acknowledged by all pertinent actors, club officials often categorically deny that racial discrimination is much of an issue, fearing their club may be stigmatized as racist and, as such, endure the economic repercussions that stem from the loss of the all-important sponsors and/or reduced audiences. To this end, it has been reported that racially abused players are sometimes advised against taking any kind of action, legal or otherwise, to challenge discrimination in the game. The right kind of publicity, one that makes good use of a club's anti-racist profile nevertheless has the potential to both generate profit for the club and promote the agenda of anti-racism organizations. The combination of media influence and the near-celebrity status of certain clubs and players render the game of football as the ideal platform from which an effective and purposeful anti-racist campaign can be launched. Moreover, the commercialization of the game has recently encouraged "clubs to provide free entrance to schoolchildren from districts with relatively high minority ethnic populations, and so make some return from merchandise and refreshments or tickets that would otherwise have remained unsold. In such circumstances the promotion of anti-racism or multiculturalism within the game coincides with the financial interests of clubs in a manner that seems only to benefit both."[28]

Simply put, the already unenviable task of anti-racism organizations becomes all the more complex, given the presence of a hidden agenda that frustrates anti-racists aiming to expose the decay of sport, yet satisfies the game's officials that seek to preserve the integrity and values of football. Along similar lines, it is only reasonable to assume—regardless of the genuinely constructive contribution of anti-racism organizations in eradicating racial discrimination from the game of football—that it is difficult to define or, for that matter, appreciate the intrinsic worth of anti-racism campaigns in football due to their imperfect relevance to prejudice in society as a whole. Advancing the same line of reasoning are Garland and Rowe who argue that

> the gains made by anti-racists, significant though they have often been, are likely to be of limited benefit to society more generally. Given that this might appear a controversial statement it is important to stress that it in no way implies criticism of the motivation or appro-

ach of many of those involved in campaigns and strategies across the country. As has been argued throughout this text, many of their achievements have been remarkable in the context of a sport usually noted for its insularity and conservatism and, while many agencies have sought the credit for the general process of anti-racism in the game, it should be acknowledged that much of the success is due to the grassroots involvement of countless committed individuals. The limited scope with which anti-racism within football can be transferred to society more generally relates to the nature of the problem, rather than the efficacy of activists. Since diverse racisms can be identified in complex social formations the potential for anti-racism confronting the problem in a unitary manner is limited.[29]

Evidently, the world of football appears to have a different view of racism from society and, therefore, a different approach and understanding of this phenomenon altogether. The game's culture does not always coincide with that of society as a whole, thus the need to adopt suitable yet distinct measures when addressing common problems, in particular when they emanate from one sector of society but have the ability to change form and erode others too. What is essential in grasping the complex relationship between racism and football—particularly so to members of anti-racism organizations—is first realize that many forms of racist conduct during a football match border on the ritualistic aspects of the game and, second, to appreciate the fact that rival fans need to distinguish themselves from the opposition. Both features are central to the construction of fan identity and therefore should not be confused with the more prevalent forms of racial discrimination that currently disturb European societies.

However, the above should not suggest that what a football stadium "provides to its fans is a phantasm or a mirage. Rather, it is the arena for the embodiment of particular forms of social life, that have their own routines and cultural modes of expression. In short the football stadium provides one context in which local identity can be ritually defined, regardless of the changes taking place in its immediate environment and patterns of migration."[30] Advancing their argument, Back, Crabbe and Solomos add that

> what we have demonstrated here is how acts that appear to be blind hate possess a rationale and a structure. This enables us to understand how particular black and overseas players are isolated within the logic of what we refer to as a structure of antipathy. Here racism becomes part of a series of other sources of hostility that together culminate in vicious and hateful acts. We would argue that it is necessary to unpick these recondite processes in order to explain how racist abuse is directed at some potential targets and not others. Equally, it enables us to explain how racial abuse of opposing players can coexist with a professed love and glorification of black players who are wearing the home team's shirt. The other point that we hope we have made conclusively is that popular racism is always nested within the

context of particular local contexts and needs to be seen as part of the flow and rhythm of football matches. Here the game and the expression of racism within it is analogous to an unfolding social drama whose plot is always uncertain. This is why it is so difficult to predict when racist responses will occur because they are always a product of the interplay of forces (on the pitch and in the stadium) that cannot be foreseen. Yet at the same time, we suggest that the patterns we have documented here are the product of an underlying knowledge structure that isolates players and targets them for racist abuse.[31]

It is within this context that the infamous incident involving Spanish coach Luis Aragones and French superstar Thierry Henry needs be discussed. Days before an international friendly match between the national football teams of Spain and England in Madrid in October 2004, Aragones's unorthodox attempt to motivate Spanish international Jose Antonio Reyes by calling his French teammate at Arsenal "black shit" made the headlines in the two countries and beyond. Without delay, as you would have thought, an assortment of media agents, players, managers, officials, fans, anti-racists of all sorts and pretty much every virtuous man interpreted Aragones's remark, appropriately so, as innately racist. Despite the fact that one cannot possibly disregard this interpretation, it is imperative that we assess to all intents and purposes the causes that attacked the dignity of the talented French striker. To begin with, the seemingly racist context of the attribute "black," in connection with the phrase in question might have been an innocuous reference to Henry's skin color and thus his ethnic background. In line with Gilroy's critique of Miles, regarding the use of the term "race," the word "black" alone is unlikely to generate or even encourage discrimination. Likewise, the word "shit," though vulgar perhaps, cannot be ascribed racist connotations, no matter the context. In other words, neither "black" nor "shit" seem to infringe the notion of political correctness whatsoever. Employing the method of inductive reasoning, therefore, we can only assume that what seems to have insulted the French football player, as well as the all-pervading anti-racists, was the appalling effect of the combined use of "black" and "shit," though the author maintains certain reservations.

As far as clubs are concerned, they seldom reject the essence of anti-racism campaigns, but seem reluctant to embrace them for they paradoxically perceive these campaigns as possible causes of racism. Given the likely consequences that racial discrimination is thought of bringing about at club level, it is hardly surprising that club officials consider such campaigns a menace, perhaps even more so than the phenomenon they were designed to combat in first place. Interestingly, "support can, sometimes reluctantly, be articulated for anti-racist initiatives despite the point that this is often merely a rhetorical gesture. This was illustrated by a community officer at a small football league club who told us how he had taken a letter offering support to the Let's Kick Racism out of Football campaign to the club chairman for his signature. The chairman responded by stating 'I'm not signing that. I'm a racist,' to which the community officer replied, 'Well, sign it anyway,' which he duly did."[32] Even though clubs acknowledge the likely consequences of racism within football, "the need to maintain a positive public profile encourages them to deny that racism is a feature of their club—or if it is, then it is one caused by extremist hooligan outsiders who are not 'real football fans.' Collectively this leads to a situation whereby there is a broad consensus that racism exists within the sport, and yet an equally widespread insistence that the difficulties are primarily elsewhere—somebody else's concern."[33]

Justifiably, this lack of understanding only has the potential of hindering the attempts of anti-racism organizations to rid football of bigotry. Even when clubs commit themselves to the ideals of such organizations, the relevant community projects they usually carry out only serve to highlight the very same lack of understanding, as their officials fail to take notice of minority communities' need to retain their cultural diversity (the right to be different), while also maintaining their right to equal treatment. Yet not all clubs suffer from a racist following, which only further complicates the mission of anti-racism organizations. There is no doubt that "the frequency, and to some extent the form, of racism in football grounds varies greatly between clubs. Shared codes of ritual behaviour hold true for all clubs but as we've argued each fan culture exhibits distinct forms of prescribed formal behaviour and symbolism. In order to understand the range of racist activity one needs to examine the relationship between processes of racialization and the collective ritual and symbolic practices that give any particular fan culture meaning. In this sense differences with regard to the level and intensity of racism need to be understood in terms of the way racist practices are nested within the ritual and collective symbolism of each fan culture."[34] The fact remains, however, that racism is a problem to society as a whole, not just football, or, indeed, any other section of society alone. To eradicate racial discrimination from the popular game, the cooperation of local and national authorities and particularly the agencies devoted to the effective assimilation of all ethnic minority communities is imperative.

Anti-racism in football revisited

The authors cited in the previous section of this chapter published their work at the beginning of this decade to fill an important gap in the relevant literature, at the same time as the anti-racism organizations presented in this book boasted a small number of years campaigning in the field of football. While the experience of the same organizations is nowadays significantly enhanced, at least in terms of the activities carried out every year, some of the authors' findings continue to haunt the popular game, particularly in Britain.

One of the much debated issues regarding racism in football, as already mentioned in chapter 2, pertains to the ambiguous role of extreme right-wing parties and movements. While some scholars claim that the relevant information available is either in short supply or simply unsubstantiated, others consider the extreme right too significant a factor to ignore. Garland and Rowe support the latter view and argue that "the extreme right have targeted football in Britain for three main reasons: to further their political programme, to generate and sustain international networks of the far-right, and as potential means to attract new recruits."[35] Despite the gravity of their account, the main question that emerges from the above is whether anti-racism organizations are sufficiently equipped to challenge the agenda of the extreme right. The reliability of Garland and Rowe's assertion notwithstanding, the risk of the extreme right exploiting the vast popularity of the game to advance their propaganda by converting an otherwise ordinary football stadium into a political arena—to disseminate relevant information or recruit new members—simply cannot be afforded. Surely anti-racism organizations employ the same properties of the game to raise awareness against racial discrimination and xenophobia; nonetheless, the question remains: who is louder and, perhaps, more successful? Taking into consideration the fact that an almost insignificant number of fans come from ethnic minority backgrounds, in fear of racial abuse, the same xenophobic-like environment of a football ground that persuades scores of non-white supporters against attending matches probably encourages extreme right elements to take a more active stance in promoting the sort of racial discrimination that surrounds us. Without a doubt, countering the effects of extremism in football is, indeed, a daunting task for any anti-racism organization that seeks to increase ethnic minority attendance.

As far as black fans are concerned, Back, Crabbe and Solomos "developed an argument about the scope of black inclusion in football fan culture and its limitations, be it by the defining centre of English football fan culture or the variegations of local patriotism and its normative structure. The nationalisms of the neighbourhood and the circumscriptions of Englishness we outlined here offer black fans passports to entry that are always issued with specific terms and conditions. These circumstances are largely restricted to black males who perform and participate in class-infected forms of hegemonic masculinity."[36] No matter what criteria black fans have to fulfill so as to become an integral part of a club's fan base, there is definitely much scope for anti-racism organizations to develop similar tactics, again, in order to improve the attendance rates of members from ethnic minority communities. The sheer presence of many gifted black football players and their use as role models should suffice for convincing black supporters, at least, to restore their faith in the beautiful game, reclaim their rightful position on the terraces and enjoy the festive atmosphere of a football match away from racial discrimination. Yet for black fans to recover their place in football's culture, black football players must make great strides to first vindicate their righteous place in the game and then to improve conditions in non-playing career opportunities.

Needless to say, institutional racism too needs be defeated before football rids itself of racism. To this end, Back, Crabbe and Solomos asked themselves a rather interesting question that one could raise again today, almost a decade later, for nothing has changed much since—even the answer remains the same. Their attention-grabbing question, dilemma rather, is as follows: "If black players can pull on the England shirt, is it possible that one day there could be a black manager of England?"[37] Even though the question seems genuinely philosophical—one that necessitates much debate and careful consideration—the answer is nothing but pragmatic. A short but comprehensive "no" would suffice. The much disputed decision of the English Football Association to appoint Sven Göran Eriksson as England manager would probably side well with the above argument, yet a more recent incident speaks volumes in our defense. Having first enjoyed a commendable football career, Paul Ince did succeed in becoming the first black premiership manager, though quite belatedly. In the summer of 2008, Ince took charge of Blackburn's dressing rooms, but was fired a few months later after a really poor spell at the club. Some may recall Ruud Gullit at the helm of Chelsea and later Newcastle United or even Jean Tigana at Fulham; however, it becomes apparent that their foreign background somehow preceded the dark color of their skin. It is worthy of note that conditions at lower divisions, though more promising for black managers, only improved in 1993 after the appointment of Edwin Stein at Barnet.

Institutional racism is, beyond any shadow of doubt, *the* most pressing matter that anti-racism organizations ought to concern themselves with, should their campaigns ultimately be crowned with success. Writing at the turn of century, Back, Crabbe and Solomos revealed that "the administration and management of football has remained predominantly white in its composition. This stands in stark contrast to the changes in the racial and ethnic makeup of the players."[38] Once more, the situation has hardly altered, since "the underrepresentation of blacks and Asians in administrative positions at football clubs and local football organizations, including their absence from the English Football Association"[39] persist to this very day. Anti-racism organizations may prove extremely successful in raising awareness about racism; educating fans regarding the perils of racial discrimination, offering players from ethnic minority backgrounds equal opportunities, inspiring the most prominent governing bodies to adopt relevant legislative measures, even at supranational levels, drawing the authorities' attention to anti-social phenomena in football, and even succeed in removing racist chanting from football grounds permanently, yet they will have by no means defeated racism unless racial discrimination is tackled at institutional level too. Racism is certainly not confined to terraces, but stretches over football's premier institutions. What is more, institutional racism, in terms of football, serves no purpose other than preserving the game's white qualities, unmistakably at the expense of all the other "races," the existence of which we dismissed earlier in this chapter.

All things considered, the theory and practice of anti-racism are poles apart, since the campaigning of all pertinent actors is rarely free of obstacles, with problems usually stemming from either an apparent lack of understanding of what racial discrimination entails or the lack of concern that sadly characterizes certain fans, players, managers and club officials, as well as football's local, national and supranational governing bodies. What is truly essential in eliminating racism from football is the good use of the game's unique qualities and the heartfelt commitment of high-ranking officials at all levels to the ideals and values that sport, in general, defends. Otherwise, anti-racism organizations will be better known for their likely contribution to the eradication of racial discrimination from sport, probably because they were at some stage denied the opportunity to utilize all available means, no matter the amount of literature devoted to the subject under examination.

Notes

1. John Solomos, *Race and Racism in Britain* (London: Macmillan Press, 2nd edition, 1993), 17.

2. Jochen Blaschke and Guillermo Ruiz Torres, *Racism in Rural Areas*, Final Report, Study for the European Monitoring Centre on Racism and Xenophobia (Berliner Institut für Vergleichende Sozialforschung Mitglied im Europäischen Migrationszentrum, 30 November 2002), 14.

3. Blaschke and Torres, *Racism in Rural Areas*, 25.

4. Solomos, *Race and Racism in Britain*, 194-195.

5. Solomos, *Race and Racism in Britain*, 195.

6. Robert Miles, *Racism after "Race" Relations* (London and New York: Routledge, 1994), 28.

7. Miles, *Racism after "Race" Relations*, 59.

8. Kenan Malik, *The Meaning of Race: Race, History and Culture in Western Society* (London: Macmillan Press, 1996), 101.

9. Miles, *Racism after "Race" Relations*, 103.

10. Solomos, *Race and Racism in Britain*, 18.

11. Miles, *Racism after "Race" Relations*, 2-3.

12. John Solomos and Les Back, *Racism and Society* (London: Macmillan Press, 1996), 105.

13. Solomos and Back, *Racism and Society*, 109.

14. Floya Anthias, "Diasporic Hybridity and Transcending Racisms: Problems and Potential," in *Rethinking Anti-Racisms: From Theory to Practice*, ed. Floya Antias and Cathie Lloyd (London and New York: Routledge, 2002), 22.

15. Cathie Lloyd, "Anti-Racism, Social Movements and Civil Society," in *Rethinking Anti-Racisms: From Theory to Practice*, ed. Floya Antias and Cathie Lloyd (London and New York: Routledge, 2002), 63.

16. Lloyd, "Anti-Racism, Social Movements and Civil Society," 76.

17. Alastair Bonnett, *Anti-Racism* (London and New York: Routledge, 2000), 4.

18. Bonnett, *Anti-Racism*, 10.

19. Solomos and Back, *Racism and Society*, 1.

20. Miles, *Racism after "Race" Relations*, 42.

21. Paul Gilroy, *There Ain't No Black in the Union Jack: The Cultural Politics of Race and Nation* (London: Unwin Hyman, 1987), 22.

22. Bonnett, *Anti-Racism*, 45.

23. Les Back, Tim Crabbe and John Solomos, *The Changing Face of Football: Racism, Identity and Multiculture in the English Game* (Oxford and New York: Berg, 2001), 107-117.

24. Jon Garland and Michael Rowe, *Racism and Anti-Racism in Football* (Basingstoke and New York: Palgrave, 2001), 5.

25. Garland and Rowe, *Racism and Anti-Racism in Football*, 6.

26. Garland and Rowe, *Racism and Anti-Racism in Football*, 108.

27. Garland and Rowe, *Racism and Anti-Racism in Football*, 110.

28. Garland and Rowe, *Racism and Anti-Racism in Football*, 180-181.

29. Garland and Rowe, *Racism and Anti-Racism in Football*, 193.

30. Back, Crabbe and Solomos, *The Changing Face of Football: Racism, Identity and Multiculture in the English Game*, 43.

31. Back, Crabbe and Solomos, *The Changing Face of Football: Racism, Identity and Multiculture in the English Game*, 132.

32. Back, Crabbe and Solomos, *The Changing Face of Football: Racism, Identity and Multiculture in the English Game*, 165.

33. Garland and Rowe, *Racism and Anti-Racism in Football*, 190.

34. Back, Crabbe and Solomos, *The Changing Face of Football: Racism, Identity and Multiculture in the English Game*, 96.

35. Garland and Rowe, *Racism and Anti-Racism in Football*, 88.

36. Back, Crabbe and Solomos, *The Changing Face of Football: Racism, Identity and Multiculture in the English Game*, 101.

37. Back, Crabbe and Solomos, *The Changing Face of Football: Racism, Identity and Multiculture in the English Game*, 285-286.

38. Back, Crabbe and Solomos, *The Changing Face of Football: Racism, Identity and Multiculture in the English Game*, 37.

39. Christos Kassimeris, *European Football in "Black and White": Tackling Racism in Football* (Lanham and Plymouth: Lexington Books, 2007), 87.

Chapter Eight

Conclusion

Lina Tsoumpanou

The sheer fact that today's European Union comprises an admittedly impressive twenty-seven member states suggests that a rather thorough process of integration is in effect, vertical as well as horizontal, which undoubtedly renders interdisciplinary approaches to cross-cultural phenomena imperative. While taking into consideration that European integration is widely considered *sine qua non*; nevertheless, little attention is devoted to those social aspects that best exemplify the significance of assimilation. For this reason, the European Social Survey is often employed for the purpose of interpreting the attitude of the European population with regard to key institutional policies, at both national and supranational levels, so as to better comprehend, among others, the concept of diversity. Given that a staggering thirty European states will take part in the fourth round of this bi-annual research, the data collected seldom fail to reveal forms of discrimination, thus stressing that integration is far from complete.

European history is replete with national rivalries, regional conflicts and political turmoil to an extent where racial stereotypes were oftentimes overemphasized for the cause of promoting a distinct impression of national identity. What triggered a process of nationalistic fervor—clearly evident from the unparalleled savagery of the Second World War—was the essence of supremacy, cultural or otherwise. Sadly, such disturbing views have yet to be eclipsed from an assortment of ideologies and movements pertaining, albeit not exclusively, to the extreme right. Contemporary phenomena such as social exclusion, xenophobia and racism have come to haunt modern Europe and blemish the continent's cultural background in a manner that defies its more reputable qualities, even though it remains perfectly in line with certain features of its less-than-innocent historical past.

The vision of the European Union ever since its inception reflects a long-term goal of securing lasting peace among all European countries by promoting further social, economic and political integration. The European Union was structured with a unique international model of supranational schemes in mind, concerning policies relevant to matters that reflected the interests of its member-states. The ultimate goal is to create a common future for a variety of populations coming from different cultural backgrounds that will ensure their peaceful, harmonious co-existence. Although there was great skepticism regarding the potential loss of national identity, the European Union succeeded, gradually, in promoting European Union citizenship without replacing national citizenship per se. The key for achieving this was based upon the promotion of the term "multi" at all levels (multi-national, multi-regional, multi-lingual, multi-racial and multi-cultural society); nevertheless, the most important element has been the European Union's persistence on the respect of fundamental rights and freedoms.

Despite the sense of optimism that guides the European Union to further integration, the revival of nationalism is often attributed to globalization and the inequalities that stem from it. Looking back in history, one can trace many instances of propagandistic incidents at the expense of ethnic minorities, usually victimizing alien cultures during economic crises. Immigrants are nowadays not always welcomed by their host countries, even though the relevant government will, more often than not, grant them certain rights, as new forms of racism—less clear than traditional forms of the past—seem to have appeared in Western societies. Naturally, these phenomena of xenophobia account for the exclusion of people who are understood to be culturally out of the ordinary. In this respect, integration is perceived in terms of maintaining homogeneity and, therefore, safeguarding the cultural values of the host country, rather than recognizing the inherent right to differentiate.

Not surprisingly, xenophobia is employed in political discourse, too, by parties aiming at promoting relevant stereotypes for the sole purpose of expanding their electorate. The media often sustain such stereotypes and clichés—thus contributing to xenophobia—albeit, perhaps, unintentionally, since coverage of immigrant-related incidents usually attract much public attention. Extreme right parties are more inclined to racist rhetoric, though not exclusively, as evident in the case of the National Front in France, Italy's *Lega Nord*, the *Vlaams Blok* in Belgium, Austria's *Freedom Party* and the *Pim Fortuyn List* in the Netherlands, to name a few. Sadly, the aforementioned parties not only enjoy relative electoral success, but also appear less reluctant to devote part of their campaigns to xenophobic propaganda by targeting immigrants, habitually stressing the negative cultural impact of the latter upon society. The tragic events of September 11 and the "war on terror" that followed soon after produced the necessary grounds for a number of governments and relevant actors to develop undemocratic practices that violate human rights, obliterate the essence of fundamental values and constitutional principles. Alarmingly, certain politicians adopted an anti-Muslim stance in an attempt to emphasize issues denoting to internal security. Likewise, public opinion occasionally reveals racist undertones that advance a sense of social exclusion at the expense of ethnic minorities across Europe, just as anti-Semitic acts have recently witnessed an increase.

The sheer size of black communities in Europe should provide, theoretically, ample evidence to document the continent's thriving integration process; however, the rise of race-related acts of violence, insufficient anti-discrimination legislative measures and the apparent lack of basic rights all serve to indicate that members of these communities are, by and large, considered second-class citizens. Indicative of social exclusion were the violent 2005 riots in Paris, when the French capital was almost literally under siege, thus epitomizing the government's inability to redress such racist phenomena. While one may question the prospect of a truly diverse European Union, nevertheless, European Social Survey findings suggest that the majority of the European Union citizens are open to concepts pertaining to diversity. Interestingly, the legislation that is nowadays available to combat discrimination remains vague and largely ineffective. Although anti-racism legislation, at national and supranational levels alike, would help eliminate the omnipresent perils of racist conduct, legislation alone is inadequate. What is imperative beyond doubt is raising awareness about racism, or else harmonious multicultural societies in Europe shall never materialize. Education and specifically designed teaching material, for example, can be properly utilized to promote diversity in schools, just as sports—football in particular—have the capacity to promote equality and combat discrimination of all forms and at all levels.

It is precisely in this context that the football-oriented anti-racism organizations discussed herein have designed their campaigns in an attempt to eliminate football's modern plague. The capacity of education to raise awareness about certain anti-social phenomena—whether the audience comprises schoolchildren or football fans—and the overwhelming ability of football to promote integration provide sound instruments in the campaign against racism. Despite the captivating environment that characterizes the two central European countries, Austria and Switzerland was last summer dominated by football as they hosted the 2008 European Championship. Among the various events and activities organized by Football Against Racism in Europe (FARE) and its partners were the anti-racism messages delivered by the captains of the four semi-finalists prior to kick-off. On the occasion, the football pitch was decorated by two enormous "Unite Against Racism" banners, with the two contesting national football teams suitably placed in between. Sadly, Euro 2008 did not escape racism, as indicated in a report compiled by FARE observers and submitted to Union of European Football Association (UEFA) officials. It is imperative, therefore, that all football governing bodies and other pertinent actors form a common front to rid European societies of racism and other forms of discrimination. Making good use of the game's mass appeal must surely enhance the continent's prospects for a far more colorful and diverse setting.

Despite the likely success of anti-racism organizations in the field of football, quantifying their overall achievements is obviously impractical simply because such an assessment would require a number of tangible statistical information, not to mention data pertaining to racist incidents related to football and the parties involved. Equally problematic, of course, is the denial of racial discrimination in the game, a view shared by many involved in football. Yet the most alarming aspect of racism in football is that this phenomenon is in a constant state of flux, therefore sustaining its threatening posture vis-à-vis the beautiful game, while also continuing to intimidate members of ethnic minority communities. In this respect, anti-racism organizations ought to adapt their tactics accordingly, so as to monitor more effectively what is already quite a multifaceted phenomenon. Those involved in anti-racism campaigns should consider, perhaps, combining forces with academic networks so as to address racial discrimination comprehensively. A certain degree of familiarization with the relevant theoretical background of their tenacious adversary is likely to enhance the anti-racism organizations' knowledge about intolerance, more generally, as well as the prospects for even more successful campaigns against racism in football. While it is certainly not suggested that those involved in football-related anti-racism campaigns devour scores of books devoted to the study of "race relations" theories, a better understanding of the phenomenon of racism should, hypothetically, improve the nature and scope of their relevant activities.

On the other hand, anti-racism organizations are not merely concerned with raising awareness about intolerance. Quite a substantial part of their initiatives involves a great deal of educational material and schemes that never fail to impress on account of their edifying properties. Football is, of course, an integral part of such activities owing to its qualities, particularly if intended for schools. Kick It Out encourages the involvement of schools in their annual Week of Action by organizing school competitions, while also involving teachers to a great extent regarding the citizenship curriculum. Likewise, Football Unites, Racism Divides delivers programs of anti-racist education, usually concentrated on issues pertaining to citizenship, to local schools and colleges, as well as to young people who wish to work in a youth and community work setting. Football Unites, Racism Divides has worked with the Institute of Citizenship in developing curriculum materials. They also maintain a Resources and Information Centre devoted to anti-racism that includes books, DVDs, posters, magazines, teaching packs and exhibitions. Finally, Show Racism the Red Card, too, has developed anti-racist educational resources for schools and organizes annual school competitions and educational workshops. The educational projects of Kick It Out and Football Unites, Racism Divides stand out, for they offer similar educational services to prisons as well. Equally significant are the exhibitions held by the aforementioned organizations regarding the overall contribution of black football players to the development of the game.

Projects developing links between clubs and their local communities are of key importance to all anti-racism organizations. Kick It Out is probably better known for its annual Week of Action, a nation-wide campaign against racism in football that seeks to redress the kind of exclusion that some groups witness. The Community Day, organized jointly by Football Unites, Racism Divides and Sheffield United, has a very similar agenda but is held at local level. The role of local authorities is also central to the success of these campaigns, for reaching out to community, particularly ethnic minorities, is often more effective when the former are involved, as campaigns then attain the all-important official acknowledgment that is usually required for a successful outcome. Recommending to clubs that they introduce equal opportunities policies and race equality standards are an essential part of the anti-racism organizations' agendas too. As you might expect, all anti-racism organizations discussed herein adopt appropriate tactics to attract the attention of not only ethnic minority communities but, more specifically, asylum-seekers and refugees as well. The Unity Cup Festival organized by Kick It Out, for example, is an attempt to engage displaced people in football and to combat social exclusion. For the record, the under-representation of the Asian community in the game of football is a comparatively similar issue. Needless to say, clubs play a rather considerable role, too, not merely because they are indeed the most prominent agents of the game. Their players are suitably utilized as exponents of anti-racism, always within the context of what characteristics turn a footballer into a proper role model, championing their ideals on and off the pitch.

Despite whatever features may distinguish the campaign of one anti-racism organization from another, in sum, their activities actually differ little, probably because their adversary is much the same. It is hardly surprising, therefore, that the anti-racism organizations examined in the preceding chapters all join forces to combat racial discrimination in football at a European level under the auspices of the Football Against Racism in Europe network. As already mentioned, the pan-European campaigning of Football Against Racism in Europe, successful as it is, is closely related to the kind of cooperation that epitomizes the relationship among all anti-racism organizations across the continent, especially those devoted to the game of football or sports more generally. Beyond any shadow of doubt, the eradication of racism from football depends much on the coordinated approach of all pertinent actors. Clearly enough, any lack of coordination would result in nothing more than an imperfect defeat of prejudice in the game.

No matter the degree of collaboration among all anti-racism organizations or the harmonization of their activities, it is certainly difficult to establish with accuracy whether racist incidents in football are nowadays any less frequent on account of these organizations coming to life. Their sheer absence a few decades ago may account for the expansion of racism over the game of football, yet it is almost impossible to determine the magnitude of the same problem today. Neither the founding of these anti-racism organizations nor the multitude of football governing bodies involved can be considered ample evidence for the success or not of anti-racism campaigning across Europe. Even the relatively recent interference of the European Parliament and the subsequent legislative measures adopted cannot possibly ascertain the extent of severity of racial discrimination in the game at present. Instead, it appears that racism in football is these days an ephemeral phenomenon that rarely evades the parameters of what is deemed a sudden occurrence that all pertinent actors seek to remedy, though in a manner that can bring about as temporary an improvement as the means utilized. Furthermore, it is imperative that racism in football is addressed not only in terms of a societal problem that infiltrated the world of sport. For the most part, it is a problem that manipulates the versatile culture of the popular game to express itself in an equally resourceful fashion.

While racial discrimination is, indeed, a societal problem, there is no evidence to suggest that the racist incidents that occur in football are in any way triggered by events in society. Intolerance in society and football alike is expressed in a variety of forms that hardly correspond to one another, for racism in football comes across resembling a wholly different issue, a distinct phenomenon for that matter. Without any doubt, one could hold accountable whatever football and its culture epitomize, ranging from the fans' identity and their need to distinguish themselves from their rivals to the misinterpreted philosophy behind the game's values and the associated conviction that football facilitates social exclusion. Surely foul language and offensive gestures are determining characteristics of what fan culture stands for, at the same time as extreme right-wing parties and movements are keen to exploit football's vast popularity to advance their xenophobic agendas. Yet the above cannot merely justify the existence of racism in football. On the contrary, an imperfect, biased, understanding of football as outlined in the previous lines only serves to oversimplify an admittedly complex phenomenon, thus disguising racism all the more—that much is revealed in the earlier chapters. It would be more accurate, perhaps, to suggest that while football does not necessarily encourage racism, the mob-like environment that best describes conditions on the terraces and the related anonymity it presents gives an adequate explanation for the occasional racist outburst. Undetectable in huge crowds, some supporters—not essentially racists—seize the opportunity to express the passion for the club they follow in the most unfathomable ways, sometimes even defying the norms of society by throwing off their masks to put across what are widely perceived as anti-social or offensive remarks, though not in an intrinsically racially prejudiced context.

Yet we do not deny the presence of racism in football, unlike others deeply involved in the game. Denial is, probably, the most intriguing aspect of this phenomenon and, quite possibly, the main reason that it persists. Failure to improve our understanding of the problem's extent will certainly condemn the game of football to a prolonged state of nausea, until racism becomes a deep-seated evil too intricate to dispose of. Exactly because it is exceedingly difficult, and ambitious, to foretell whether racism will ever be eliminated from football, it would make more sense, perhaps, to suggest that the future for anti-racism organizations in football will become overwhelmed by a unremitting process of readjustment as they maintain their relentless campaigning in many different shapes and forms—always in conjunction with the constantly changing nature of racism itself.

Index

About the Contributors

Christos Kassimeris is assistant professor in political science and heads the Department of Social and Behavioral Sciences at European University Cyprus in Nicosia. Before joining European University Cyprus, he was teaching European Integration Politics (BA) and International Relations of the Mediterranean (MA) for three years at the University of Reading. He holds a PhD in political science, an MA in international security studies and a BA in sociology from the University of Reading.

Kurt Wachter studied social anthropology and African studies in Vienna and Cape Coast. He works at the Vienna Institute for Development and Cooperation as project coordinator of the Football Against Racism in Europe network since 1997.

Susanne Franke has long served as a member of the Schalker Fan-Initiative and has chaired the organization since 2006. This is an honorary post, as she is employed elsewhere. She holds a PhD in English studies and an MA in English studies, American studies and prehistory from Ruhr-Universität in Bochum.

Jacek Purski has studied journalism at Wyższa Szkoła Komunikowania i Mediów Społecznych and works for the Never Again association (*Nigdy Wecej*). He has been project coordinator of "Let's Kick Racism out of Stadiums" for the past five years.

Danny Lynch is media and communications officer at Kick It Out.

Ruth Johnson has been managing the Resources and Information Centre of Football Unites, Racism Divides since 1997 and has written anti-racism poetry as part of the "Chantwriters" group during Sheffield's "Off the Shelf" festival of reading. She holds an MSc in information management from the University of Sheffield and a BA (Hons) in communication studies from Sheffield City Polytechnic.

Ged Grebby holds a BA (Hons) in geography from North Staffordshire Polytechnic and has served as regional official of the Youth Against Racism in Europe campaign for four years before becoming chief executive of Show Racism the Red Card in 1995. He is much involved in the development of the campaign's strategy, establishing links with other similar organizations and fundraising activities. Other than improving educational resources and liaising with football clubs, he is also overseeing the work of the Scottish Development worker and project worker.

Lina Tsoumpanou was a research associate at the European University Cyprus and national co-coordinator of the European Social Survey before joining the Research Promotion Foundation as scientific officer of the European Research Programmes and International Cooperation Unit. She holds an MA in Euro-Mediterranean studies from the University of Reading, a BA in international relations and European studies from Panteio University and a BA in philosophy, pedagogics and psychology from the National Kapodistriako University.